Washington Money-Go-Round

Jack Anderson

Elliott & James
PUBLISHING

Production Supervisor: Sheryn Hara
Production Assistant: Lana Plitman
Editors: Vicki McCown, Ivy Truesdell, Luke Dawson
Jacket design and layout: Ron de Wilde
Text design and layout: Shael Anderson
Cartoonist: Christopher Miller

Dedication:

TO THE UNKNOWN TAXPAYER

Acknowledgments:

I am indebted to my associate Aaron Karp,
without whose capable reporting this book would not have been possible.
Special thanks also to my colleagues Daryl Gibson and Dale Van Atta
for valuable research and editing assistance
and to my partners Jan Moller and Michael Binstein
for their help in bringing an idea to fruition.

Table of Contents

INTRODUCTION TO WASHINGTON MONEY-GO-ROUND

THOMAS A. SCHATZ, PRESIDENT, CITIZENS AGAINST GOVERNMENT WASTE

The American people believe that more than half of the money they send to Washington simply goes down the drain, a perception that puts government waste near the top of every taxpayer's list of grievances. But it is rare that the profligate spending in the nation's capital are catalogued in a way that can be understood by everyone who bears the government's burden of taxes and regulation.

Over the past decade at Citizens Against Government Waste (CAGW), I have been privy to just about every story regarding excessive government spending, and I am almost never surprised by new abuses of our tax dollars. But my eyes were opened by the impressive litany of waste, fraud and abuse in "Washington Money-Go-Round."

As he has done so often in his 50 years of exposing scandals and waste in Washington, Jack Anderson has written in a manner that will entertain, enrage and enrapture readers. The raw nerve touched by "Washington Money-Go-Round" should get every American up off their couch and out onto the streets demanding that our elected officials end the insanity that will bankrupt our country.

I have been privileged to work with two American icons, J. Peter Grace and Jack Anderson. They co-founded CAGW over a decade ago to alert the country to the perils of government waste, abuse, fraud and mismanagement. For years, Peter and Jack shouted from the rooftops about what would happen if we didn't pay attention to the way Washington was misspending our money. Millions of taxpayers heard the message, and 600,000 joined our cause.

But the cause is much larger than a single organization—it affects each and every one of us. That's the case Jack makes in this book, and that's why it is required reading for anyone who cares about the fate of the United States.

Just who is responsible for the massive waste, fraud, abuse and mismanagement in the federal government—and the resulting deficits and debt? The answer to that question is fundamental to our children and grandchildren's future and will determine whether America will remain the world's foremost economic power.

This book is necessary for senior citizens who know that the benefits they are receiving through Social Security and Medicare won't be there for their children and grandchildren unless significant changes are instituted. It's vital for baby boomers, who were angered enough by the war in Vietnam to march in the streets, yet don't want to spend the time thinking about why both parents must work just so the salary of one can pay taxes. Boomers don't want to contemplate the fact that they are all guilty of child abuse by leaving a massive deficit and debt to their children and grandchildren. "Washington Money-Go-Round" is essential reading for Generation Xers, more of whom believe in UFOs than in Social Security, and who will never receive back from the government what they pay in taxes.

In example after example, "Washington Money-Go-Round" lays out what's wrong with the federal government's handling of our money. But more than that, the book challenges people to do something about the waste and tells them how to go about getting a better return on their tax "investment" in government.

CAGW, with Jack Anderson as its chairman, has for the past decade been saying that there are hundreds of billions of dollars going to waste each year in Washington. Certainly, I have confirmed that impression before audiences all over the country; when asked if they believe that the government can cut 25 percent of its budget without endangering the Republic, virtually no one disagrees. That would amount to $400 billion out of the $1.6 trillion annual budget. While that may seem like a massive number, it's no less than what many companies have done to survive amidst fierce international competition over the past several decades. And after reading "Washington Money-Go-Round," no one will doubt that improved stewardship of our tax dollars can go a long way toward achieving those savings.

The size of the problem was recently confirmed by the House Government Reform and Oversight Committee. In its September 1996 report, "Federal Government Management: Examining Government Performance as We Near the Next Century," the committee concluded that "public perceptions of pervasive waste, fraud and mismanagement in the Federal Government are unfortunately accurate." In short, the committee found that hundreds of billions of dollars are being wasted "in the near term on cost overruns, program delays, delinquent payments, loans, grants and unfulfilled contracts." The committee said that the fault lies in "[p]oor financial management, wasteful procurement and inventory practices, sloppy contract management, personnel abuses and manipulation of personnel rules, silly or even harmful rules and regulations."

By devoting greater resources to good management practices, and eliminating the waste, the federal government could save those hundreds of billions. "Washington Money-Go-Round" provides a blueprint to cut this waste and restore a positive vision for the future.

PROLOGUE

WELCOME TO
THE RAT RACE

O n the day that Thomas Jefferson was inaugurated third
president of the United States, he arose in a small Washington rooming house, dressed himself plainly and walked
like an ordinary citizen to the site of the inauguration ceremony.
There he delivered a speech whose themes were the subordination
of government to individual rights and the glorification of free
expression. Then he walked back to his boarding house.

When Jefferson entered the dining room, he found all seats at
the tables were occupied; no one was asked to give up a seat and
none offered. Accepting the democratic principle of first-come,
first-served, Jefferson went up to his room without his dinner.

He was not a clodhopper, unused to the amenities. He was one of the world's sophisticates, a man of wealth, the master of a great plantation. But in his public capacity, Jefferson was determined to set an example of simplicity and subservience. He presented himself not as the master, but as the servant of the people.

Sixty years later, this concept of the American republic was still sufficiently in vogue that a British ambassador could be shocked by coming upon Abraham Lincoln in the White House shining his own shoes. "In Britain, we don't shine our own shoes," the ambassador said.

"Well, whose shoes do you shine?" Lincoln responded.

Lincoln would often answer the White House door. He would travel on foot to the various departments of government to deliver his instructions and get their reports. For recreation he did not retire to kingly estates across the continent as did the czars, kaisers and recent presidents. During Lincoln's entire presidency, he spent only 55 days away from the White House, and most of those days were spent visiting the front. Lincoln contented himself with riding on horseback alone around Washington, unprotected, even though he had been shot at and knew men were out to kill him.

It was painful for Lincoln to refer to himself as "the president," and he would go through great circumlocutions to get around that phrase. He signed his letters "Your obedient servant." Though sometimes forced by events to assume almost dictatorial powers, he was one with Jefferson in glorifying not the government of majesty and omnipotence we see today, but, as every schoolchild knows, the government "of the people, by the people and for the people."

In my 50 years in Washington, I have seen little of that subservience among public "servants." Washington was all atwitter to behold Jimmy Carter walking down Pennsylvania Avenue to his inauguration in 1977. With dozens of limousines at the president's disposal, including the one that trailed him down the street that day, the gesture had more to do with image making than genuine humility.

There is still an occasional member of Congress who will sleep on a cot in his office rather than spend his money on a Capitol Hill apartment. But he can do that only because the taxpayers spend their money subsidizing the House gym where he showers and the dining hall where he eats and the parking lot where he keeps his car. There is little humility in the gesture, and no public penury in the end.

The common theme I have observed is one of aggrandizement and usurpation. The growth of material perquisites has become the sign of greater power over the public dollar. I thought, naively, that the madness had reached its peak during the Nixon administration. Picture Martha Mitchell, wife of Nixon's Attorney General John Mitchell, keeping her own office and staff, with FBI agents ironing her frocks and government limousines and chauffeurs at her beck, while her husband presided over the plan to break in, burglarize and wiretap law-abiding citizens.

Would that the insanity had ended with the shame and purging that resulted from the Watergate scandal. Instead, the disrespect for the American people lives on in profligate spending, creative excuses or even outright lies to cover malfeasance, and a federal government that reaches into far corners of our lives in a way that no founding father ever envisioned. The driving power behind it all is the primacy of re-election of the few over the welfare of the many.

Our $1.6 trillion federal budget is a monument to greed. There is the greed of politicians who spend your money in such a way that it guarantees their re-election. There is the greed of bureaucrats who will do anything to perpetuate their fiefdoms. And—please take this personally—there is the greed of everyday Americans who have become so soft on the government dole that they can't imagine going back to a world where people relied on themselves before they held out their upturned palm to Uncle Sam.

I am not ashamed to admit that as a lad I swallowed great doses of "simplistic" patriotism from which I still get periodic twinges. I was brought up to respect the government and its processes, but I was also taught the primacy of the spiritual over

7

the temporal and the importance of self-reliance and individual effort. We the people, by our own freedom of will, were supposed to place limits upon the proper sphere of government. We cultivated our natural skepticism toward the claims of omniscience and omnipotence which politicians are wont to make.

Our Founding Fathers were so repulsed by the notion of an omnipotent federal government that they devoted most of their deliberations on the Constitution to the subject of how to keep the president and the Congress out of your lives. They settled on the Tenth Amendment which mandates that any power not expressly given to the federal government in the Constitution belongs either to the states or the people.

What happened?

By degrees, we Americans got what we paid for—Big Government.

During the Watergate scandal, my colleagues at the Washington Post, Bob Woodward and Carl Bernstein, got some advice from their infamous source "Deep Throat": "Follow the money."

Those are words to live by for a journalist trying to get to the root of most stories. When historians write the tale of the 20th Century, they will find it was the money—the squandering of it, the manipulation of it, the love of it—that bought us the top-heavy nation the Founding Fathers feared.

Fifty years ago, I arrived in Washington to join the staff of the feared and respected political columnist Drew Pearson. He called his column the "Washington Merry-Go-Round." Neither he, nor later I, ever saw anything about the operation of the federal government that caused us to change the title. Yet Drew believed that informed people could make a change for the better. From him, I borrow my hope for the future and my title, "Washington Money-Go-Round."

CHAPTER ONE

WHAT GOES UP
DOESN'T ALWAYS COME DOWN

I've never met a milkman from Kansas City, but I've been writing to him for five decades. This mythical milkman is my American "everyman." I have visualized him and targeted my writing to him when I have attempted to explain the fumblings and bumblings of the federal government in my newspaper column. It is one tactic that has forced me to focus outside the Capital Beltway. (My apologies to the "milk-persons" of Kansas City and the "every-persons" of America, but I am an old man with old habits that are hard to break.)

My milkman wants to know what happens to his money when it arrives inside the Beltway, but he is hard pressed to find out. His representatives in Congress talk with bloated self-importance of "sequestration" and "supply-side economics" and "budget reconciliation" and "continuing resolutions." They brag about "budget cuts," but as far as the milkman can determine, the care and feeding of the federal government keeps getting more expensive. He is sure of that, even though he rarely sees any mention of the bottom line. Where did his taxes go and who made the decision?

Baaah-loney

There's some woolly reasoning going on in the Agriculture Department that's costing the taxpayers more than $5.5 million a year. It's called the "unshorn lamb" program and it pays sheep ranchers for each lamb they don't shear. (There's also a $40 million-a-year program to encourage production of wool, but that's another story.) The reasoning behind the unshorn-lamb program was that it kept the 'wool pulling' industry in business. Wool pullers strip the pelts off dead lambs. Trouble is, there are almost no wool pullers practicing these days, so the program is a big waste of money.

Washington Merry-Go-Round
November 29, 1982

My milkman figures if he can keep his own books straight, he ought to be able to understand his government's books. But the federal budget is not a family checking account, nor is it a big-business ledger.

If the federal apparatus were a family, the people spending the money would be the same people who sweat to earn it and their respect for the bottom line would be affected by their sweat. If this were a big business, the object would be making money for the shareholders, not serving the needs of 250 million people.

Instead, the federal budget is one-of-a-kind, the mother of all bank accounts. It amounts to about one-quarter of the total domestic economy every year. You could take just the amount that constitutes the federal debt, about $5 trillion, and buy up most of the private businesses in the nation.

There is no chief executive officer sitting atop this huge empire, nor is there a mother or father balancing a checkbook. When it comes to understanding how the federal budget works, the big secret is that no one is in charge. That's the way the Founding

Fathers designed it. They structured a system of checks and balances (although "balance" is a misnomer when it comes to the bottom line) between the president and Congress, allowing neither to dominate the process.

The Founding Fathers couldn't know that by 1996, 60 percent of the federal budget would be out of the control of Congress. That is the mandatory spending determined by promises made and debts incurred—Medicare, Medicaid, Social Security and interest payments on the national debt. The arduous annual congressional budget process covers only the remaining 40 percent, called "discretionary funding."

That process of discretionary spending begins in January of each year when the president painstakingly draws up his budget proposal. Abraham Lincoln might have had time to shine his own shoes, but the modern president is too busy running for re-election and making the world safe for democracy to attend to mundane chores, including writing the budget. Instead, he relies on the Office of Management and Budget to tell him where the money should be spent in the next fiscal year, which begins October 1. And the OMB relies on the various agencies of government to figure out how much money they will need to continue next year to do whatever it was they did last year.

The bureaucrats call this technique "current services" budgeting, or "if it ain't broke, don't fix it." Of course, the problem with this approach is that it frequently is broke, and there is little room in the process for introspection about possible repairs. Occasionally, if taxpayers raise a howl, the word will filter up to the president that the nation probably could get along without federal helium reserves or tree-planting grants for small businesses or a tea-tasting board, and the programs might be eliminated.

More often, the constituency that hovers around every government program—the people who stand to profit from its continuation ad infinitum—are the squeaky wheels that the politicians hear. My Kansas City milkman is no match for those lobbyists who inhabit "Gucci Gulch," the corridor outside the House Ways and Means Committee.

President Jimmy Carter had the not-so-novel idea that perhaps the federal government shouldn't base its budget on the assumption that current services are worth perpetuating. The notion of zero-based budgeting—starting from square one each year and having to make a fresh defense of every program—was making the rounds in the state and local governments where Carter had cut his teeth. As president, Carter decreed that the federal bureaucracy could jolly well do the same. The result was a nightmare of federal navel gazing that threatened to bring the bureaucracy to a grinding halt. Even the most rabid of budget reformers had to admit that the zero-based budgeting on a mammoth federal scale was unworkable. The bureaucrats responded with a blizzard of paperwork eagerly justifying their own jobs. Members of Congress—themselves experts at the practice of job retention—had neither the sophistication, nor the time, nor the political will to sort through the mess.

The bureaucracy gratefully returned to the current services method, well aware that it is a crude baseline on which to build a $1.6 trillion budget. How, for example, does one estimate what it will cost next year to replicate the same level of services provided by the military this year? Does the president consult with Saddam Hussein to make sure he has no plans to invade Kuwait next year? Do the Joint Chiefs of Staff ask the folks in Bosnia if they will all learn to live together peacefully next year? For that matter, can the Federal Reserve guarantee what interest rates will be next year or can the OMB promise a specific rate of inflation?

Grossly handicapped by the whims of the economy and the unpredictability of human nature, the president must nevertheless send his budget to Congress and, at that point, kiss his proposal goodbye.

The budget process on Capitol Hill resembles the Japanese kabuki dance. This is a traditional Japanese drama which can best be described as an elaborate pretense. The actors wear lavish wigs and makeup. They go through ostentatious motions, singing and dancing with stylized poses and gestures.

This is exactly how members of Congress perform when they prepare the federal budget. Like the kabuki dance, this annual ritual has become an art form—an elaborate performance that distorts reality. The congressional performers hide behind masks that put false faces on the facts. Their stylized statements and ritualistic movements are all part of the great pretense. But let me tell you what really goes on behind the scenes.

The president's budget, laden with necessity and fantasy, hits the halls of Congress in early February and is parceled out to the House and Senate Budget Committees for hearings. The important thing to remember here is that the president's numbers mean absolutely nothing. He has no power to spend your money. Only Congress can do that.

> ### Congress vs. common sense: match-point
>
> During the grueling budget debate, members of Congress had a lot on their minds—like whether to cut medical care for the elderly or day care for infants, and by the way, where to put their new tennis court. The Senate already has a tennis court in the Dirksen Senate Office Building. But the poor members of the House don't have any place to practice their ground strokes on the taxpayers' dime. Apparently a few members of Congress decided it was time to remedy the situation. They have ordered the architect of the Capitol to draw up plans for a House tennis court, either in the courtyard of one building in the Capitol complex or on the roof of another.
>
> *Washington Merry-Go-Round*
> *October 30, 1990*

The way Congress doles out the money is so baffling as to discourage all but those driven by profit motive from participating in or even following the process. The budget committees in each chamber scribble numbers all over the president's budget, send it to the House and Senate floors for passage, put their heads together to merge the House and Senate versions, and then pass a "concurrent budget resolution." At this point it is mid-April and the budget still means next to nothing. Congress has decided what it would like to spend money on and put a limit on how much money it will spend. Incredibly, Congress hasn't actually authorized the spending of the money, and the president never signs this resolution. Yet already you folks outside the Beltway are being pelted with verbiage from your representatives on Capitol Hill taking credit for championing vital services to your community and slashing wasteful spending on other communities.

In phase two, the budget resolution is turned over to an array of congressional committees with authority over various agencies. These committees debate whether the money proposed in the budget resolution will actually be spent on the programs as suggested. They write authorizing bills that the House and Senate must pass and send to the president for his signature. For example, the House and Senate Armed Services Committees decide which Pentagon programs will be funded for the coming year. Then those committees draft the bill that okays the spending. Still the budget process is not finished. The agencies of government don't yet have the right to draw money out of the federal till.

In phase three, the House and Senate Appropriations Committees and their subcommittees review each of the authorization bills passed in phase two and decide how much of the money each of the lucky programs will actually receive. The appropriations committees have the real power in the process. In spite of all the dealing and dickering that has gone before, these committees can decide to fund programs that have not been authorized or to leave approved programs high and dry without any money. This conveniently allows your senator or representative to take credit for approving a federal goody for you and at the same time vote against funding for that goody.

The edicts of the appropriations committees are sent to the full House and Senate for approval as separate bills divided by functions (for example, an education appropriations bill) and then to the president for his signature. Now we have a budget.

The meanderings that began with the president's budget proposal can thus be summarized in terms a family can understand:

Phase One: The Anderson family budgets $2,000 for a vacation this year.

Phase Two: The family decides to go to Disney World.

Phase Three: The Andersons decide we can afford to take only three of our nine children and we vote on who must stay home. (In the wondrous world of federal budgeting, the family would borrow enough money to take everyone and let the grandchildren pay it back later.)

As complex as the whole process is, it has been worse. Before 1974, appropriations subcommittees considered the budget wish lists of the agencies they governed. The decisions of all the subcommittees were then thrown into a hopper and—voila!—a federal budget. This would be the same as all nine Anderson children writing individual letters to Santa and then sending my wife, Olivia, and me to Toys-"Я"-Us to fill the orders, no questions asked. It may happen that way in some families, but it's no way to run a family or a government.

The Congressional Budget and Impoundment Control Act of 1974 reordered the process to begin with budget committees in the House and Senate and filter down from there. The filter of committees can be both a blessing and a curse. Democracy demands a high level of input to make sure the majority is kept happy. But the sad history of the American budget has been that more input means higher spending.

Up until 1877, the spending authority in Congress was kept tightly in the hands of one appropriations committee in each house. Then, in a series of laws, Congress decided to parcel out the decision making to the special interest committees with jurisdiction over individual functions of government. It wasn't quite the equivalent of giving the fox the keys to the henhouse; it was more like giving the hens the keys to the grain silo. The committee members tended to develop mild to severe cases of "clientitis"—a propensity to look fondly on the programs they supervised. These special-interest committees were more likely to insist on bigger funding for their pet projects than the appropriations committees that had looked at the big picture had suggested.

By the turn of the century, the new system was breaking the budget. Spending went through the ceiling. Seeing the error of its ways, the House went back to a single committee system in 1920 and the Senate followed suit in 1922. For the next decade, Uncle Sam operated in the black. But in a series of budget "reforms" beginning in the 1930s, the spending authority began to be dispersed again. As a result, today 17 committees have some right to determine how your money is spent.

The 1974 reform law tried to give that power back to the budget committees, but the real wheeling and dealing still goes on in the appropriations subcommittees, and they still suffer from costly clientitis.

The 1974 act also created the Congressional Budget Office (CBO) so members of Congress could have a staff of their own number crunchers to tell them when the president's number crunchers at OMB were trying to pull a fast one. The new law also imposed a timetable on the whole process. Without a calendar, Congress occasionally let the decisions slide into the next fiscal year. While Congress dickered, agencies went ahead with business as usual, spending money that hadn't been authorized on programs that hadn't been approved.

The law now forces Congress to meet deadlines, or at to least go through legal contortions to get around those deadlines while the taxpayers look on in horror at the spectacle of a federal government on the brink of default. If Congress can't reach agreement on a budget by October 1, the federal equivalent of New Year's Day, then it can pass temporary "continuing resolution" laws to keep business running as usual without a formal budget in place for the fiscal year. Or Congress can choose as it did twice in 1995 and 1996 to shut down the government—tell all but essential employees to go home because nobody has the authority to pay the bills.

Each side in the partisan budget battle hopes such a drastic measure will force the other side to its knees. More often than not, the ones forced to their knees by a brief government shutdown are the outsiders—the little contractor who counts on a steady stream

Who's watching the waste watchers?

Is there no endeavor of the federal government so intrinsically worthwhile that it can't be perverted into yet another wasteful boondoggle? Apparently not. Recent reports from the President's Council on Management Improvement say the government spent $250 million and 5,800 staff years in 1984 identifying areas of potential waste, fraud and abuse—but the great bulk of the areas had already been identified in routine internal checks by the agencies involved. It's fine to watch waste, but who's watching the waste watchers?

Washington Merry-Go-Round
June 13, 1996

of payments from the federal government to keep a business afloat, or the welfare mother waiting for news about a government job, or the family that drove from Florida to Washington only to find that the Smithsonian museums were closed for the week. Members of Congress still get their paychecks, bureaucrats get a few days off for which they will be paid later when the budget is finally approved, and the average taxpayer learns just how easy it is to get along without the federal government.

Ideally, the tortured process comes to a merciful end long before October 1, and once again the wheels of the federal government are greased for another year.

CHAPTER TWO

BALANCING THE CHECKBOOK

The American ideal has always been this: that we will leave our children a better life than we had.

Mine is the first generation of Americans to violate that trust. It began innocently enough in 1981 with an optimistic new president who told us we could have more without paying more.

I liked Ronald Reagan personally and voted for him twice. After the cheerless and demoralizing Carter administration when America seemed awash in inflation and overshadowed by indecision, I warmed to Reagan's "Morning in America" attitude. We could cut taxes, put people to work, restore our reputation as a superpower, and stare down the "Evil Empire" of communism, all without breaking a sweat.

It seemed almost miraculous the way Reagan turned the nation around in the 1980s. Yet in the end it was no miracle at all. The Republican president and Democratic Congress put it all on a credit card. We knew it was happening, but we were enjoying it too much to protest.

The national debt—the total amount still owed by Uncle Sam from past borrowing—was $785 billion when Jimmy Carter left office. The deficit—the difference between what Uncle Sam collected in taxes and what he spent—was $79 billion in Carter's last budget. His claim to fame may be that he was the last president who gave us a deficit that could be expressed in double digits and a national debt that was only billions. Reagan's average budget deficit was more than $180 billion. When he left office in a blaze of popular adulation, the national debt was $2.6 trillion. No wonder it was such a great party!

Then we woke up to "Morning in America" with a hangover. Congress, under Democratic management, not only cut the taxes and appropriated the money that Reagan requested but rejected spending cuts that he also requested.

Today the debt ceiling, the amount of debt Congress has given itself the right to accumulate, is $5.5 trillion. We should reach that ceiling by the end of 1997, and then Congress will have to vote itself a longer line of credit. If the debt were evenly divided among Americans to pay back today, your family's share would be $40,000.

In 1996 the federal government spent $1.6 trillion to do its job. That's 1.6 plus 11 zeros. It is nearly impossible for the average person to fathom that much money. Congress counts on that bafflement to keep you from screaming, "Enough!"

If the total federal budget were counted in miles instead of dollars, it would take us from the Sun to Pluto, round trip, 222 times with more than 15 million miles left over for getting lost. Looked at as a slice of the total U.S. economy, the money spent by Uncle Sam in a year is 22.3 percent of the total output. When you add state and local government spending, the bureaucracy accounts for 35 percent of the gross domestic product.

A national credit report

Debt and deficit spending were not invented in the 1980s. The Revolutionary War left the United States nearly $75 million in debt. The War of 1812 brought the total to $123 million. These were big numbers for a new nation, but borrowing to finance war was not unheard of, nor was it considered rash.

By 1835 the debt was paid off. In fact, the Treasury had a $19 million surplus and a big problem. There was no provision in the Constitution for disposing of excess funds. Congress couldn't simply cut taxes to compensate the people. There were no income taxes until 1915. Uncle Sam got what little money he needed in those days from selling public lands in the West and levying customs duties.

Within two years after paying off the war debts, the government had nearly $40 million burning a hole in its pocket. Congress decided to spread the money out among the states. They had to call it loans because the Constitution had not allowed for block grants, but the states were not expected to repay the money.

Too bad, because Uncle Sam could have used it later. Along came the Civil War and, for the first time, the national debt had to be counted in billions instead of millions. With prudent post-war budgets, the $3 billion debt was slowly reduced to less than $1 billion before the start of World War I. But the U.S. debt was never again zeroed out. World War I left us $31 billion in the hole; the Great Depression made it $43 billion; World War II put us $242 billion in the red. (Here's an eye opener: The total accumulated debt at the end of that war was just about the same as the amount Uncle Sam borrowed in 1996 alone, which was $241 billion.)

The debt has grown steadily in this century, but payments on the debt, when seen as a percentage of the gross domestic product, did not consistently outrun the booming economy, at least not until the 1980s.

"Supply-side economics" was the buzz that resounded so pleasantly in our ears in those days. There were a few spoil-sports, like George Bush who called it "voodoo economics," but we ignored him and eventually he became a convert too. When he left office, the total debt was $3.3 trillion.

Here is the crux of supply-side economics: If you cut tax rates, the economy will respond with such boundless enthusiasm that the federal Treasury will overflow with the bounty from more people working and making more money and paying more taxes. Reagan's economists were telling us we could have more for less.

The endless parade of chinless leaders

Why can't Congress simply cut the waste from the federal budget and eliminate the deficit? Fiscal enemy No. 1 is the bureaucracy. Bureaucrats rarely solve problems. That would eliminate their jobs. Instead they study and perpetuate problems. Fiscal enemy No. 2 is the leadership. Political leaders at all levels refuse to make hard decisions that might pain their special constituencies. They put off needed remedies until the next person's term, and the next person has no more courage than the last.

Washington Merry-Go-Round
July 20, 1990

The tax cuts came so fast and furiously in the early months of the Reagan administration that Americans, especially wealthy America and corporate America, had their heads spinning with delight. In three years, Reagan cut individual income taxes by 25 percent and thus deprived the Treasury of $754.4 billion. David Stockman, Reagan's budget director, had the job of coming up with spending cuts to match the tax cuts. It wasn't an easy task given the fact that the president never met a military appropriation that he didn't like and was also loath to mess with Social Security. Most of what Stockman unveiled as budget cuts turned out to be smoke and mirrors.

Stockman looked back on the fiasco years later and called himself an "incubator of shortcuts, schemes and devices to overcome the truth." If the numbers couldn't be made to crunch by themselves, then the Reagan accountants simply changed their economic projections and based their anticipated savings on the best of all possible outcomes. Thus was born the ever-cheerful budget baby, "Rosy Scenario."

Those optimistic forecasts were necessary to mask the amount of money Reagan was pouring into the Pentagon to break the back of the Soviet Union. The reason the United States won the Cold War was not military superiority. It was the illusion of might, an illusion purchased with borrowed money. Quite simply, we didn't outfight the Soviets; we outspent them.

When Reagan was president, I had occasional access to the White House. I remember now—and look back with more cynicism than I had then—how he explained to me his strategy of winning World War III without firing a shot. Reagan's advisors had told him that the Soviet Union was on the skids financially and that one more push would break the "Evil Empire." The president's weapon was one that never worked, was never fired, was never even tested. Yet the illusion of a threat was enough. The weapon was the costly Strategic Defense Initiative, or "Star Wars," a fantastical Rambo in space that could, according to its billing, disable whatever the Soviets launched at us.

Under Reagan the Pentagon was not above falsifying some of its reports on the potential of the Star Wars system just to spook the Soviets. It worked. The Soviets broke their own economy trying to keep up with us in the arms race. Even after Soviet leader Mikhail Gorbachev decided it was time for his country to drop out of the race, his military commanders went on spending the money anyway.

With hindsight it is easy, perhaps even correct, to say that the Soviet Union would have collapsed eventually anyway. The inherent folly of communism would have brought down the economy without the pressure of an arms race. What the arms race did was leave Russia so distressed and unstable that its recovery is still uncertain.

It didn't leave the United States in the black either because voodoo economics never delivered on its promises. Given the track record of supply-side thinking under Reagan, it was folly for presidential candidate Bob Dole to promise a 15 percent across-the-board income tax cut during his 1996 campaign without an equal cut in spending. Those who favor tax cuts at any cost dusted off their old Rosy Scenarios and tried to prove that supply-side economics would work if given another chance. Sad experience should teach us that whenever a politician begins to talk of tax cuts, without specifying an equal amount in enforced spending cuts, then rationalizing will soon follow. When you hear the words "supply-side," you may assume the speaker is in deep denial.

Cooking the books, Washington style

There is a popular misconception that Reagan did, in fact, cut spending. Any president or member of Congress can boast that they have cut spending, even as you watch the total budget shoot through the ceiling. Blame it on the current services method of budgeting—the method by which next year's budget is projected based on this year's budget plus a slight increase for inflation.

For example, if a particular program cost $80 billion to run this year, then it might cost $85 billion to run in the same fashion next year. But the president submits a budget saying he can run the program for $83 billion instead. Presto! He has just "cut" the budget by $2 billion. By the same magic, if the president's budget asks for $85 billion, but Congress finally agrees to only $83 billion, it's a budget "cut," even though you, the taxpayers, will be asked to come up with $3 billion more.

Some government economists have even figured out how to call a deficit a surplus. They figure if the deficit is, say, $200 billion, but the interest on the debt that same year is $220 billion, Uncle Sam is actually spending $20 million less on real operations than he gets in revenues. Another budget cut! That may allow an economist to sleep better at night, but for us average taxpayers, our government is still $220 billion deeper in the hole.

While Ronald Reagan was enjoying the twilight of his administration, the illusion of budget cuts began to fade and Congress slapped itself in the face. Thus was born the Balanced Budget and Emergency Deficit Control Act of 1985, better known by the names of its sponsors, the Gramm-Rudman-Hollings Act. This much ballyhooed law set a worthy goal: By 1991 Uncle Sam would clean up his act and no longer spend more money than he took in. (The last year he had done that was 1969, but that was strictly sleight of hand. That year Congress decided to count the Social Security Trust Fund as regular tax revenue so they could hide the fact that the Vietnam War was running up the debt.)

Gramm-Rudman set specific, dwindling deficit ceilings for every year through 1991 (later hedged to 1993) and laid down the law: If the ceiling is breached, then Congress will have to make across-the-board spending cuts. That was called "sequestration," a fancy term meaning "Nobody gets any money until we figure out how to balance the budget." Lawmakers patted themselves on the back and took credit for having won the deficit battle. End of discussion.

Unfortunately, there were a few things that Congress hadn't anticipated, like the savings and loan bailout, and the Persian Gulf War, and the unpredictable ups and downs of the economy. Oh yes, there was also the one big thing that lawmakers chose to ignore—their inability to control their own profligate spending habits. Every year, Congress and the White House found ways to inflate the means. They danced delicately around the deficit targets they had so proudly hailed in

Snow-job

Scientists at Kirtland Air Force Base, N.M., recently attended an annual three-day "ski conference" at Snowbird Mountain, Utah. The bill—$9,100 for the 14 people attending, at $650 a head—was picked up by the Air Force Weapons Laboratory. The ostensible purpose of the junket was to attend a conference on quantum space electronics conducted by two professors from the Universities of Arizona and New Mexico. But the daily schedule left plenty of time for the slopes: Breakfast at 7 a.m., conference program at 7:30 a.m., skiing at 11 a.m. Dinner came 6 1/2 hours later, followed by another business meeting at 7:30 p.m.

Washington Merry-Go-Round
February 7, 1984

Gramm-Rudman. They projected rosy revenues. They removed the cost of the savings and loan bailout and the Postal Service debts from the books. They borrowed from the Social Security Trust Fund and called it revenue. They paid the military one day early on the last day of the fiscal year so the expense wouldn't appear in the new year's budget.

The lesson of Gramm-Rudman was that fixing a deficit target is a bad joke. The economy is simply much more powerful and capricious than the great minds of Congress can contemplate. It is the real dog, and the federal government is merely the tail that gets wagged. To assume that the tail can control the economic dog is folly.

Senator Phil Gramm called the law that bore his name "a bad idea whose time has come." But by 1990 it was obvious Gramm-Rudman was a foolish idea whose time had come and gone. That year Congress scrapped Gramm-Rudman and passed the Budget Enforcement Act (BEA) with a more realistic premise—that Congress could only be held accountable for the things it could control, the discretionary spending programs. It cannot control entitlement spending such as Social Security or Medicare because that would mean mandating how many people are allowed to grow old or get sick.

BEA looks at the budget as two parts. There are discretionary programs; BEA put spending limits on those to keep Congress from borrowing more money to rachet up the programs. And there are "PAYGO" (pay-as-you-go) programs, such as Social Security, which are supposed to pay for themselves through earmarked taxes. Under BEA, if Congress wants to be more generous with entitlements, like awarding increased retirement benefits or higher Medicare reimbursement, it must pay for its generosity with new taxes in the same year. In other words, entitlements must be "deficit neutral." BEA doesn't reduce entitlement spending. It just keeps Congress from borrowing money to pay for it. Under BEA, discretionary spending has dropped about two points as a percentage of the total economy. That has been the price we pay to carry the burden of entitlements.

In spite of Gramm-Rudman and BEA, the deficit continued to rise, outpacing the rosy projections every year. Take 1991 for example. The original Gramm-Rudman law proclaimed that by then the deficit would be zeroed out. A "Son of Gramm-Rudman" amendment added a little breathing room and said the 1991 deficit would be only $64 billion. Then the BEA said $245 billion would be more realistic. But, in reality, the deficit that year was $270 billion. So much for good intentions.

The deficit has come down slightly during the Clinton administration, but that has had little to do with self-control and more to do with inevitable cuts in the defense budget after the Cold War, the sale of assets from defunct savings and loans, and economic growth.

The current mandate in Congress is to balance the budget by 2002, an admirable goal that is once again based on an unrealistic assumption: that Congress can set an arbitrary deadline for a balanced budget and somehow wag the economic dog. Another built-in assumption that has proven unworkable is that the two major political parties can agree on enough budget cuts to reach balance. Their bickering in the 104th Congress led to two partial shutdowns of the government and a budget that was finally approved six months into the fiscal year.

There is no reason to believe that even if Congress did manage to achieve a balanced budget in the magic year of 2002, it would stay balanced, especially with the pending retirement of the baby boom generation that will overwhelm the Social Security and Medicare budgets.

Do we really need a balanced budget?

All borrowing is not equal. There are good deficits and bad deficits. A bad deficit is one that outpaces the economy as a whole. That never happened to the United States during a period of peace and prosperity until the 1980s. Like a family that borrows more than it can responsibly repay, we have become less creditworthy.

Economists don't like it when someone compares federal deficit spending to a family bank account. In part they are correct in saying the two are apples and oranges. A family that takes out a mortgage for a new house or a company that borrows money to build a new plant is not engaging in deficit spending. It is making an investment. The family members hope the house will serve their needs, save them rent in the long run, and then turn a profit when they sell it. A company works on the assumption that the new plant will increase productivity and allow business to grow.

Even state and city governments don't call it "deficit spending" when they issue bonds (go into debt) to build new schools or run utility lines to new neighborhoods. They call it "capital improvement." And the capital budget is never mixed with the operating budget. That is why you don't hear much talk of deficit spending at the city council meetings. Your city is in debt, but that debt is kept in a separate set of books.

The federal government doesn't have the same luxury. There is no such thing as a capital budget when Uncle Sam wants to build a new interstate highway or a battleship. It comes out of the operating budget, and if that means borrowing money, then the government is said to be operating in the red. Thus some borrowing makes sense.

The problem is, Uncle Sam has borrowed far beyond the limit that can be justified for capital improvements. When the family starts running up the credit card for groceries, when the CEO takes out a loan to pay salaries, that is deficit spending.

Breaking out part of the federal budget as a capital account is not as easy as it sounds. Some things that pass for investment on the federal level would not be considered investments in a home or business. A federally funded research project or jobs program may be an investment in that it may boost the economy, but you can't

Royal rip-off

Perhaps the most incredible case [of Medicare fraud] is that of the 'Welfare Queen' of Illinois. Investigators have found that she first posed as a surgeon and billed the state for performing an open heart operation. Then she turned around and posed as the heart patient and collected for paying her phony doctor bill. Finally, she submitted a bill for an additional $16 a day as the heart patient's private nurse.

Washington Merry-Go-Round
April 14, 1975

depreciate research or jobs on the books. Plus, much of the capital investment the federal government pays for, including highways and other infrastructure, doesn't ultimately belong to Uncle Sam but is turned over to state and local governments. That's another barrier to carrying the expense as a capital investment on the federal books.

The General Accounting Office has offered one solution that may be almost too fine a tool for politicians who are more comfortable with the blunt-instrument approach to spending. The accountants at the GAO think Congress could differentiate between "consumption spending" and "investment spending." The first burns money to meet an immediate need, such as food stamps. The second makes a difference for the long haul, such as a high-tech research lab. But in our lawmakers' haste to oil the squeaky wheel, the quick fixes often get preference over real solutions.

Federal debts are also different from family or corporate debts in that the money circulates within its own system—the giant U.S. economy. If a family or a company borrows money, it must go outside itself to do that. Someone else gets the interest. But with federal debt, we are both the borrowers and the lenders. We, the taxpayers, borrow the money and repay it later with interest. We are also the lenders, the private citizens who buy Treasury bonds. If we, the lenders, want to cash in our bonds, then we, the borrowers, ante up more taxes to pay ourselves back. The amount of money in circulation remains the same and is not lost to the American economy as a whole. (The exception is when the lenders are foreigners and the interest paid to them goes back home with them.)

Deficit spending can be your friend, but it's a friend you don't want hanging around year after year. By spending more than it collects, the government can infuse the economy with the stimulus it might need to snap out of the doldrums. Thus stimulated, the economy theoretically would generate more activity which would produce bigger profits and higher wages which would increase tax payments. The Congressional Budget Office estimates that every percentage point of unemployment will add $50 billion to the deficit. So spending more to create jobs may pay dividends in the long run.

On the other hand—and I have heard it said there is no such thing as a one-handed economist—reducing the deficit is the best move the government can make to increase private savings which lead to private investments which stimulate the economy. The United States consistently lags behind its international trading partners in the level of private investments. Twenty years ago, private investments accounted for 17 percent of our gross domestic product. Now it is down to 14 percent and dropping. This can be attributed, in no small measure, to the appalling amount of money tied up in federal debt. The statistics may be mind-numbing, but the result is stark enough—degraded quality of life for our children.

From deferred tax to economic dampener, the deficit as a vicious circle

With an open line of credit, the federal government has no incentive to spend prudently. And if anyone needed to shop around for bargains, it's Uncle Sam, who is losing 14 percent of his budget every year to interest on his debts. Federal borrowing ties up a significant portion of the U.S. economy in relatively nonproductive, noncreative pursuits—bureaucracy, waste, welfare, interest. More of your money ends up in the hands of Congress instead of being left in your wallet to spend at your discretion. This federalizing of the national wealth puts a damper on the creativity, enthusiasm, ambition and innovation of the private sector. We are all homogenized by one, great, government spending machine.

A deficit is simply a deferred tax. The more we borrow now, the more our children and grandchildren will be spending as interest on our debt rather than putting their money into the programs they will need to maintain their quality of life. We are asking them to pay tomorrow for the frills we are not willing to give up today.

Worse, Uncle Sam is the most upstanding borrower in the bank and he crowds the others out. Imagine a line of companies, entrepreneurs and individuals waiting for approval of loans for the most admirable of causes—new construction, capital investment, local schools—all things that would be a shot in the arm to the economy. Then along comes Uncle Sam who has the full faith and credit of the taxpayers backing every penny he borrows. Sam goes to the head of the line and others don't get their money. There is a finite amount of money in the American economy to be loaned, and every cent that the federal government borrows is another penny lost to private borrowers.

With open-ended authority to borrow and spend, the federal bureaucracy, it would seem, has forgotten what it means to be thrifty. For example, President Clinton's Labor Department, under Secretary Robert Reich, decided in 1995 to encourage baby boomers to save more money for retirement. (The irony of the federal government telling the taxpayers that they aren't saving enough money was apparently lost on Secretary Reich.) Thus was launched the "Retirement Savings Education Campaign," which by some estimates may have cost you taxpayers as much as $2 million.

The government bought advertising on billboards and television and in newspapers. A public relations firm was paid $250,000 to come up with ideas. The Labor Department spent $8,000 just to move a stage to enhance television coverage of the kickoff event at which Secretary Reich complained, "Americans are not saving

How to get paid hard cash for doing hard time

It is no secret that the Social Security system has been milked dry to pay all the benefits that Congress keeps adding. But there is something that the Social Security Administration would prefer to keep secret: It pays out millions of dollars each year in disability and survivor benefits to convicts . . . An inmate at the Indiana State Reformatory, for example, was convicted of murdering his 5-year-old stepdaughter and sentenced to life imprisonment. In 1968 he applied for Social Security disability benefits on the grounds that his record rendered him unfit for society and he was therefore unable to work. He has received some $12,000 a year for the past 12 years.

Washington Merry-Go-Round
June 2, 1980

enough." All the money for this boondoggle came from the department's Pension and Welfare Benefits Administration, which at the same time was slashing its budget to investigate fraud in your private pension funds.

Similarly, when Vice President Al Gore published his report on reinventing government, the printers used expensive glossy paper and three colors of ink. The standard government printing job is done on recycled paper with one ink. The fancy printing came to nearly $170,000. The normal cost would have been about $55,000. And the name of that report? "Creating a Government that Works Better and Costs Less."

Small wonder that Americans are panicky about deficit spending. Their money is no longer just bleeding; it's hemorrhaging. Before they are bled dry, they've raised a howl that is reverberating in Washington.

This has created an unhappy predicament for the politicians who inhabit the temples of government. For decades they've hustled votes by heaping more and more benefits on their constituents. Now the burden of all these benefits is too heavy for the taxpayers to continue bearing.

But the politicians can't take back the benefits, which have now become entitlements in the public mind. By cutting entitlements, politicians risk antagonizing large blocs of voters who have become accustomed to those benefits.

As always, our elected leaders would prefer, if they could get away with it, to postpone any painful problems until the next fellow's term. But, increasingly, the budget pressures can't be put off. When all the postponements run out on them, the politicians invariably attack the budget with a meat ax, slashing numbers but avoiding specifics, so they can escape blame for cutting anyone's particular benefits.

These across-the-board cuts leave it to the bureaucrats, who are being cut, to decide what to cut. They become surly over the cutbacks, which threaten their status quo. So they usually keep their wants and cut the public's needs—a process that slashes too much muscle and leaves too much fat.

Then it's the citizens' turn to become surly. But they feel powerless to stop official mismanagement and misconduct; they become apathetic and succumb to the notion that nothing can be done about it anyway. More and more is left to the authorities, but no one trusts them to perform.

Voters who are turned off usually don't turn out. This increases the alienation between politicians and voters. Candidates can't afford to court voters who don't vote. So the candidates turn to the special interests, which have axes to grind and cash registers to tend in Washington. Those who finance politics expect a return on their investments. Thus members of Congress can no longer support an issue just because they believe it's right. They can't afford to alienate their backers whose power over them increases as citizens withdraw from the democratic process.

Is the situation, then, hopeless? Of course not. But the first thing citizens must do, in the words of the late Lyndon Johnson, is "lift up the cow's tail and look the situation straight in the face."

CHAPTER THREE

A DOLLAR IS A TERRIBLE THING TO WASTE

M y father, Orlando Anderson, was too busy keeping his family afloat to dabble in politics. It's a shame because he knew what to do when he got hold of someone else's money.

A friend told me of encountering my father on a Salt Lake City street corner one snowy holiday evening. Dad was toting a Christmas tree on his shoulder and glaring at the change in his hand. "That fool gave me 25 cents too much," my father grumbled. "Now I've got to go all the way back to return it."

Imagine an assembly of the president's Cabinet when they look over the tax receipts for the year. The president shakes his head and grumbles, "Those fools gave us $25 billion too much. Now we've got to give it back."

Contrast that fantasy with this reality.

In 1989 Congress appropriated $8 million to build schools for Jewish refugees who left North Africa to settle in Paris. Senator Daniel Inouye of Hawaii put the Parisian schools in the federal budget that year because one of his campaign contributors asked him to. It was that simple. Congressman David Obey of Wisconsin, chairman of the House committee that agreed to the expense, defended it in the spirit of compromise.

"It was only a lousy $8 million," Obey said.

A lousy $8 million?

Yes, but it was my lousy $8 million, and yours, and hundreds of other Americans'. My entire tax bill and the taxes paid by a good share of my community in the Washington, D.C. suburbs were flushed down the toilet with that one wasteful appropriation. At least they would have been, had Congress not been shamed into rescinding the appropriation after a public outcry.

Instead, my money probably paid for first-class airline tickets for cows that were flown to Europe that year in an "Export Enhancement Program." Or I might have paid for part of the cost of a $25,000 study to find the best spot to build a new workout gym for congressional staffers. Or my taxes may have paid for a going-away party for a regional Federal Reserve bigwig. It's also possible that my taxes went straight to the federal accountants—the worker bees who ferret out all the possible ways the government can waste money. They need about $200 million a year to fund that search.

I don't know how much Congressman Obey pays in annual taxes, but I'm sure it doesn't amount to a lousy $8 million. So where do he and so many of his fellow lawmakers come up with the boneheaded idea that $8 million is chump change?

Sadly, it is the conclusion they reach mindlessly when they have $1.6 trillion to spend every year. Think again of the total budget as 222 round trips from the Sun to Pluto. That lousy $8 million wouldn't get us one-fourth of the way to Mercury, the closest planet to the Sun. The taxes paid by the average American would barely get our rocket off the launching pad.

What combination of carelessness, arrogance and fuzzy-headedness has brought our Congress to the point where a million dollars wasted here or a million dollars misspent there is not worth breaking a sweat? The same lawmakers who crow when they pass a tax break that puts $8 back in your pocket will dismiss $8 million with the wave of a hand.

Postcards from Porkville

The culture of waste is so pervasive that it permeates even the smallest corners of the bureaucracy. It is trickle-down economics at its worst. Here are just a few of the ways your tax dollars have been squandered and mismanaged. I've plucked these examples at random from the massive waste pile that lies stinking under the noonday sun:

• The Secret Service is in charge of tracking down counterfeiters of U.S. currency; but those federal agents aren't talking about one of the most devastating counterfeit print runs ever that stemmed from sheer political stupidity. Counterfeit $100 bills, called supernotes because of their high quality, are floating around the world, threatening the stability of the dollar overseas. These notes are so good that the Federal Reserve, which normally makes American banks swallow the loss when they mistakenly accept a fake bill, is reimbursing the banks for these.

Why are these supernotes so convincing? Because they come off U.S. Mint printing presses given to Iran before Islamic fundamentalists overthrew our ally, the Shah of Iran.

The Shah wanted to print pretty money. President Richard Nixon and his major domo, Henry Kissinger, catered to the Shah's every whim because he was controlling oil prices for them and their friends in the oil business. So when the Shah asked for a high-quality currency press, he got one. He also got American master engravers to train Iranian printers—tradesmen who were left behind when the Shah fled Iran and the Ayatollah Khomeini took over. Since then, $100 bills printed on those presses have been used to finance the Iranian war of terrorism against the United

States. The bills circulate widely in the former republics and satellites of the old Soviet Union where the Iranians do much of their weapons shopping.

It wasn't until the early 1990s that U.S. officials figured out what was going on. The recent redesign of the $100 bill is in part a campaign to thwart the counterfeiters, but it is too little too late to save the taxpayers from the expense of making good on the bad bills.

• Millions of dollars each year are lost in the ether because Congress refuses to stand up to a loud group of Cuban-Americans in Florida. The money is squandered on TV Marti, a U.S. Information Agency TV station that keeps trying, but failing, to broadcast propaganda to Cuba. TV Marti's signal has always been jammed and will always be jammed by Fidel Castro who is having the last laugh. No matter what technology USIA uses to broadcast the signal, it is lost. USIA wants to spend $1.2 million to switch from VHF to UHF in yet another attempt to outsmart Castro, but it won't work. Castro can get more jamming equipment with little effort and cost. TV Marti lives on because Cuban-American activists who want to harass Castro at any cost have intimidated Congress and the White House.

> ### *The toast of waste town*
>
> Slippery fingers cost the government hundreds of thousands of dollars. According to one internal survey, 48,000 pieces of government glassware are broken each year. These cost the taxpayers $127,000. And $100,000 worth of glassware vanishes each year.
>
> *Washington Merry-Go-Round*
> *April 12, 1979*

• During a four-year period of the Reagan administration, for each $1 spent on housing projects for the poor, the hard-up tenants saw only 34 cents in benefits. During the same time span, the Department of Housing and Urban Development decided to classify Beverly Hills as a "distressed" city eligible for federal aid because more than 20 percent of the housing stock there was built before 1940. They may call that "distressed" in Allentown, but in Beverly Hills, that's called "old money."

• A group of Justice Department attorneys inspected their new offices in 1994 and pitched a fit over what they discovered. The new digs were 30 square feet smaller than their old offices. So the never-used offices were ripped out and rebuilt. The cost of the reconstruction, plus the rental of temporary quarters for the petulant lawyers, was $237,000. Creating a suitable work space for this bunch didn't stop there. The taxpayers bought them a $5,000 mahogany planter to decorate the lobby. The office boss had a personal bathroom in his office, but his new water heater stopped working. The heater had been sealed behind a tile wall, but the plumber offered to take out the tiles, fix the heater, and install an access door for future repairs, all at no charge. No thanks, the bureaucrats said. The access door would look "chintzy." So a brand new heater was installed in a nearby closet for $1,680. (By the way, these were bankruptcy lawyers.)

• In 1994 Congress appropriated $15 million to build a foot-bridge from New Jersey to Ellis Island, the gateway for millions of immigrants at the turn of the century. The reason for the bridge was to save tourists the $6 it takes to ride the ferry.

• The United States owns 3,000 pieces of property in foreign countries. The real estate is worth about $12 billion, and some of it is ripe for selling. For example, in Tokyo one of the U.S. Embassy residences was appraised at about $92 million in 1990. The State Department estimates it could replace the house with a new one for $3.8 million. Okay, that still sounds like high living for a government servant, but I'm willing to take savings wherever I can find them. In spite of being told repeatedly about the potential for big real estate profits from its Tokyo holdings, Congress hasn't bothered to sell the old house.

• The National Endowment for the Arts gave an "artist" more than $6,000 for a film of people throwing paper and burning gasses out of airplanes. What was thrown away was money from your pocket—the gasses were courtesy of Congress.

• The National Institutes of Mental Health gave a $97,000 grant to a group of scientists so they could study behavior patterns and interpersonal relationships in a Peruvian whorehouse.

• Long after smallpox had been wiped out, the federal Office of Smallpox Eradication was still humming along spending $1.2 million a year collecting data on nutrition.

• The Department of Housing and Urban Development got $675 million to give away in Urban Development Action Grants in the 1970s. But the standards for what constituted a poor community in need of urban renewal were so broadly written that tens of millions of dollars were spent on constructing fancy hotels—a Hilton, a Hyatt Regency and a Marriott. Now you can pay $100 a night or more to stay in a hotel that you helped build to help the "poor."

• Ronald Reagan's Cabinet members loved the privileges of rank. In the early 1980s, the taxpayers were spending more than $100,000 a year to keep a private dining room operating for Transportation Secretary Drew Lewis. Interior Secretary James Watt spent $9,000 entertaining guests, sometimes at a national historic mansion at Arlington National Cemetery where the doors were locked to the public. Commerce Secretary Malcolm Baldridge ordered his oak-paneled dining room expanded for $12,000. Attorney General William French Smith needed $80,000 a year to run two dining rooms in his office complex, one for formal occasions and one for "working" meals.

• The Federal Labor Relations Authority spent $150,000 remodeling the director's office in the early 1980s. The taxpayers filled the office with Barcelona chairs, Tunisian rugs, drum tables, a serving bar and more. Three floor lamps alone cost nearly $800.

• In 1991 Congress allotted $6 million to upgrade the subway system that runs under the Capitol. You, the taxpayers who pay the bills, can ride this cute little train, but be prepared to be thrown off if a member of Congress needs a seat. Also, you may have to wait a few minutes before the train leaves. A special bell signals the operator to hold the train if a member of Congress is on the elevator headed for the subway.

• In 1994 alone, Congress spent $800,000 on calendars to give away to constituents. Lucky you if you got one of these. At least you got a return on your investment.

• When Denver built a new airport in the early 1990s, the Federal Aviation Administration paid more than half a million dollars to compensate its Denver employees for the costs of moving closer to work. Some of them moved farther away but got the money anyway.

• The Law Enforcement Assistance Administration was one federal giveaway that lasted two decades before Congress recognized it as a waste of money. In 1972 several Florida law enforcement agencies used a $350,000 LEAA grant on an education program to urge citizens to call police if they saw or heard anything suspicious. The University of California got $293,700 in LEAA money to study what a great idea it would be to publish a law enforcement encyclopedia. They didn't actually publish the book for that amount of money, mind you. They just looked at the possibility of publishing it. Some of the local police agencies didn't spend their LEAA grants. They just invested them—millions of dollars worth—in U.S. Treasury bills, so the federal government ended up paying interest on its own money.

> ### There has to be a catch
>
> Who says Congress can't economize when it wants to? Why, just the other day our penny-wise legislators decided to change the backing of the two-year House wall calendars from cardboard to a less rigid material, for a savings of $250,000.
>
> *Washington Merry-Go-Round*
> *December 12, 1985*

• The cost of the savings and loan scandal was supposed to top out at about $215 billion. But in 1996 the Supreme Court added another $20 billion when it ruled that Congress had unfairly used accounting gimmicks to try to clean up the mess—gimmicks that had plunged more healthy savings and loans into financial trouble. Congress would like to lay the blame for this fiasco on savings and loan owners who took too many risks with their depositors' money. Some of those operators are in jail where they ought to be. But the full weight of the blame rests with Congress itself, which willy-nilly passed the law deregulating the thrifts, thus giving them a license to gamble.

• Dan Quayle's favorite mantra when he was accused of being a lightweight in the Senate was to repeat the words, "Job Training Partnership Act." It was a jobs program invented by Quayle and Senator Ted Kennedy, which they boasted was a boffo success. During its first eight years of operation, the JTPA trained seven million people to do something, anything, for a living, at a cost of $15.5 billion. But repeated audits of the program show it might have been a better idea just to give the trainees the cash. Most of them ended up in jobs that paid less than $5 an hour, and their ability to hang on to even those jobs was not impressive.

The vultures that circle government giveaways found every opportunity to take advantage. Training contracts went to companies that inflated their profit margins and exaggerated their costs. One contractor put trainees through a 129-day program to teach them how to wash cars.

• Taxpayers are footing the bill for college tuition amounting to more than $6 billion a year in student loans. Almost a third of the nation's college students have their fingers in this jam jar, and about 15 percent of the borrowers will default when it's time to pay up. The students are not even required to have a high school diploma before they get a federal college loan, and much of the money goes to pay for vocational training in low-wage jobs such as bartending and cosmetology. The banks that lend the money take little risk because the federal government insures the loans, giving the banks 98 percent protection against loss. That means the banks have no incentive to be careful about which schools of "higher learning" get the tuition money. Since 1992 Congress has been experimenting with direct loans from the federal treasury to students, bypassing the banks. In principle it's a good idea, but the overhead costs of this new approach are running more than $400 million a year.

• Federal workers are paid a premium, 125 percent of their regular pay, if they have to work on Sundays. Incredibly, they get the Sunday premium pay even when they take vacation or sick leave that includes a Sunday. In 1993 a federal appeals court declared that the government had to pay the premium, even when the employee was off. As a result, requests for vacations that fell on Sundays went up as much as 3 percent in some federal agencies. In five agencies audited by the General Accounting Office, this Sunday premium pay cost the taxpayers $146 million in just one year. Of that, $18 million went to employees who didn't really work on the Sundays for which they were paid because they were sick or on leave.

• The Immigration and Naturalization Service has inspectors whose job is to search for illegal immigrants on luxury cruise ships. These "inspections" involve a few hours of work and many more hours of relaxation in exotic ports of call. In one year alone, those inspectors took 1,615 cruises while collecting salaries totaling $218,000. Why the inspectors can't check citizenship documents at the port is a mystery to me. The cruise lines pick up the fare for the inspectors, which poses a blatant conflict of interest because the inspectors have the power to fine their hosts $3,000 for each illegal alien found aboard.

• The National Institutes of Mental Health wastes precious tax dollars researching an ever-expanding list of silly syndromes, disorders and other dubious dementia. NIMH spent four years and $757,560 studying "young men's risk for dysfunctional intimate relationships." Another $161,913 was spent studying Israeli reactions to SCUD missile attacks during the Persian Gulf War. Another $104,055 NIMH grant went to study how people communicate through facial expressions. That grant proposal sagely noted, "It can be difficult for people to control their facial expressions because they cannot see their own faces."

• The Internal Revenue Service has a new $125 million headquarters building in Maryland. The price allows $700,000 for commissioned art work, including a sculpture for a private garden for IRS personnel. The garden and the sculpture, according to the specs, are supposed to help give the workers a "sense of place." Somebody should remind them that their "place" likely will be at the end of the unemployment line if any of the current proposals for a flat tax become reality.

• The National Aeronautics and Space Administration can put a man on the moon, but it can't seem to get a commercial airline ticket for its top administrators. A 1994 inspector general's report charged that NASA officials spent $5.9 million a year flying around the world on NASA airplanes instead of taking cheaper commercial flights.

You've got to give a little to get a little

The Department of Housing and Urban Development, which is asking Congress for $1.7 billion to implement a homeless strategy, cannot be accused of giving its own workforce a free ride.

"Regrettably, we must inform you of a two cents per month increase in the quarterly parking fee," read a screaming flyer with "NOTICE" stamped six times. "Please increase your quarterly payment to $75.63."

One "hard-hit" HUD employee said it costs "more money to Xerox the flyer and pass it out" than HUD will recoup with the increase. A HUD spokesperson said the flyer corrected a mistake and "it saved a lot of confusion. The last thing you want is to get some hassles."

Washington Merry-Go-Round
July 7, 1994

President Clinton issued a directive restricting the use of government aircraft by executive branch officials, and the Office of Management and Budget has a rule that says government planes can be used only if no commercial airline service is available within a 24-hour window of travel. Yet NASA bigshots keep using NASA jets, apparently unable to interpret airline flight schedules that often offer commercial flights that arrive at almost the same time.

When pressed for an explanation, NASA officials said they wanted to eliminate "the potential occurrence of problems resulting from over-booking, flight cancellations, delays, missed connections, lost luggage and other time-consuming complications which commonly occur with commercial travel." In other words, the kinds of problems you, the taxpayers, face every time you board an airplane.

• When freshman Congresswoman Carolyn Maloney first arrived in Congress in 1992, she looked for the most wasteful program in government so she could study it as an example of how the budget process ought not to work. That's how she found the $2.5 million Civilian Marksmanship Program that had kept showing up in the federal budget since 1903. It was conceived in the wake of the Spanish-American War after the armed forces complained that too many of the new recruits couldn't shoot straight. In the 1990s the money has been used to distribute 40 million rounds of free ammunition to gun clubs and Boy Scout troops.

Even the Pentagon didn't want the program anymore. But when Maloney introduced legislation to cut back funding, she was blocked at every turn. It seems the program had a supporter more powerful than the Pentagon—the National Rifle Association. But in 1996 Congress at last drove a stake through the heart of this money sucker. Its functions were sent over to a private, nonprofit corporation that has to raise its own money for operations. What a concept.

• The Army Corps of Engineers never met a bucket of concrete it didn't like. The corps' solution to the flood control problems of the nation for the last three decades has been to build tens of billions of dollars in dikes, levees and channels to force the nation's rivers into a straightjacket. This rearrangement of nature has frequently made flooding worse by encouraging people to build where they shouldn't and by discouraging cheaper, more natural means of coping with inevitable floods. The average annual loss from flood damage in the United States is $3 billion, making a mockery of the corps' flood control projects.

The Clinton administration showed some signs of wanting to get the federal government out of the local flood control business and make communities pay their own costs, but Congress has not cooperated. Next time you're in Washington, drop by the offices of the House Public Works Committee. Its oak-paneled walls are lined with pictures of dams and bridges that benefit the few at the expense of the many.

• You may never sink your toes into the sands of a New Jersey beach, but you will pay $1.7 billion to keep that sand intact before the Army engineers are finished spending your money on this boondoggle. The beach restoration project covers 33 miles of the New Jersey coastline, and the corps aims to keep enough sand on those beaches to make tourists happy. This is a losing battle against Mother Nature involving as many as 34 truckloads of sand hauled in to pour on every one foot of shoreline. If you have a chance to get to the Jersey shore, you can stand on the sand you bought and watch your money wash out to sea.

• The average private company in the United States has one car in its motor pool for every 100 people on the payroll. But not Uncle Sam. The ratio in the government fleet is one car for every 10 employees.

• Uncle Sam spends about $2 billion every year on furniture and bric-a-brac. Even when agencies are forced to cut back on the services they are mandated to provide, they don't scrimp on ambiance. For example, in 1991, when the Federal Deposit Insurance Corporation was threatening to run out of money for its primary job—insuring bank deposits—it spent $31,274 on rubbing its brass statues with oil, $177,000 on art work, and $6,210 on coffee mugs.

• The U.S. Board of Tea Experts cost taxpayers $200,000 a year until it was finally and painlessly put to death in 1996. The job of the federal tea tasters for decades had been to decide which imported teas were not tasty enough for Americans. Their work had nothing to do with safety or health, only with taste. Unfortunately, six days after President Clinton put the tea tasters out of business, he signed a law creating a national Popcorn Board to set standards for that neglected food. Apparently, Americans cannot be trusted to make their own decisions about such weighty matters.

• The Department of Energy lost three laser printers valued at $6,400. After 22 months they were inexplicably found locked in a toilet stall in a DOE office building.

• Americorps was the showpiece of President Clinton's Corporation for National Service which was set up in 1993. The point was to encourage charity and volunteerism, but the "volunteers" seem to be getting a big chunk of the charity. An audit by the General Accounting Office revealed that the volunteers were costing the taxpayers as much as $31,000 a year each for stipends (translation: salaries) and payment of their outstanding college loans. Some of the uniforms for the volunteers were running $1,474 per year per person. Americorps also spent your tax dollars to produce politically partisan newsletters and to promote Clinton's legislative agenda.

• The federal bureaucracy is forbidden by law from using your money to lobby Congress for more money for more operating funds, but a mere law doesn't stop them. In 1996 the Agriculture Department used a tactic honed by politicians and lobbyists—the focus group. Agriculture, which administers the food stamp program, convened groups of voters to ask them a wide range of questions about how their government was functioning and how they felt about some proposed changes in the food stamp program. Then they took the information to Congress. The only two places where focus groups were used were Kansas and Indiana—the home states of the senator and congressman who chair the Senate and House committees with jurisdiction over food stamps.

> ### Row, row, row your boat ...
>
> The Coast Guard provides free, non-emergency services to nine million recreational boaters, including yacht owners. If a yacht develops an engine problem, the Coast Guard will tow it to the nearest repair yard—at the taxpayers' expense.
>
> *Washington Merry-Go-Round*
> *June 10, 1985*

Other Clinton administration departments used your money to lobby for the president's agenda. Employees of the Veterans Administration got notes in their pay envelopes urging them to oppose the Balanced Budget Act. The Labor Department paid for an 800 phone line to solicit support for a minimum wage increase. The Environmental Protection Agency published tracts urging opposition to some parts of the GOP Contract With America.

• In 1995 the National Endowment for the Humanities spent more than $4 million on a bit of navel gazing called the "National Conversation on Pluralism and Identity." The money financed a series of discussion groups to "provide Americans of diverse backgrounds across the nation with opportunities to engage in sustained and informed conversations about what it means to be an American." But that's not all. For your $4 million you also got, of course, research projects. These studies were supposed to "place questions about American pluralism and identity in critical and historical perspective." In one grant, $125,000 paid the tab for a group of school teachers in Maine to spend three weeks studying "the role of photography in forming an American identity."

• Congress and the White House have their very own Commission of Fine Arts that advises them how to spend your money on paintings and sculpture. This advice costs nearly $1 million a year in salaries and overhead—before a single piece of art is commissioned.

• The Office of Government Ethics spends nearly $8 million a year making sure members of Congress don't violate the public trust. This failed enterprise needs no further comment from me.

These random boondoggles illustrate the many ways that the federal bureaucracy wastes your money—through fraud, greed, mismanagement, carelessness, ineptness, overregulation and attempting to do for people who can do for themselves.

A call to action

In my 50 years of reporting on the doings of Washington, I could have focused solely on exposing how the federal government squanders your money, and it would have filled a library of books. But there came a time, in 1984, when I was no longer content to sit on the sidelines as a harpy.

Early in his administration, Ronald Reagan set up the President's Private Sector Survey on Cost Control, popularly known as the Grace Commission after its chairman, industrialist J. Peter Grace. Its mission was to show how to rein in government spending. Before the work was finished, 161 business executives and 2,000 volunteers had donated their time and resources—valued then around $75 million. The Grace Commission issued its report in 1984. It was nothing less than a formula for reinventing government.

The reaction, as I could have predicted, was what I call the "Starling Effect." Periodically, a new device is tried out in Washington to shoo the starlings from the eaves of government buildings. The startled birds rise, fluttering and twittering, then settle back after the alarm has faded. Much the same effect is produced on the federal establishment when new deficiencies are exposed. It causes sudden flapping and fluttering. Then everyone settles back to business as usual.

The men and women who put their heads and hearts into special commissions are supposed to politely pack up and go home and be grateful for the honor of having served. But J. Peter Grace was not that kind of man; he was a certified curmudgeon. He showed up in my office, growling about the ways of Washington. He had uncovered massive government waste, but he seemed to be the only person who wanted to get rid of it, he snorted. There were at least two of us, I told him.

We decided to form an organization, Citizens Against Government Waste, which would rise from the ashes of the defunct Grace Commission. This was not welcome news to the politicians and bureaucrats in Washington—to have Peter Grace and me together as thorns in their side. Peter led our crusade until the day he died in 1995, and I have tried to carry on.

In CAGW's first decade, our efforts helped save the taxpayers billions of dollars. The officials who are supposed to serve the public, elected and appointed alike, have turned out to be our worst enemies. In the process, I have learned some valuable lessons about what is wrong with our model of democracy and how it evolved into a culture of waste, fraud and abuse.

A molasses tidal wave called "Reform"

First and foremost, Uncle Sam is a slow learner. The wheels of American government turn so slowly they remind me of Al Gore's self-deprecating joke told at the 1996 Democratic National Convention. Gore said if you used a strobe light on him, it might actually appear as though he were moving. Such is the pace of government.

People may be shouting warnings from all sides, yet government just plods along doing its business as usual. Even financial catastrophes such as the savings and loan debacle, or world-reshaping events such as the end of the Cold War, seem to have little impact on the government's day-to-day spending habits.

For example, in 1982 the Grace Commission, found that the government was using 332 incompatible accounting systems to keep its books. The commission recommendation was the only sensible solution—to consolidate them into one accounting system. More than a decade later, President Clinton's own attempt at reinventing government, the National Performance Review, found 287 accounting systems still operating. This snail's pace of reform wastes billions of dollars annually.

It reminds me of the tale about two hunters in Canada who bagged six deer and dragged them back to the small airplane that

Reach out and bilk the government

Commerce Department employees spent a total of 18,000 staff days on improper personal telephone calls in 1985, according to the department's inspector general. This cost the taxpayers an estimated $3 million. "Over the years, a permissive attitude has developed that allows, if not encourages, (telephone) abuse," the inspector general noted. "Practices that are strictly forbidden by the regulations have become, in some employees' minds, a right." Most of the personal calls were to family members, but many were to banks, horoscope services and dial-a-porn numbers.

Washington Merry-Go-Round
January 15, 1987

had brought the hunting party to the wilderness. The pilot objected, "We can't load all those deer on this plane. They're too heavy."

But the hunters pressed him. "We flew up here last year and we bagged the same number of deer and got them on the same size of airplane without a problem."

Their arguments wore the pilot down and he let the hunters load their deer. The plane took off, soared briefly, sputtered and crashed. The two hunters dragged themselves out of the wreckage.

"Where are we?" said the first.

"I don't know, but I think we're about 20 miles farther south of where we crashed last year," said the second.

In like fashion, the federal budget crashes each year, and instead of dumping some of the load, Congress takes pride in having made it an extra 20 miles.

Top-level officials in the General Accounting Office told me something privately that they will not say publicly—that the federal government's financial management system is haywire and that it has been haywire for as long as anyone can remember.

It wasn't until 1994 that Congress mandated that every federal agency have its books audited by the GAO, and those mandated audits did not begin until 1996. Until then, the only federal agencies that had ever been independently audited regularly were only those that had a fiduciary mission, like the GAO.

Would you buy stock in a private company that never had its books audited by an outsider? You could not because the Securities and Exchange Commission, a federal agency, requires all publicly traded companies to open their books to independent auditors. Yet, as an American taxpayer, you are an involuntary stockholder in a $1.6 trillion-a-year business that has never been audited.

Most federal agencies live in mortal fear of the new requirement for audits because they can't answer simple questions like, "How many computers have you purchased this year and where are they now?"

Admittedly, the Anderson family operates on a far smaller scale, but we know when something is dear enough to keep track of.

At least in one aspect of family life—producing children—our ratio is on a par with the federal scale. If someone asked me "How many children do you have and where are they now?" I could immediately answer the first question, nine, and within a few hours I could get the answer to the second question. The problem with the federal bureaucracy is that nothing is personally valuable enough to the bureaucrats to warrant tracking. Somebody else paid for it so, "What, me worry?"

The ultimate payback—an IRS audit

Once the GAO starts auditing all the federal agencies on a regular basis, the worst offender is likely to be the nation's bill collector, the Internal Revenue Service. GAO auditors have told me they can't wait to get their red pencils into the IRS books regularly. This agency responsible for tax collections can't even tell you realistically how much it is owed because it can't efficiently keep track of which taxpayers are dead or alive and which of the living ones have any more blood to be squeezed out of them.

Repeatedly in its annual reports to Congress, the GAO has singled out the IRS as one government operation "especially vulnerable to waste, fraud, abuse and mismanagement."

During the past 25 years, the IRS has twice attempted and failed to modernize its antiquated tax processing systems. Its managers are so muddleheaded that its motto ought to be "Let the taxpayer beware." About 50 percent of the letters the IRS sends out this year challenging the way you prepare your tax returns will end up being incorrect. And about 40 percent of the time, when the IRS attempts to levy a penalty on you, the tax man is wrong and you are right. Those mistaken overcharges add up to a $5 billion attempted shakedown of taxpayers every year.

Once when GAO auditors had the chance in 1993 to peek at the IRS' books, they found a video display terminal that was worth $752 but was entered in the inventory as a $5.6 million asset. At the same time, the tax agency was paying $36,000 for a maintenance contract on a computer that no one had touched for three years. And there was the small matter of $797 million in seized assets which the IRS wasn't sure were still around. If you try to claim those kinds of expenses on your business tax return, you can expect an IRS auditor to visit you—in your prison cell.

When the government finishes wasting the money you hand over, you can count up the additional money you waste just by complying with the Draconian tax code and the demands of the IRS. It costs taxpayers $150 billion a year in time and professional advice just to figure out how to honestly pay their taxes.

Ironically, the United States could save money by spending some money—investing in a better accounting system and state-of-the-art technology. One GAO accountant compared the current state of federal bookkeeping to a family trying to manage its budget using only coins—no bills, no checks, no credit cards.

Computer-generated pork

After President Clinton took office, he got a cook's tour of the White House and was appalled at what he saw. The mansion is mired in the stone age, technologically speaking. Clinton couldn't fathom how primitive some of the communications and computer systems were compared to what was available on the market.

How can that be when the federal government spends more than $20 billion a year on new technology—not to mention the billions more that is spent keeping the old systems up and running?

Clinton had put his finger on a problem that is bigger than he ever could have imagined. Nearly every agency head in the federal government must have muttered "Amen" to the new president's lament because they, too, lack the critical information required to manage and control the behemoth bureaucracy. Compared to the private sector, the federal government's systems are lagging seriously behind.

Take health care, the centerpiece of Clinton's 1992 campaign. With 36 million Americans uninsured and countless others under-insured, it is nothing short of scandalous that Medicare mistakenly paid out more than $1 billion for services already covered by other insurers. The reason was bad data.

Imagine a commercial bank with records so mangled that it keeps loaning money to customers who are already in default on previous loans. Yet that's what happened at the Department of Education, when it gave millions of dollars in new loans to students who were already in arrears.

Similarly, the cleanup of the savings and loan debacle produced a scandal within a scandal. The Resolution Trust Corporation was responsible for processing more than $400 billion in assets from failed thrifts. But it bungled its own management on a scale worse than the thrifts in its charge.

At the Bureau of Indian Affairs, which has a budget of more than $2 billion, the accountants had a problem keeping track of their inventory. At one point they overstated the value of their inventory by $538 million. That will happen when you list the value of a chain saw as $99 million, a television as $96 million, and a typewriter as $77 million.

Even when an agency attempts to cure these record-keeping problems, the cure can be worse than the disease. The Veterans Benefits Administration undertook a modernization program aimed at speeding up claims payments to veterans. But it didn't look before it leaped into a $94 million investment—an investment that trimmed, at the most, 12 days off the average 151 days it took to process a claim. Anyone but a member of Congress would consider that a dubious return on the investment dollar.

For federal employees, I am champion of the top 3 percent, bane of the bottom 3 percent

Lest I am found guilty of bureaucrat bashing, let me clear the record here. I have built a career on gleaning secret information from dedicated and concerned federal workers, usually pretty low on the food chain, who saw a wrong and wanted to right it. Much of the information I disclose here came from people who blew the whistle on their employers. In fact, when government workers are surveyed, they complain that from one-quarter to one-half of their fellow workers are unnecessary to the operation. They know where the flaws are, and no one is more interested in reforming the system than the people who have to work within it.

An encouraging sign that the bureaucrats still have their heads on straight came in 1996 from, of all places, the CIA. When CIA Director John Deutch tried to spend $10 million on volleyball courts and exercise equipment for his employees, they rose up in protest. They said they would rather have the money put into the tools they needed to do their jobs better.

The slackards and money grubbers on Uncle Sam's payroll are exceptions to the rule, yet they are so skilled and so dedicated to their perfidy that they have managed to turn the federal piggy bank on its head and the money keeps spilling out.

CHAPTER FOUR

SMART BOMBS AND DUMB BUDGETS

I nside the Pentagon it was known as file "MIL-C-44072C." After six months and 175 hours of research, development and assembly, the final product emerged—not from the hangar, but from the oven.

It was the Pentagon's official recipe for fudge brownies and oatmeal cookies.

There were instructions on the texture of the brownies ("firm, but not hard") and the moisture count for the cookies ("not more than 3.5 percent"). The bakers couldn't use just any old shortening. It had to have "a stability of not less than 100 hours as determined by the Active Oxygen Method in Method Cd 12-57 of the Commercial Fats and Oils chapter in the Official and Tentative Methods of the American Oil Chemists Society."

The walnuts "shall be of the small piece size classification; shall be of a light color; and shall be U.S. No. 1 of the U.S. standards for Shelled English Walnuts. A minimum of 90 percent, by weight, of the pieces shall pass through a 4/16-inch diameter round hole screen and not more than 1 percent, by weight, shall pass through a 2/16-inch diameter round hole screen."

Holy Betty Crocker! Not only do we have a 22-page brownie and cookie recipe, but the scandal inside this scandal is that we have a U.S. standard for Shelled English Walnuts!

The saddest part of this story is that the Army's explanation for the overdone recipe almost makes sense: "If you don't write everything exactly to the letter, somebody is going to cut a corner so that they can save a penny. You have to make them so detailed that contractors can't cut a corner on it."

But this brought a response from then-director of the Office of Management and Budget, Phil Lader: "It's a culture which tries to stop somebody from doing something bad and therefore makes it impossible for anybody to do anything especially good. Every action, specification and supervisor was put into place to avoid or correct something wrong. Each one action made sense individually, but the aggregate of all this is duplication that knots the whole system."

When the 22-page recipe was passed around a meeting of President Clinton's National Performance Review staff, there were gasps of disbelief. One committee member slapped his palm to his forehead and said, "How in the world could we have gotten to this point?"

How, indeed?

Sacred cows and pork-fed generals

The Pentagon has gotten to this point by having too much money to burn in the first place. The defense budget is so tied to our patriotic heartstrings that we cannot mothball a stockpile of bombs without someone crying that God and country are in danger of extinction. On Capitol Hill, military appropriations are held sacred. Members of Congress, who challenge ever detail of a $50,000 anti-poverty project, will approve a $50 million Pentagon proposal with no questions asked. Result: Staggering amounts have been lavished on armaments that should have been scrapped or never should have been built in the first place.

The defense budget is also such a massive part of our national economy—$264 billion spent in 1996—that we cannot close a military base or cancel a submarine contract without upsetting the tenuous economic balance of cities, even entire states. Weapons that are no longer needed to defend the nation against the Soviet superpower are critically needed, instead, to provide jobs in key constituencies. Increasingly, the defense budget is becoming a multibillion-dollar jobs program. In 1996, for example, congressional leaders submitted an unprecedented request to the Pentagon for detailed information on how many jobs another $15 billion for more military projects would create in whose congressional districts.

Not military needs, but economic benefits now drive most defense procurement. Each weapons system is supported by a formidable lobby, composed of the military branch that operates it, the contractors who manufacture the component parts, the workers who put the parts together, and the members of Congress whose districts enjoy the financial rewards. The test has become not whether a weapon is worth the cost, but whether its production will benefit the right constituency.

The top brass also order pet weapons that turn out to be impractical or obsolete. They rush ahead with new, unproved weapons, often changing the design in the middle of production. (The Pentagon was in such a hurry to use the C-5A cargo plane that it rushed to production before the new plane was fully tested.

The result was 12 more years of tinkering to fix the wings, at a cost of $1.3 billion)

Every miscalculation, every wrong hunch, every revised blueprint runs up the bills that are charged to the taxpayers. The military warehouses, meanwhile, fill up with spare parts for canceled and antiquated systems.

The Pentagon's prodigal spending and sloppy bookkeeping have encouraged defense contractors to engage in all manner of malfeasance, misfeasance and nonfeasance. The taxpayers have lost billions through subtle deception and outright fraud.

The military art of skinning the taxpayers is an old tactic. Thirty years ago, for example, the Chinese didn't possess a single missile that could hit the U.S. mainland. Yet President Lyndon Johnson was pressured into ordering a $5 billion anti-missile system that had no purpose except to shoot down China's nonexistent trans-Pacific missiles. The people who promoted the $5 billion boondoggle were the defense contractors whose fear of China was in direct proportion to the size of the contracts they expected to receive.

Generals roughing it at the bar

At last, a story about Pentagon procurement in which the military has actually <u>saved</u> money—and it's the pits.

So far this year, the armed services have put in requisitions for $340,914 worth of red, pitted maraschino cherries—without stems. "I can guarantee you there isn't any fat in this deal," said Bob Ungar, executive vice president of International Fruit Products in Ft. Wright, Ky., which supplied 28,084 cases of cherries in pint jars, at a total cost of $295,467. He said cherries with stems—the kind used in whiskey sours at officers' clubs—cost a lot more than the stemless variety used to garnish salads.

Washington Merry-Go-Round
July 1, 1985

The overdone fudge brownie or the $600 toilet seat are just symptoms of the problem. As one top GAO auditor explained, "It's like the doctor saying you have a cough, but he doesn't ask you if you smoke." The Pentagon wakes up one morning and finds itself with a $436 hammer in the inventory. An almighty howl is raised, but it will happen again because there is no mechanism for telling the generals that they could have met the same specifications with a $10 hammer from their local hardware store.

The Pentagon's procurement standards are so arcane that they consume 250 million hours of paperwork each year. It takes 100,000 staffers, making $5 billion a year, to process all the Pentagon's procurement paperwork. By one estimate, those regulations cost the Defense Department $50 billion a year to monitor and enforce.

For a six-month period in 1991, the staff of the Strategic Defense Initiative program (SDI or "Star Wars") kept track of the paperwork and hours it took to keep up with the demands from the secretary of defense for documentation on the purchases for just one of the SDI programs. They counted 75,000 hours spent by government workers, 250,000 hours spent by contractors, $22 million in expenses, and more than a ton of paper in supporting documents. (I can't pass up the opportunity to note that this is truly a case of the pot calling the kettle black—the dubious Star Wars program complaining about Pentagon waste.)

One study compared the number of accounting transactions used by the Navy and by Ford Motor Co. to pay for a purchase. Ford used three transactions. The Navy used 35.

Once a purchase is made, the Pentagon can't give an accurate accounting of its inventory and often can't even tell how much money it owes contractors. In a nine-month period audited by the GAO in 1993, the overpayments to defense contractors added up to $1.4 billion. The Pentagon knew about its miscalculated benevolence because most contractors were honest enough to report the overpayments. In one case, a single contractor sent back 540 checks for $135 million. Another contractor tried for nearly two years to persuade the Pentagon to take its money back—$670,000. Finally, the company sent a check to the Defense Department, which promptly returned it.

In the mid-1980s the GAO issued a series of white papers on financial management in the federal government. At the time, the Air Force brass thought they had set a sterling example of how money ought to be handled. So they cheerfully submitted their books for a GAO audit. The generals got a nasty surprise. The Air Force's figures were off by billions of dollars. Their inventory procedures were, in the word of one GAO insider, "wacky." They couldn't reconcile their cash; they had lost track of office equipment and weaponry; they were using scores of different accounting systems that didn't communicate with each other.

Fiction, nonfiction and Navy fiction

Here are a few examples of the waste that results from poor bookkeeping and unwise planning by the armed forces.

The Pentagon has a 10-year supply of uniforms, mattress covers and tents valued at a whopping $1.8 billion—all in mothballs. Some of the items are so ancient as to be suitable only for a re-enactment of the Normandy Invasion. The Defense Logistics Agency has a stockpile of 5,100 hospital robes just in case anyone needs them. They've been on hand for 40 years. A defense depot in Tennessee packed up 2,930 cold-weather undershirts and put them in storage in 1952. The style was declared obsolete in 1981. Only 12 of the shirts were ever unpacked.

The Navy spent $3.7 billion on parts for deactivated ships because no one told the Ships Parts Control Center that the ships had been phased out. Similarly, in 1990 the Army bought nearly 1,700 pieces of equipment—spare parts for missiles and tanks—that cost $67 million. All the while, $184 million worth of the same parts were already gathering dust in Army warehouses.

The Pentagon doesn't always hoard its useless inventory. Oh, no, sometimes they sell it—like the 40,000 turtleneck shirts bought by the government for $5 each and then sold at auction for a penny apiece.

Also, you can't pull the wool over the generals' eyes every time. Sharp-eyed Pentagon shoppers noticed in 1990 that one company had charged the taxpayers $999.20 for a pair of pliers. The generals demanded an immediate rebate and the contractor cheerfully complied. When Uncle Sam is the customer, he's always right. In this case, he got a refund of $333.20. That brought the price of the pliers down to a bargain $666.

Haven't the generals ever heard of Sears?

This isn't a new story. Twenty years ago while thumbing through some Defense Department procurement documents, I found that the Pentagon was spending $314,000 a year on rawhide holsters specially made for Colt .45 handguns, yet the military hadn't bought any Colt .45s in more than 30 years. I also discovered that the Navy had purchased 65,000 pairs of sunglasses for 33,000 aviators, and each pair of glasses was supposed to last three years. At the Naval Air Station in Pensacola, Florida, one group of flyers got 12 pairs of sunglasses each (this was Florida, after all), plus four flight jackets ($50 each), three pairs of boots ($21.50 each), and six pairs of gloves ($11.50 each).

If we could lay all the armed services collectively on the psychiatrist's couch, the diagnosis would certainly be an obsessive compulsion to shop. Plainly and simply, they are living beyond your means. And it's high living, with swivel chairs, plush rugs and fancy frills.

Never mind that it takes more generals and admirals to man the Pentagon today than were needed to command 10 million men and wage war on two fronts during World War II. The real contrast is in their living style. Inside the Pentagon, the military brass now roost happily among their status symbols. Their standing is determined in exacting detail by their office acreage, rug plushness, furniture array and limousine service. They are known, too, by their dining, parking, and washroom and

How to make money in publishing

A major Energy Department contractor charged the government $30,000 for a "nuclear legislative handbook" that consisted of publicly available, photocopied material arranged in a looseleaf binder.

Investigators for the House subcommittee on energy conservation and power said the material copied for the handbook included profiles of lawmakers, a digest of nuclear energy legislation and a compilation of legislators' voting records on nuclear issues.

But the profiles were lifted whole from a book published by Congressional Quarterly; the legislative digest was available free from the subcommittee itself; and the voting records could have been obtained easily from the Energy Department's own legislative liaison office.

What really appalled the investigators was that only six copies of the looseleaf handbook were produced over a three-year period—at $5,000 each, one of the most expensive photocopying jobs in history.

Washington Merry-Go-Round
August 31, 1984

elevator privileges. Whether they sip water from a silver decanter, brown plastic jug or water fountain in the corridor is another sign of their status.

But a Pentagon official's immediate domain, the office, provides the real clues to his or her importance. Is it large enough, say, for a football scrimmage? Is there a trim of woodwork around the walls? What color is the rug, and how deep do you sink in it? Does the office contain a king-size desk? A flag stand? A sofa suitable for taking naps? These are the things to watch for.

I also recall a huge hullabaloo a few years back over who should be allowed to embellish their hats with scrambled-egg designs. At the time, no one below a Navy captain or an Army-Air Force colonel could wear this cherished scroll. Then the Navy opened the privilege to commanders, causing Army-Air Force majors to demand equal hat privileges.

The most coveted symbol of Army status is tenancy in one of the cavernous, barn-like houses along "Brass Row" at Fort Myer, Virginia, within easy limousine distance of the Pentagon. But wherever the generals and admirals hang their brass hats and whatever the manpower limitations, they always seem able to spare enough enlisted bodies to wait on tables, mow their lawns, and perform other menial chores. GIs living in substandard housing have complained to me about pruning roses and hanging decorations for debutante balls for the daughters of the big brass.

To keep the officer corps in doodads befitting their rank, the Pentagon also spends billions on trinkets that are hardly necessary to defend the nation. That is woeful enough, but the Pentagon also has a propensity for paying more than the trinkets are worth.

A makeover of the Army Missile Command's quarters for visiting VIPs cost $71,000. The money bought beds that cost $1,000 each. They were covered with $518 bedspreads. The accessories—blankets, dust ruffles, pillow shams—cost another $712 per bed. If the bigwigs' toes got cold in the middle of the night, they could pull up a $400 quilt.

Officers' clubs constitute another gilded rat hole for pouring money down. At Mildenhall Air Force Base in England, a $70,000 remodeling project mushroomed into a $2.2 million renovation complete with marble, solid oak paneling and gold-plated chandeliers. The club at Scott Air Force Base got an equally pricey facelift—$2.4 million—which paid for, among other things, a 12-by-18-foot carpet that cost $20,823. The Air Force said the carpet was necessary to "enhance the aviator image."

Before auditors caught them, officials at Tinker Air Force Base in Oklahoma tried to use money from the B-2 bomber program to move and expand their skeet-shooting club at a cost of $772,000. Only 24 of the 7,000 airmen at Tinker were members of the club.

Because Air Force Chief of Staff General Merrill McPeak didn't like the look of officers' uniforms, he spent $1.5 million on fashion designers who produced prototypes of new threads. The result would have made our warriors look like glorified airline pilots, stirring a sartorial revolt.

While military bases around the country braced for closings and cutbacks, 24 generals at Bolling Air Force Base near Washington, D.C., gave high priority to the installation of remote-controlled gas fireplaces in their quarters. Cost: $36,000. The generals already had wood-burning fireplaces to ward off any chill, but officials at the base invoked a rationale amounting to environmental patriotism: "The air quality in D.C. is receiving much scrutiny at this time and the gas fireplaces are clean-burning, thus supporting the EPA clean air regulations. And they do not require chimney sweeping."

Air Force Chief of Staff Michael Dugan lost his job in 1990 when he boasted too openly to the press about plans for attacking Saddam Hussein's forces during the buildup for the Persian Gulf War. But that wasn't all Dugan lost; he also lost a fancy house the Air Force was remodeling for him at Ft. Myer, Virginia. The limit that the Pentagon was normally allowed for sprucing up a general's quarters was $25,000. But for Dugan, the brass got a congressional dispensation to exceed the limit by leaps and bounds. How big a leap? $196,010. Unfortunately for Dugan, it was his replacement who got to enjoy the digs.

At Bolling Air Force Base, sources tell me that the top brass try to keep up appearances there with little success but much spending. The base has all the charm of a railroad yard, yet in one year alone Bolling spent at least $400,000 on aesthetic improvements, much of it devoted to officers' quarters.

Some waste is for the birds

We have frequently likened the federal bureaucracy to a "fuddle factory" where the workers are so confused that they act in opposition to one another. Consider this recent example:

The U.S. Fish and Wildlife Service will spend about $250,000 this winter to keep migratory birds out of the Kesterson Wildlife Refuge near Fresno, California. Human scarecrows will be used to fire amplified popguns around the clock from off-road vehicles to scare birds away. The reason:

A drainage system built by the Reclamation Bureau to carry chemical-contaminated irrigation water from Central Valley farmland to the sea was never completed. So the toxic water now ends up in the marshes of the refuge, and migratory birds must be scared off lest they poison themselves.

Washington Merry-Go-Round
November 12, 1984

One of the most outrageous stories of military waste I have ever uncovered was not the most expensive, but it takes the prize for sheer stupidity. It happened in 1989, during Jordanian King Hussein's visit to Washington. His host, President George Bush, decided to take him on a tour of George Washington's Mount Vernon estate. From Mount Vernon, the king, the president and the entourage were to sail a few miles up the Potomac River and dock at Bolling.

The base was pitched into a royal fever. Groundskeepers were dispatched to do a rushed landscaping job. Some GIs were handed cans of paint and told to paint the dock where the president's boat was to stop in a matter of hours. The crew had already begun painting when somebody figured out that the paint would still be wet when Bush and Hussein walked the planks. Since it wouldn't do to have the king and the president sticking to the dock, the painters were abruptly called off. But they did spray the grass at the last minute with a chemical to make it look a deeper shade of green. Fortunately, both heads of state kept off the grass.

Compared to the multibillion-dollar defense budget, the foolishness at Bolling was a mere coin collection plate. But the Pentagon has wiped so many collection plates clean that the waste has become monumental.

All military bases around Washington—because they could host a visit by the president or a chief of staff at any minute—are kept in a state of red carpet readiness. None is more ready for a VIP alert than is Andrews Air Force Base, where the president's planes are hangared, where members of Congress begin and end their junkets, and where visiting heads of state plant their feet on U.S. soil.

To leave a pleasing impression, the Air Force gave Andrews a $9.5 million facelift in the early 1990s. "Leaders from around the world gain their initial impressions of the United States Air Force and our nation as they transit Andrews," a base spokesman defended the expensive makeover. Unsightly overhead power lines were buried and other aesthetic touches added.

With Andrews dressed up, dignitaries can now get a first impression of a wealthy country that throws money away on frills. Then their second impression comes on the drive between Andrews and downtown Washington where they see how the taxpayers of that wealthy country live—many in poverty, some victimized by crime, some sleeping on steam grates in the doorways of boarded-up buildings. Burying a few utility lines won't change that.

Across the Potomac River at the Army's Fort Myer, a group of officers' wives embarked on their own spending spree during the Persian Gulf War. Their mission was to remodel the visitors' suites at a cost in round numbers of $900,000—all without the knowledge of Congress. Apparently, the decor of the old visitors' suites didn't suit the tastes of the officers' wives.

They spent $90,000 on new furniture, though the suites had been refurnished about 10 years earlier and were hardly subject to rough wear and tear by visiting dignitaries. For each bathroom they purchased a solid brass cup holder ($99.38), a solid brass bathroom faucet ($352), a soap dish ($93), a toilet paper holder ($81), and a bathrobe hook ($43). One of the auditors who looked into the shopping binge after it was all over told me, "We've got the $100 cup holder to go with the $600 toilet seat."

The remodeling was conducted with all the urgency of the Persian Gulf War. The requisition orders for the furniture were marked "Code 3," a designation usually reserved for wartime emergencies or natural disasters. That designation allowed the buyers to avoid competitive bidding, which added about $35,000 to the cost.

When it was all over, the base commander pronounced the project "quite well done." But he admitted he had learned a lesson. "Ensure the perception that the taxpayers are getting their money's worth." Given the $350 bathroom faucet, the taxpayers might have had the perception that they got soaked.

One Air Force general spent $75,000 to build an avenue of 50 flagpoles on his base. When someone complained, the general assigned the same unit that installed the flagpoles to investigate whether they were a waste of money. The investigators concluded that no money had been wasted because the flags were top-of-the-line. Apparently waste is not waste if it's high-quality waste.

When the Army ROTC decided to enhance its image by changing its name to Army ROTC Command, $300,000 was spent promoting the new name. About 60,000 cadets and 5,000 officers got new shoulder patches and a regimental crest.

Underground artists

I tweaked the Navy's nose in 1982 when I reported that not all the Navy's painters were slapping gray paint on battleships. I had discovered there was also a staff of skilled artists whose only job was to paint portraits, landscapes and favorite ships to grace the walls of admirals and their friends.

This corps of artists, reminiscent of court painters of the Renaissance, produced original oils of whatever subjects struck the admirals' fancy. When I saw the logs of their projects, I found references to paintings of wildlife, a bullfighter, a dog and even a belly dancer—the sort of art work that sailors used to get from tatoo parlors.

Included in the files were thank-you notes from the admirals to the painters: "Thanks so much for touching up the picture of my brother-in-law." "The painting that you have done of my home is something I will always treasure." "Just a note to tell you how

thrilled everyone in the office is over the painting of Mount Fuji."
"It goes without saying that you clearly exploded your talents in
the production of my dear mother's portrait."

Before I ever learned of the existence of this school of artists,
Navy investigators had already done a secret probe of the operation
and recommended it be shut down. That recommendation was
ignored. The investigators left a note in their files: "The authority
for performing this function is
unknown, the legality is question-
able, and revelation outside the
Navy is potentially a subject of
public criticism."

Right on all three counts.
When I revealed the existence of
this perquisite, the public criticism
burned the Navy. But instead of
going after the generals who took
advantage of this boondoggle,
the investigators fixed their sights
on me. They forced the artists to
fill out a questionnaire which
demanded whether any of them
had talked to me. "How did you
become aware of the article?" the
questionnaire asked. "What is
your opinion of the article?"

> ## We can't spare the money, we should strike it from the budget
>
> For the past 18 years, the Air National Guard has held an annual bowling tournament in Nashville, Tennessee. Two thousand people attended last May's tournament. And at least 431 of them flew in from such faraway points as Chicago, Milwaukee and Suffolk, New York —at the taxpayers' expense. In all, 18 separate round trips were made in government planes at a cost of $110,000. Though the junkets were all passed off as "training missions," a confidential Pentagon memo in August 1979 warned that such flights are "extremely difficult to justify."
>
> *Washington Merry-Go-Round*
> *April 14, 1981*

The inquisition turned out to be short-lived. After I inquired
about the questionnaires, the Navy destroyed them.

Move over, MGM

The Pentagon has, in the past, fancied itself to be a movie
maker as well as a patron of the arts. I learned in 1980 that old
generals didn't always fade away. Sometimes they were kept alive
on film at taxpayer expense. Until the practice was exposed, film
technicians were employed at Norton Air Force Base in California
to do a "This Is Your Life" kind of movie for retiring generals,

often narrated by celebrities such as Jimmy Stewart and Tennessee Ernie Ford. The films cost tens of thousands of dollars.

Putting an end to the film biographies, however, did not end the Pentagon-Hollywood connection. Every year the military reviews requests from filmmakers to use airplanes, battleships and tanks as movie props. Sometimes the Pentagon charges filmmakers for the use of these props, but the charge does not come close to covering the expense in manpower and equipment.

The Pentagon figures these movies are an investment in recruitment. The decision as to which of the movies will be subsidized by the taxpayers comes down to image—will the movie amount to a recruiting poster for the armed services? The Pentagon's favorite was "Top Gun." But the generals declined to cooperate with Oliver Stone on "Platoon," or with Sylvester Stallone on his "Rambo" series (too negative), or with Clint Eastwood on "Heartbreak Ridge" (too much profanity).

I can only imagine where the censors were when the Navy agreed in 1989 to turn over the U.S.S. Missouri to Cher, free of fee, so she could make her video "If I Could Turn Back Time." Navy officials defended themselves, saying the video was done "at no additional cost to the government" because the sailors were on their own time. And why not? The Navy had to beat back the number of sailors eager to spend their Fourth of July holiday cavorting as a chorus line on the deck of the proud battleship while Cher, in a fishnet G-string, straddled the Missouri's 16-inch guns. There had not been so much excitement about a film made on the Missouri since the ship hosted the 1945 surrender of Japan in Tokyo Bay.

Cher's video was so risqué that MTV—a cable music video channel not normally known as an arbiter of good taste—wouldn't show it until after 9 p.m. Navy veterans were embarrassed that their service would stoop so low, but the Navy offered no apologies. Instead, it deemed the video to be a "subliminal advertisement of the Navy seeing Cher aboard a battleship with sailors." I can't argue with the "subliminal" claim.

Smoke and mirrors

The Pentagon is almost as adept at making excuses for bad decisions as it is at keeping the cost of those decisions under wraps. In the late 1980s, some Air Force generals got it in their heads to renovate their Pacific headquarters in Hawaii. The cost was $5 million, something Congress might have balked at. So the generals didn't bother to ask. Instead they billed the massive remodeling project as a series of smaller "maintenance" jobs which did not need congressional approval. Part of the ruse involved redrawing the wings of the huge headquarters building on real estate maps so they looked like 14 separate buildings. And, instead of putting the work up for bid (that might have drawn attention to the project), the Air Force shipped 500 of its own handymen to Hawaii on "temporary duty." Officially, the mission was called a "training project."

If the military has figured out how to spend money without the blessing of Congress, the legislators are equally adept at burying boondoggles in the defense budget that the Pentagon doesn't want. It is a favorite place for hiding pork barrel projects. George Bush once complained that the defense budget ought to be "more than a piggy bank for people who want to get busy beating swords into pork barrels." Occasionally, the Pentagon and Congress are partners in pork barreling—as happened when the Air Force wisely farmed out construction of its new C-17 cargo plane to contractors in several states. The technique assured that several members of Congress would be feeding at the barrel.

Four-star bread and circuses

The Morale, Welfare and Recreation fund (MWR) on any military base is the place to look for creative bookkeeping. This is money raised from the profits on sales at the PX stores. It is supposed to be used to improve the lot of soldiers and their families; it's intended for day-care centers, bowling alleys and other recreational facilities—especially in areas where commercial recreation is limited.

But, at a time when 6,000 military families are on food stamps, the Pentagon is pouring millions of dollars a year from the MWR funds into high-end sports like golf and skiing that are too pricey for enlisted people.

In 1989 I reported that officials at Andrews Air Force Base used MWR funds to buy and maintain a Mercedes-Benz reserved exclusively for a four-star general who visited the base a few times each month. Tooling around in a Mercedes instead of a military Jeep certainly boosted the general's morale, but I doubt that it cheered the foot soldiers.

The Mercedes story pales, however, when compared to the string of military golf courses built with MWR funds. The military has so many golf courses that, in 1985, Congress banned the construction of any more. The order has been skirted by a variety of accounting tricks. Mind you, there is nothing inherently wrong with a golf course; the taxpayers don't begrudge the troops playing a little golf between wars. But the armed forces invade the greens as if they were military objectives.

Myrtle Beach Air Force Base in South Carolina spent $646,000 on golf course construction without congressional permission. Yet the nearby city of Myrtle Beach is the golf course capital of the United States. Dozens of courses are within putting distance of the air base.

Andrews Air Force Base has not one but three 18-hole golf courses which have an elite clientele of military brass, members of Congress and the duffer-in-chief himself. The newest course was built in 1996 for $7 million at a time when more than 300 children were on a waiting list for the crowded day-care centers on the base. While bulldozers were smoothing over the land for the fairways, the GAO was busy investigating the day-care crisis at Andrews. Frantic parents wanted to know why the MWR funds

---

Shorthand for waste

The federal government recently shelled out $60,000 to determine which typewriter of the highest quality could be purchased for the lowest price. The tests were then pronounced "inconclusive."

Washington Merry-Go-Round
May 25, 1981

---

weren't put to better use for a new day-care center, which would have cost $5 million.

Andrews officials continued to defend the new golf course as "a great boost for morale as well as a sound business decision." But calling that golf course a "sound business decision" is somewhat like calling a 50-foot putt a "gimme." By the Pentagon's own estimate, it will take 10 to 20 years for the course to pay for itself, let alone turn a profit. (By the way, there are 19 other military golf courses within an easy drive from the Pentagon.)

These excesses with the MWR funds cannot be brushed off, as apologists have tried to do, as an extravagance with the soldiers' own money. The cash in the MWR fund does not cover all the expenses and the fund is subsidized with about $1 billion in tax money each year.

In one creative bit of accounting, the Pentagon has put money into the MWR funds from the sale of recyclable materials such as paper and cardboard that are collected on military bases. The recycling programs are supposed to pay for themselves, plus environmental and safety projects. If there's any money left over, it can be added to the MWR fund.

But money that should go back into the Treasury from the sale of military surplus is now going to pay for golf courses. Military bases routinely sell items that are specifically excluded from the recycling program and do not reduce the waste stream—crashed aircraft, jet engines, vehicles, aircraft and ship parts, electrical components and unopened containers of oil or solvent.

About 90 percent of the recycling program's proceeds come from items that wouldn't otherwise end up in the dump. The Norfolk Naval Base in Virginia, for example, sold $769,000 worth of F-14 aircraft brake parts. The Tooele Army Depot in Utah received almost $2 million from "recycled" Army all-terrain vehicles.

These were items you paid for in the first place, but when they were sold, nobody offered you a rebate. With the Pentagon's happy definition of "recyclables," small wonder that the annual profits from recycling jumped from $1.5 million to $37 million in just 10 years. And those numbers don't count all the recycling money, since some bases also hold their own property disposal sales instead of selling the material through regional disposal offices. This makes the exact amount of money that bases are raking in—and subsequently spending on MWR activities—nearly impossible to track.

Meanwhile, you faithful taxpayers recycle your cans and newspapers, but nobody gives you a golf course in return.

The tale of the Warthog prince

Tales of golf courses and chandeliers get the blood boiling, but they don't begin to match the money lost through poor planning and outright fraud in the production of big-ticket weapons systems favored by the Pentagon. Those stories fill your daily newspapers—the B-2, the C-17, Star Wars.

One lesser known fiasco involved the lowly Warthog—evidence that the top brass will sideline perfectly useful weaponry because it isn't fancy enough.

During the Persian Gulf War buildup, I found out that the image-conscious Air Force secretly opposed deploying the A-10 Warthog attack planes to the Gulf because they were too slow and ugly. The Air Force had tried to name the planes "Thunderbolts" when they first came off the assembly line, but the nickname "Warthog" stuck. The Army was more fond of the A-10 than the Air Force, whose pilots flew them, because the A-10s destroyed tanks more reliably than the sleek F-16s. Defense Secretary Richard Cheney sided with the Army and ordered the Air Force to send in A-10s.

The performance of this humble plane became the Cinderella story of the allied air forces, surprising even proponents with its effectiveness and versatility. And the A-10's chief opponent, Lt. Gen. Charles A. Horner, who was in charge of Central Command Air Forces during the war, had to eat crow. "I take back all the bad things I've ever said about the A-10s," Horner admitted to his staff. "I love them. They're saving our asses!"

Army officials were relieved at General Horner's mea culpa. "We would be in serious trouble if they hadn't come," an Army officer at the front told one of my reporters during the war. "They are THE major weapons between us and the Iraqis, and we're counting on them to take out a huge number of tanks before they get to us."

Air Force generals and pilots always favor glamorous, high- and fast-flying jets. But the Army needs slower, heavily armored planes to provide close air support for their troops. The Warthog has a maximum speed of 450 miles per hour; in contrast, the F-16 can fly more than 1,100 miles per hour. Before the war, top Air Force officials lobbied Congress to get rid of the Warthogs and modify the F-16s to take their place. The cost of the modifica-

Double dipping

When a blizzard hit Massachusetts in 1978, the state was declared a disaster area and government emergency funds flowed in. One snow job perpetrated by a small business-man in the Bay State was recently discovered by General Accounting Office watchdogs. It seems the man reported his Cadillac destroyed by the storm. He not only got a loan from the Small Business Administration to replace the Caddy; he got a grant from the state to replace the same car.

Washington Merry-Go-Round
February 26, 1981

tions was estimated to be $3 million per plane, well over $1 billion for the whole fleet.

Then the uncomely Warthogs performed unexpected feats in the Persian Gulf War. They knocked out Scud ballistic missile sites, artillery, supply points, radar installations, surface-to-air missile sites and rescued a downed Navy pilot. One even won an unexpected dogfight with an Iraqi helicopter.

Sweeping waste under classified carpets

Evaluating the A-10 was quick work because its budget is out in the open. Not so with an estimated $14 billion of the annual defense budget which is kept secret for national security reasons— the so-called "black budget." Some big-ticket military purchases, such as the B-2 Stealth bomber, begin in the black budget and remain in the shadows until they can be unveiled to the public.

The Air Force is the biggest secret spender, putting 40 percent of its procurement budget into hidden purchases. In the name of patriotism, generals will routinely lie about the existence of these programs, sometimes even after they become public knowledge—like the Aurora spy plane designed as a replacement for the trusty old SR-71 Blackbird. The Air Force still refuses to acknowledge so much as the existence of the air base where its secret projects are housed—Area 51 in Nevada—even though hundreds of people flock to work there every day and it is on the Defense Department's own unclassified maps.

There is a legitimate need for secrecy for weapons development. But the same secrecy that protects our military technology also breeds incompetence and fraud. A prime example is the National Reconnaissance Organization—the black-budget agency that builds spy satellites. Until 1992 the name of this organization was not even spoken out loud. Evidently, that was not all that was left unspoken. In 1993 Congress learned through the grapevine that NRO was building itself a new $300 million office complex using funds that had been skimmed from its satellite operating accounts. Then in 1995, Congress found out that the NRO was hoarding nearly $4 billion that had been budgeted but unspent. The NRO director was fired and others were scolded. That's all. Don't expect to see the $4 billion in the form of a rebate in your tax returns. The Pentagon speedily spent it on U.S. missions in Bosnia and elsewhere.

When some members of Congress first wanted to make public the exact amount of the money in the NRO slush fund, CIA Director John Deutch declined. He said the public did not understand NRO's mission and, therefore, "would not have the correct impression of NRO." In other words, the amount of the slush fund would look scandalous.

Over the years, the brass have become experts at blowing away your money despite repeated efforts to teach them a little thrift. In 1981 Frank Carlucci, then deputy defense secretary, was anointed to be the general in command in the war on waste. He pinpointed the problems: changing specifications after awarding a contract so the price goes up; buying the item with the most bells and whistles even though it may not be the best buy; and centralizing the buying authority, thus creating countless layers of bureaucracy that made the shopping process slower and more costly. Carlucci apparently forgot his own report when he later became defense secretary because nothing changed.

Even after the Soviet empire collapsed and the Cold War ended, obsolete programs that should have been terminated were hoarded and expanded. Neither Congress nor the Pentagon had the political will to order major cutbacks. In an act that passed for political courage in Washington, Congress and the president recused themselves from making the decisions about which unneeded military bases would be closed. Instead, they turned that problem over to an independent Base Closure and Realignment Commission (BRAC) which took the heat. BRAC made the decision to close 243 domestic bases, and Congress deliberately gave itself only the power to say yes or no to the whole package. The lawmakers said yes and then immediately began doing damage control in the devastated communities, claiming the whole thing wasn't their idea.

The Cold War may be over, but the Pentagon budget planners haven't gotten the news.

CHAPTER FIVE

EASTERN TIME   CENTRAL TIME   MOUNTAIN TIME   PACIFIC TIME   WASTED TIME

SOME THINGS NEVER CHANGE

Since the founding of America, public servants have been loose with the people's money. There has always been work for the enterprising muckraker who, if he's cantankerous enough, will spare no one—not even George Washington, who was so devoted to our fledgling democracy that he refused to accept a salary as commander of the Revolutionary War armies.

Nevertheless, I conducted a belated investigation of Washington's finances. His expense ledger—a brittle, yellowing document kept in a vault at The National Archives—reveals that the more things change, the more they stay the same.

Our first president stands tall as a man of granite integrity so honest that he couldn't lie to his father about a vandalized cherry tree. Yet Washington, within his legal rights and with congressional permission, racked up a personal expense account during the eight-year Revolutionary War that would be the equivalent of $22.5 million today.

When General Washington presented his bill in July 1783 to Congress, few eyebrows were raised. The Comptroller of the Treasury not only did not quibble with the sum but sent a letter, thanking this hero of the Revolutionary War and complimenting him for displaying "that degree of Candor & truth . . . which invariably distinguish all your actions . . . ."

Never look a gift horse...

When Washington accepted command in 1775, he was roundly praised for refusing to accept a salary. In his acceptance speech, he generously proclaimed:

"As to pay, Sir, I beg leave to Assure the Congress that as no pecuniary consideration could have tempted me to have accepted this Arduous employment (at the expence of my domestic ease and happiness) I do not wish to make any Profitt from it. I will keep an exact Account of my expences. Those I doubt not they will discharge, and that is all I desire." (Spellings all original.)

Congress must have thought it had struck a bargain with the great general. They had offered him a salary of $500 a month, that would be equivalent to $25,000 a month today. If this seems generous, it would hardly compensate him for a job that would put him atop the list of traitors to be hanged by the British.

Congress should have insisted that Washington take the salary.

On the eighth day God created pork...

He was accustomed to fine living, having accumulated wealth that was multiplied when he married Martha Custis, the wealthiest widow in Virginia in that day. He went off to war, as befitted a Virginia gentleman of his stature, in grand style.

The total sum of Washington's expenses in the dollars of his day came to $449,261.51. That amount included the 6 percent annual interest that Washington charged for personally loaning the government the money for his expense account until he was reimbursed.

On General Washington's first day on the expense account, he spent a whopping $7,845—or $392,000 in today's money—for five horses and a top-of-the-line chariot known as the "Phaeton." That would pay for a small fleet of luxury cars today. But it is less than we pay today for an armored Presidential limousine—and much less than the outlay to whisk the President around in Air Force One. Still, in Washington's time, it was a royal sum for a chariot and horses.

One of the finest horsemen of his time, Washington was a good judge of horse flesh, and throughout the war he always paid more than top dollar for his mounts—to his relatives, as it turned out. While Washington was as lucky as he was courageous—frequently jumping into the thick of the battle and having his coat or hat but not himself shot up—his expensive horses were not so lucky. Even in the earlier French and Indian War, two horses were shot out from under him.

Two things are evident from Washington's "Household Expenses" during the war. One is that he kept what he bought on the public dime. A large collection of books, maps, telescopes, dishes, cutlery, tablecloths, a pair of bearskins and other items he bought on the expense account as "necessaries" ended up at Mount Vernon after the war. Apparently, the concept of a government surplus auction had not yet caught on.

The second thing is that neither Washington nor his servants must ever have lowered themselves to bargain for their goods.

To be sure, many merchants of his day took advantage of the war to practice some major price gouging and war profiteering. One of the best evidences of merchant inflation when they saw Washington coming was a single purchase on page 41 of the Expense Account book. The November 1781 purchase, a month after the British surrendered at Yorktown, had much more detail than Gen. Washington usually included, to wit:

"To John Likley's Acct. for 20 lbs. of Tea—it being for Public use."

Now there's no question that the troops deserved a celebration as the government's treat. There's also little doubt tea was more expensive in 1781 since the Bostoners had chucked some of it overboard years before, and many refused after to pay the taxes on the imported tea. But few of us would fail to gasp at the equivalent price of $23,400 for such tea today, or $1,170 a pound.

A third of the total eight-year expense account fell under the generic title of "Household Expenses." Washington preferred the lack of specificity in his account book. His four favorite words in the book were "etcetera" (rendered "&c &c &c" by Washington), "sundry," "severals" and, most favorite of all, "Ditto," often shortened to "Do."

Washington's "Household Expenses" totaled $157,330, the equivalent today of $7.87 million—enough to keep Washington, his household, and his general staff in champagne and caviar.

It's not a dumping ground, it's a library

Despite ample office space, members of Congress find that they don't have enough room to store all the paperwork they accumulate. So the General Services Administration has provided more than 60,000 cubic feet of space at its National Records Center in suburban Maryland for storage of the legislators' old papers. There's no limit to the space an individual member of Congress can commandeer, and some have filled more than 1,000 cubic feet with documents.

This paper dump costs about $50,000 a year to maintain, and Rep. Clarence Miller, R-Ohio, has suggested that much of this could be saved if his colleagues would bother to go through their files and keep only what's necessary.

Washington Merry-Go-Round
May 21, 1980

Just how high on the hog did they live? Beginning in 1777, General Washington's expense account got less and less specific— listing, for instance, $10,000 ($500,000 in today's dollars) to a certain colonel who spent the money on Washington's behalf in September 1780. No other explanation was offered.

Food, of course, was high on the scale of household expenses. Washington savored the finest foods, insisting on a French chef to cook them. The general gained 28 pounds throughout the war. His military larder must have overflowed with eggs, milk, pears, limes and various berries. The government was also charged for ice cream, an expensive novelty in that day. I prefer to believe none of these purchases were made during the dark days when the starving soldiers of the Revolutionary Army were reduced to eating the bark off trees and roasting shoe leather for meals.

General Washington's wartime wine cellar must also have been the pride of the continent. During his first year under siege (August 8, 1775, to March 19, 1776), he expended at least $6,160 ($308,018 in today's dollars) for alcohol. That's a staggering bar bill even by today's standards, amounting roughly to $38,500 a month on booze.

The general, who didn't drink much, must have entertained lavishly. He was strictly a one-bottle man, holding his consumption to a bottle (usually of imported Madeira wine) at a sitting. He was never known to be drunk.

The commander in chief should have been well groomed for battle. He listed $500 (or $24,975 today) paid to barbers during the first year of the war. Even two centuries later, a barber bill of roughly $2,000 a month would demand a close look at a general's coiffure. But perhaps Washington's barbers not only attended his coiffure but also his teeth. (Barbers were often dentists in those days.) Washington is known to have had a series of toothaches and extractions during the Revolutionary War. The least the military could do was pick up his dental bills. (The false teeth came later. His preferred set was ivory, but he also had sets made of hippo, cow and human teeth. Contrary to popular myth, he never had a wooden set.)

When they say all expenses paid, that meant...

One of the most intriguing entries on his household expense account was "Washing." Maybe his laundry was sent out. He listed at least $1,141 (or $57,031 today) that he spent on washing between 1775 and 1781.

I raise a delicate matter at this point: The money could have gone for more than just washing. Journals of Washington's day make it clear that it was acceptable at the time for gentlemen to visit the washerwoman or her daughters for services other than washing. There was no scandal attached to this practice.

A letter from one of Washington's earthy friends, Congressman Benjamin Harrison (father and grandfather of two U.S. presidents), offered the general "pretty little Kate, the Washerwoman's daughter" for his pleasure. There is no record of acceptance by Washington, and it's possible the letter was a British forgery—the disinformation of his day.

Washington even billed the U.S. government for his charity. In January 1776 he listed a gift of $650 ($32,500 today) for "the Relief of the distressed sad Wives & Children of the Soldiers from Marblehead"—and "Ditto" for the grieving dependents in Cape Ann.

One worrisome expenditure for $301 (or $15,050 today) went to "Mr. John Dunlap" who was publisher of the most important newspaper of the day, the Pennsylvania Packet of Philadelphia. Was General Washington buying influence with the media? The paper was notably pro-war and pro-Washington. Then again, maybe he was simply paying a high price for a subscription.

Payments were also listed to two different Indian chiefs— $458 (or $22,900 today)—to keep them friendly and on the American side. Another defensible amount was billed by the general: paying out of his own pocket for spies. In his account book, the spies are never named; they're identified only as dashes. To wit: "333 1/3 Dollars given to —— to induce him to go into the Town of Boston, to establish a secret correspondence for the purpose of conveying intelligence of the Enemys movements & designs."

According to the expense account, Washington laid out $62,762 ($3.1 million today) for his spies. Compared to the CIA's budget today, that's bargain-basement espionage. One of the general's final notes in the ancient account suggests that still more black-budget debts remained outstanding after the dust of the war had settled:

"Before these Accounts are finally closed, Justice and propriety call upon me to signify that there are Persons within the British Lines—if they are not dead or removed, who have a claim upon me, for their Services in conveying me private Intelligence, and which when exhibited, I shall think myself in honor bound to pay."

And people talk about Hillary

Not the least of George's billings were for Martha's excursions to the front. Several times she traveled to the battlefield, with a full entourage and all her finery, to visit her husband—at considerable cost to the government. The last expenditure is for $27,665—an astronomical $1.4 million in today's money—for "Mrs. Washington's travell Exps. in coming to & returning from my Winter Quarters per accts. rendered."

Washington knew this needed some explanation, and he gave it:

"Altho' I kept Memms of these Expenditures I did not introduce them into my Public Accounts as they occurred—the reason was, it appeared at first view, in the commencement of them, to have the complexion of a private charge—I had my doubts therefore of the propriety of making it—But the peculiar circumstances attending my Command, obliged me (to the no small detriment of my private Interest) to postpone the visit every year contemplated to make my Family between the close of

The international language of waste

The federal bureaucrats communicate with each other in a special language that is often called "bureaucratese." We call it gobbledygook. What, for example is a "re-employed annuitant?" In plain English, it's a civil servant who retires from the government and then is rehired as a consultant at a fat salary.

Washington Merry-Go-Round
February 23, 1981

one Campaign and the opening of Another—and this expence was incidental thereto, & consequent of my self denial, I have, as of right I think I ought, upon due consideration adjudged the charge as just with respect to the Public as it is convenient with respect to Myself; and I make it with less reluctance as I find upon the final adjustment of these Accts. (which have, as will appear, been long unsettled) that I am a considerable looser—My disbursements falling a good deal short of my Receipts . . . . "

Washington starts to catch on

Maybe it's not surprising that when Washington was elected our first president, and once again offered to take no salary but expenses only, Congress respectfully declined. They awarded him a salary of $25,000 annually ($1.25 million today), and Washington later complained that it was just not enough to live on.

George certainly had no reason to be looking dour on our dollar bill. Actually, if you look closely, there's a hint of a smile on the white-haired gentleman's mouth. And no wonder.

Yet George Washington's extravagances were barleycorn compared with the lifestyles of his latter-day successors. The heady, rarefied atmosphere inside the Oval Office today, with all the homage and emoluments, could turn the head of a saint. And few men who have occupied the White House lately have been saints.

The president is surrounded by fawning servants and obedient aides. He's so pampered and so insulated by the trappings of power that he's apt to forget he is the people's servant, not their master. High fences, patrolled by armed guards and sophisticated electronic devices, keep him aloof from the public and remote from reality. Bulletproof limousines with police escorts move him over the highways. Helicopters stand ready to lift him high above the traffic snarls, above the stink of the cities and the heads of the people who live in the squalor.

Should the president wish to relax, the White House grounds offer tennis courts, a putting green and a jogging track. Inside is an exercise room and a screening room. He also has a luxury box in each of the Kennedy Center theaters and unlimited use of the Camp David resort in the Maryland mountains. Among his many other perks and privileges is free health care at the White House Health Clinic and the Naval Medical Center.

How much does it cost to maintain the president in this sumptuous style? At least George Washington left a ledger. The total today is buried in a fiscal rat's nest designed to thwart and frustrate investigative reporters. According to my press notices, I'm supposed to be a pretty good news sleuth, but I freely confess that I've tried but failed to untangle the purse strings that ensnarl the White House.

Income is concealed; services are disguised; costs are hidden. If a corporation kept books in the White House manner, the top executives would be hauled off to prison. To put it bluntly, the White House budget is a fraud obviously intended to deceive the taxpayers. It doesn't come close to offering an honest account of what it costs to maintain the president. No complete tabulation of presidential spending even exists.

The president hides his extravagances out of the taxpayers' sight in dark bureaucratic corners. White House bills are simply charged to other government agencies which don't dare reveal how much they contribute to the president's upkeep.

I've uncovered this much: The armed forces secretly pay most White House expenses. The generals and admirals are eager to scratch the back of their commander in chief. In turn, every modern president has lavished billions on defense. The money is allocated more or less equally among the services, without much regard for military efficiencies or promised economies.

Several other agencies, ranging from the General Services Administration to the National Park Service, also contribute to the president's welfare. The White House groundskeepers, for example, draw their salaries from the Park Service.

How many personal servants attend the first family? Again, no list has ever been compiled. Inside observers place the figure at about 100, counting such specialists as florists and calligraphers (reportedly, five of each). The taxpayers are expected to fuel this White House spending mill without any idea of how much it's costing them. Finding the true figures is like identifying individual ants in an ant hill.

CHAPTER SIX

WALL STREET WELFARE

I t's known by the derisive term "corporate welfare," but that's not derisive enough for the practice of giving upwards of $100 billion a year to people who have no right to be on the dole.

These aren't single mothers on food stamps or struggling families in public housing. These are the barons of Wall Street, the corporate farms of middle America and the Fortune 500 companies, all of whom would be outraged should you tell them that they have become addicted to government handouts.

Yet the shocking truth is that American taxpayers empty their own pockets to line the Gucci wallets of this class of welfare recipient through tax breaks, direct subsidies and 125 federal programs. Tax breaks alone account for $70 billion of the $100 billion a year that are lost to the Treasury through corporate welfare.

Because of the power these welfare queens and kings wield in the corridors of Congress and the backrooms of the White House, you need not expect them to suffer when the budget cuts come. Poor families legitimately receiving federal aid are told that their days on the dole are numbered. But some of the richest corporations in the country will likely continue to collect.

Betting the farm

Uncle Sam spends about the same amount of money on food stamps every year as he does on subsidies to those who grow the food. They aren't the bucolic family farmers of yesteryear, but huge agri-businesses with a welfare mentality. One boondoggle, the Export Enhancement Program, arranges for grain farmers to sell their products overseas at cheaper prices and then pays them the difference between the foreign price and the going U.S. rate. In 10 years that handout amounted to $7 billion, almost half going to three huge corporations, one of them owned by a French company.

Even the few remaining family farmers eligible for the dole are better off than the taxpayers who subsidize them. According to a 1994 Census Bureau estimate, the average farmer had a net worth of more than $1 million while the median net worth of Americans was $36,623.

Not every farmer is on the government dole, only the ones who produce specific crops and products—wheat, rice, corn, cotton, sugar, milk, honey, peanuts and others. For the amount of money that the federal government has handed over to them in the last 10 years—$370 billion—Uncle Sam could have bought nearly all the farms in America.

In 1996 Congress took a big step toward eliminating these subsidies forever, but weaning farmers from welfare will prove to be a torturous process, one which I fear may be reversed if the squealing grows too loud.

The 1996 Farm Bill set in motion a seven-year phase-out of farm subsidies which farmers accepted because the new law, optimistically called the "Freedom to Farm Act," ostensibly ends the power of the federal government to tell the farmers what and how much they can plant. For seven years, farmers on the federal dole will receive a prearranged and declining welfare payment until 2002 when the act expires. These "transition payments" will cost you $36 billion; the old subsidies would have cost you an estimated $12.2 billion over the same seven years. But when the clock runs out on the new law in 2002, it's supposed to end farm subsidies forever. And if you believe that, I have some prime swamp land I'd like to sell you.

Members of Congress patted themselves heartily on the back for this great "reform," but they exempted some of the biggest beggars—the peanut, sugar, cotton and dairy farmers. The ever-popular "conservation" program, which pays farmers not to plant anything on 50 million acres of land, also escaped reform.

Farm subsidies grew out of the muddleheaded notion that farmers are a special class that cannot be expected to suffer from the same business losses as the average entrepreneur. Certainly, the production of the nation's food supply should be closely monitored, and the federal government should have a strategy to intervene whenever the supply is threatened. But American farm subsidies have gone beyond safeguarding the breadbasket.

Consider also the guaranteed and subsidized loans from the Farmers Home Administration. At a time when Uncle Sam is paying farmers not to grow crops, he is loaning money to other farmers to start them in the business. Who are these eager young farmers? They're the ones without the capital or experience or credit history they need to get loans from banks. Nor will anyone else loan them money—except you. You're so forgiving of their shortcomings that you don't seem to mind the fact that 70 percent of the loans end up delinquent or restructured to avoid delinquency.

Crop insurance programs to buffer farmers from the whims of Mother Nature cost you $1 billion a year. Americans shell out two or three times what other countries pay for sugar and peanuts because those who grow them here have been deemed worthy of special protection from nasty foreign competition. By one estimate, protected American farm products cost you more than $11 billion a year in higher food prices. The Agriculture Department spends an incidental $118 million a year staffing 60 foreign offices to promote U.S. farm exports because farmers can't be expected to advertise their own wares. Beekeepers still get millions of dollars in price supports because it was deemed necessary during World War II to subsidize the beeswax industry for waterproofing ammunition.

Cattle ranchers have their own special brand of corporate welfare. It's called "grazing fees," and Uncle Sam's largesse with your land is scandalous. The Bureau of Land Management will let ranchers run their cattle on public land for $1.35 a head per month, while the annual price a private pasture owner will charge is closer to $10 a head. Why? Because the ranchers complain that they can't make a profit if they have to pay a fair price. Ever sensitive to the needs of the ranchers, the BLM dropped the price by 26 cents in 1996 because the price of beef went down.

Who are these poor ranchers struggling to make ends meet? One is J.R. Simplot, the Idaho potato and frozen food king with a net worth of $500 million. In one year he paid you less than $90,000 to keep his cattle on your land—though the fair market price was closer to $400,000.

Perhaps the most galling of farm giveaways, even more galling than paying farmers to grow nothing, is the Market Promotion Program that pays companies to advertise American brand-name foods overseas because they apparently can't be expected to pay for their own ads. In the past this welfare program has given $14.5 million to Ernest and Julio Gallo, $3.8 million to M&M Mars, $14.9 million to Dole (the pineapple not the politician), and $66.9 million to Sunkist. Other beneficiaries on this gravy train are McDonald's, Pillsbury and Campbell Soup. Even foreign companies with U.S. suppliers are eligible for this welfare. One Turkish cigarette company got $650,000 from this advertising fund to buy new plant equipment simply because the Turkish ambassador asked nicely. A Japanese underwear maker got $1.6 million.

The budget for these foreign ads in 1995 was $85 million. But when Congress got down to some belt-tightening in 1996, there was hope that this bit of corporate welfare would end. Incredibly, it was given $90 million and renamed the Market Access Program, perhaps in the hope that no one would recognize the same old rat hole. Defenders of this program say that for every $1 of ad money spent, $2 to $7 in business is generated in the United States. If the return is so good, then why don't the companies pay for their own advertising?

> ### Someone should be not so friendly fired at the VA
>
> The Veterans Administration's friendly lending policies are costly to the taxpayer, according to a recent investigation. The VA writes off student loans to borrowers who are obviously able to pay. For example, one loan of $638 was deemed "uncollectible," but inspectors found the deadbeat in question was able to handle a $170,000 home mortgage.
>
> *Washington Merry-Go-Round*
> *March 24, 1980*

There's pork in them thar hills

While there might be a flimsy rationale for managing the nation's food producers, what possible reason could the federal government have to continue to carry gold miners on the corporate welfare rolls? When Ulysses S. Grant signed the Mining Act of 1872, the reason was to encourage Americans to settle the Wild West. The bait built into the law was that hard-rock miners could stake their claims on public lands for a pittance and never have to pay any royalties on whatever gold or silver the rocks yielded.

The last time I checked, the West was properly settled, even overpopulated in some spots, and gold had become its own best advertiser. Yet the General Mining Law of 1872 remains in effect and more than 330,000 active mining claims are fleecing you, the owners of valuable minerals on public land. For reasons unfathomable to the rational mind, this giveaway continues unabated while Congress looks the other way. During the past three years, mining companies have extracted more than $15.3 billion in minerals from your land but have paid you only $16,000 for the privilege.

Miners can take what they want from under the ground, paying an initial patent but no rent or royalties. And if they wish, they can buy the land from the Bureau of Land Management which computes the price based on the value of the surface of the land, not the potential value of the gold or silver underneath. And because most of the valuable minerals in the West lie under worthless desert acreage or steep mountain slopes, the land can be purchased for a song. The prices top out at $5 an acre. In one year alone, the BLM sold 20 parcels of land for $4,500 total. The General Accounting Office figured the land was worth up to $48 million. Some of the more attractive BLM mountain acreage is sold for pennies, then ends up being developed for ski resorts, golf courses and condominiums when the miners are finished with it.

American Barrick Resources Corp., a Toronto company, took $8.75 billion in gold from less than 2,000 acres of BLM land in Nevada after paying a mere $5,190 for the mining rights. Then in 1994, the company decided to buy the land it was exploiting. The purchase price was $9,765. The total treasure of gold from the acreage is expected to exceed $10.2 billion. Two other companies have their eye on platinum and palladium deposits worth $4 million in Montana. They're willing to pay a full $10,080.

Those who would exercise the common sense to reform the 1872 mining law point to the fact that the BLM charges fair royalties for the oil and gas that is extracted from federal lands. It is a hefty chunk of change amounting to $4.2 billion a year coming into the Treasury.

Do you think pork just grows on trees?

Far above the welfare cheats and food stamp chiselers on the federal Christmas tree are the timber companies. No one in the newspaper business, including me, can afford a love affair with trees. So when the Forest Service tells me that a particular stand of trees is expendable and will eventually be replaced by more growth, I'm not inclined to argue. But I can't abide selling those trees at giveaway prices and then paying to pave the road for the getaway truck.

That is exactly what happens every day in our national forests. Uncle Sam spends $95 million a year building access roads to trees about to be cut. After all, the woodsmen can't carry the logs out on their backs. The Forest Service would save money if it left the trees where they were. It costs more to build the roads than the logs are worth. But the Forest Service doesn't worry because you will pay the difference. After the cost of building the roads, maintaining the forest, and undercharging for the trees, the Forest Service timber program has lost more than $7 billion in the last 14 years. For your largesse, you have 360,000 miles of logging roads that you probably will never set foot on. What is the Forest Service's excuse? The losses are not really losses because the timber program has helped to keep the forests healthy and has provided roads for recreational access.

I would be more impressed if the timber companies didn't have a such tawdry record for bid rigging and conspiracy to keep the prices down and the subsidy up.

Back in 1984 I exposed a blatant attempt by President Ronald Reagan to scrounge votes in Oregon at a loss to the taxpayers of $600 million. As it happened, timber companies came crying to the White House that they could not pay the prices they had promised for trees cut on federal land. They wailed that the market price of lumber had dropped unexpectedly. Reagan gave them an extra five years to pay at no interest. The truth, I discovered, was that the large timber companies had deliberately bid outrageously high prices for federal timber so they could drive their smaller competitors out of the market. The big companies knew full well that they would not be able to pay those prices. And they gambled that the president would forgive and forget, at a cost of $600 million to us. Such outrages didn't stop with the Reagan campaign; they continue today and every day. You can keep current of daily abuses of power and corruption with my newsletter, the Jack Anderson Confidential. It's your twice-monthly update of this book.

Two years later I discovered that some forest rangers weren't even bothering to report when they saw evidence of bid rigging. The rangers said the top brass at the Forest Service and its parent agency, the Agriculture Department, were so cozy with the timber industry that nothing would be done about the complaints anyway. One ranger overheard four timber buyers conspiring not to bid against each other. They settled the negotiations with a flip of a coin. In another case, during an auction for the right to cut a certain stand of federal timber, two of the bidders asked for a recess so they could cut a deal between themselves. While the Forest Service officials quibbled about the propriety of stopping the auction, the two bidders left the room. When they returned, one of them dropped out.

If the Forest Service were a car dealer, then the Tongass National Forest would be its Edsel. This is America's largest national forest at 17 million acres, and it costs you about $20 million a year because the Forest Service doesn't know what a tree is worth. In one year alone, you spent $44.6 million helping the timber companies clearcut and haul trees out of the Tongass, and you got $209,000 in return. One company has a 50-year monopoly contract on Tongass timber, so don't expect any competitive bidding too soon.

Congress found its conscience in 1990 and set new rules about clearcutting to protect the wildlife in the Tongass. But Alaska's congressional delegation is constantly busy trying to chip away at those rules for the benefit of the timber companies and the jobs they provide.

The Thoreau Institute estimates that if Uncle Sam were to simply charge the fair market value for all the natural resources

---

More ideas for getting rich in publishing

Ever wonder what your senator reads? Outgoing Sen. Mike Gravel, D-Alaska, recently purchased copies of "Alexander the Great," and "Celts: People Out of Darkness." He charged the taxpayers $21.55 for the two books. Sen. Lloyd Bentsen, D-Texas, apparently hoping to sharpen his speaking skills, bought "2,500 Jokes to Start 'Em Laughing" and "2,000 New Laughs for Speakers." They cost the public $14.50.

Washington Merry-Go-Round
December 15, 1980

he sells or gives away, the Treasury could pocket $21 million in the next five years. But that bit of business sense seems to be over the heads of Congress.

How much does Uncle Sam love subsidizing private businesses? Let me count the ways:

• Your tax dollars pay for much of the pharmaceutical research done in this country. But when those new drugs are ready for the market, private companies say, "Thank you very much. We'll take it from here." For example, you paid $32 million toward the research to come up with the anti-cancer drug Taxol. Then you gave the research and the exclusive marketing rights to Bristol-Myers Squibb which turned around and sold the drug back to you. (The price was $986 for a three-week supply.) What's wrong with this picture?

• Back in 1935, electricity was a luxury for rural America. So Uncle Sam came to the rescue with the Rural Electrification Administration. The REA brought power to the heartland by giving money outright or loaning it to small electrical co-ops at below-market interest rates. For the last four years the loans have been a losing proposition, costing the Treasury more than it received in interest. Rural America has had its power for more than 20 years now, but Congress refuses to turn out the lights at the REA. In 1995 Senator John McCain had a novel idea. Why not make the borrowers prove that they really need your money and that they can't borrow elsewhere? The Senate rejected that attempt at reform. The program today is no more than a giveaway to private utility companies that could and should stand on their own. Turning this boondoggle over to the private sector would save the taxpayers $2 billion a year.

• Uncle Sam must think the cutting-edge companies of America wouldn't do their own high-tech research if he didn't pay them to do it. Result: techno-pork. It's distributed by The Advanced

Technology Program which gives hundreds of millions of dollars a year in research grants to companies like General Motors, AT&T, Xerox and General Electric. Republicans in Congress tried to eliminate this giveaway in 1996, but President Clinton wouldn't bite the bullet.

• The Economic Development Administration has a noble purpose and an ignoble record for accomplishing that purpose. It was established by President John F. Kennedy to give low-interest loans and grants to America's poorest counties so they can put the money into programs that stimulate their local economy. Its ignoble fate: It has become a pork barrel for members of Congress who dip into it and extract about $400 million for pet projects that rarely target the poor and needy.

• If you liked the savings and loan debacle, you're going to love the Pension Benefit Guarantee Corporation. This 20-year-old program was intended to insure that private pensions don't go belly up. It was also supposed to pay for itself through premiums, but that has turned out to be sheer fantasy. We, the taxpayers, subsidize the shortfall when pension funds can't cover their commitments. That deficit is expected to reach nearly $18 billion in 2001. We provide the backup system for 85,000 pension plans which are supposed to disburse retirement checks to 40 million Americans. The nation's biggest employers love having your money as a fallback. They love it so much that some of them routinely underfund their own pensions, and the government accepts their flimsy excuses.

• Next time you visit Washington, be sure to take a stroll down the one-mile stretch of Pennsylvania Avenue between the White House and the Capitol. You paid for it—the street lights, the sidewalks, the landscaping, the parks. After 24 years of design and construction to beautify this mile for the benefit of the businesses that line it, the Pennsylvania Avenue Development Corporation went out of business in 1996—$150 million bled from the taxpayers and $197 million in bills still to pay.

• Congress has never formally authorized the Minority Business Development Agency which, nevertheless, has spent hundreds of millions of dollars in the last 25 years teaching businesses how to land government contracts. The most important lesson: Make sure that a member of a racial or ethnic minority is the "front" for your company. During the Reagan and Bush administrations, I learned that this agency was being used to lure prominent minority entrepreneurs to switch their allegiances to the Republican Party in exchange for development grants. If we're stuck with this agency, at least it should teach business people how to make it in the private sector, not how to squeeze contracts out of the government.

• If you can't get a business loan anywhere else, turn to the Small Business Administration. They hand out about $1 billion a year, and they won't even look at you unless you have been turned down by at least two banks. Say bye-bye to about 20 percent of your money that the SBA loans.

• You can't open your newspaper these days without reading about a national park in desperate need of more money. Our natural and historic treasures are deteriorating for lack of maintenance money. And where will Congress turn to get that money? From you, of course. Visitors' fees will inevitably rise, campgrounds will be closed, and activities will be curtailed. But don't count on that extra money you pay in fees going directly into the parks. It will disappear into the general Treasury. From there Congress may or may not decide to spend it in the parks.

Job security, military style

The Pentagon's philosophy on expenditure of public funds was made stunningly clear the other day. One of my reporters called to inquire about a contract for 300,000 laminated-plastic recipe cards to be used by bartenders at the Army's officers' clubs and enlisted men's saloons around the world.

The bids aren't in yet, but the cost is expected to run somewhere between $5,000 and $10,000. When my reporter suggested that perhaps the military pubs could get along—as they have for decades—without official guidelines, the Pentagon spokeswoman observed brightly that "even if it is wasting money," printing the recipe cards will "still be providing jobs to someone."

Washington Merry-Go-Round
September 24, 1980

And don't expect Congress to turn to the most logical source for money—the private businesses that sell overpriced hamburgers, offer rental cars, and provide hotel rooms in the parks. These concessionaires operate on a sweet deal that dates back 30 years and requires them to pay only 2.6 percent of their profits to the federal government. If the concessionaires simply paid the federal government the same 10 percent that many state parks charge, it would bring $48 million more a year into the Treasury.

Some of these contracts were given out years ago when the Parks Service was desperate to provide visitors with services. Once concession operators get their noses in the park business, it is almost impossible to get them out. The notion of competitive bidding for these contracts is a joke. Of the 1,900 concession contracts signed since 1965, only seven went to newcomers who were competing against incumbents. Smokey the Bear needs a rebate.

And Congress needs to stop using the parks budget as another pork barrel. The Parks Service continues to get higher appropriations each year, much of it paying for pet projects of lawmakers. So instead of the Grand Canyon getting trail repairs, hundreds of thousands of dollars are spent to buy and restore the home of President William McKinley's in-laws.

• You may not be a smoker; you may even think it's a disgusting and deadly habit. But you are, nevertheless, a silent investor in the nation's tobacco farms. You spend about $25 million a year subsidizing crop insurance for tobacco farms and offering agricultural extension programs to help tobacco farmers grow more crops. With their customers dropping like flies, tobacco farmers need all the help they can get.

• The Export-Import Bank has been around for 60 years, loaning money to foreigners at below-market interest rates if they promise they will use that money to buy U.S. products. Yes, you pay people to buy American. In those 60 years, the bank has lost $8 billion, but the American companies on this gravy train, like Boeing and General Electric, still get their money. Turn this baffling concept around and you have still another corporate welfare program, the Overseas Private Investment Corporation. This one loans money, even providing risk insurance to American companies that want to develop markets in foreign countries. Both of these misguided programs benefit a few American companies at the expense of their American competitors.

• You spend about $1 billion a year paying companies to ship the goods they sell overseas on U.S.-flagged ships instead of foreign ships. This giveaway dates back to 1950 when the Defense Department convinced Congress that the United States needed to have a fleet of U.S. merchant ships always ready in case of a national emergency. It wasn't practical for the federal government to build and operate those ships itself, so it simply subsidized private U.S. shipping companies to make sure they never went out of business. The result is that U.S. ships can charge more than foreign carriers because the taxpayers are paying the difference. Those American companies have grown fat and lazy on the tax-payers' green. Indeed, they probably couldn't survive if they were cut off. But no matter. The Pentagon has said for years that it no longer needs a merchant marine fleet under U.S. flag. Is anyone on Capitol Hill listening? Does anyone care?

When corporations crack open our piggy bank, what do they find? Pork, of course

This is only a partial list of corporate welfare programs sucking money from the national Treasury. Two Cabinet-level departments—Commerce and Energy—are the funnels through which much of this welfare is siphoned into corporate coffers. After carefully pondering the matter, I am convinced that shutting down both departments would rectify the notion that what's good for Wall Street is good for all streets.

First to go should be the Commerce Department, the breeding ground of corporate giveaways. With an annual budget of $3.6 billion and 35,000 employees, Commerce not only nourishes overfed companies, it has also taken on duties that overlap so many other federal agencies that all the president's accountants and lawyers haven't been able to untangle the territorial issues.

The Commerce Department's sacred mission is to promote and protect the interests of private entrepreneurs. While a few industries may need that protection in the global marketplace, the department has gone beyond basic protection to promote habitual dependence that breeds more dependence.

Sixty percent of its budget and 37 percent of its staff have settled in an unlikely place—the National Oceanic and Atmospheric Administration. While this agency has a few functions that have legitimate public interest—conservation, species protection and limited research—it has assumed the welfare mentality of its parent, the Commerce Department. NOAA promotes commercial fishing development and produces navigational charts and maps, all for the benefit of fishing companies that pay nothing for the right to haul away the bounties of the ocean. NOAA's commercial giveaways rightly should be sold on the commercial market, while NOAA's conservation work could be assumed by the Interior Department, which already duplicates some of the work.

> ### It's not waste, it's a stockpile
>
> Squirrely bureaucrats at the Energy Department spent $250,000 last year storing useless documents in a Maryland warehouse. Among the eminently junkable material discovered by DOE inspectors were such items as 90,000 copies of a 1975 pamphlet titled "Why an Energy Crisis?" and 21,000 Gas Mileage Guide Reorder Forms, also dating back to 1975.
>
> *Washington Merry-Go-Round*
> *July 5, 1980*

A subset of NOAA, the National Weather Service, is also ripe for the pickings. There are now about 300 private companies in the United States that duplicate the work of the Weather Service, providing weather forecasts to the agriculture and aviation industries. Of course, we need a federal weatherman to alert us to Mother Nature's moods so we'll know how to bundle up the kids for the school day. But citrus growers and airline companies should pay for the more detailed advice they need—which is available from private forecasting companies that have a solid reputation for efficiency. Instead of ceding commercial forecasts to these up-and-comers, the National Weather Service is spending $4.6 billion of your money on a modernization program so it can compete with them.

The ambitious freshmen Republicans in the 104th Congress tried valiantly to shut down the Commerce Department in 1995, but they were no match for the department's biggest boosters— its own bureaucracy and President Clinton who has never hesitated to use the public purse to win friends and raise campaign contributions. At the same time, Clinton wants to suck more taxes out of corporations by closing corporate tax loopholes. It's a case of whatever Uncle Sam taketh, he giveth back—closing the loopholes while opening the doors to more tax-funded subsidies.

In a tawdry bit of politicking, Commerce Department employees, with White House connivance, capitalized on the tragic death of Commerce Secretary Ron Brown in an airplane crash in 1996. They tried to link Brown's legacy sentimentally to the continuation of the department. But the taxpayers cannot afford such an extravagant memorial to a public servant. If all the corporate welfare was stripped out of the Commerce Department's budget, its few critical functions—such as the Census Bureau, the Patent and Trademark Office, and a slimmed-down National Weather Service and NOAA—could be assimilated into other government entities.

The Energy Department not only burns oil, it burns money

The Energy Department was President Jimmy Carter's creation. After two decades, it's time to say "No thanks" to this misguided gift of a misguided president. Anyone who followed my reporting on the Carter years may remember that I was no fan of his. We would be better off if we eliminated from government the last vestiges of this well-intentioned man.

Carter's notion of a Cabinet-level Energy Department arose from a contrived energy crisis. Not content to have all of us turn down our thermostats and put on our sweaters, Carter threw the bureaucracy behind his effort to counteract an Arab oil embargo. No thanks to Carter, the price squeeze was broken and the crisis dissipated. But the Energy Department has proved to be more durable.

What we have left today is a Cabinet department whose mission was supposed to be energy conservation and alternative energy research. But it now spends 85 percent of its money on other functions, including nuclear weapons development, nuclear waste disposal and wholesale power marketing. This has developed into a bureaucratic enclave with a remarkable ability to remake itself whenever it is threatened with extinction. When the oil crisis abated, the department threw itself into weapons production. Then when the Cold War ended, the bureaucrats at the Energy Department quickly shifted their emphasis to environmental cleanup. DOE's latest incarnation is as an enthusiastic purveyor of corporate welfare, turning its laboratories and budget over to private companies for research they formerly paid to do themselves.

From its humble beginnings, the Energy Department has blossomed into the largest civilian contracting agency in the federal government. But growth has not taught DOE how to manage those contracts. On any given day the General Accounting Office can check the books at the Energy Department and find numerous rip-offs by contractors. In a typical case, the contractor chosen for work at a nuclear weapons plant was so unprepared for the job that the cost of the contract ballooned from $2 million to $72 million just to repair the mismanagement. Another contractor sweet-talked DOE into leasing 58 vehicles at the taxpayers' expense although the work site covering 1.2 square miles already had 800 bicycles and 1,100 vehicles to carry its workers around.

By mistake, DOE's facility in Richland, Washington, got $30 million more than it needed for its security operations. Instead of returning the money to the Treasury, the folks at Richland spent it on other projects.

Lockheed Martin Energy Systems manages the DOE facility at Oak Ridge, Tennessee, where it is restructuring the way business is done. Admirably, the company has managed to carry out the reforms without any layoffs. But why, then, did the company need to spend $8.7 million of your money on training programs and other services for displaced workers?

DOE's Northwest Bonneville Power Administration is supposed to market electrical power from federal dams. In one case Bonneville decided to buy 20 years' worth of power from one plant for $2.2 billion. The rub was that Bonneville needed to draw on the power plant for only six months out of the year, but it grandly agreed to pay for running the plant year round.

It isn't unusual for the Energy Department to sign contracts that require the taxpayers to reimburse the contractor for equipment or money the contractor's own employees have stolen. Other contracts require the taxpayers to pay cleanup costs, fines and legal fees if the contractor violates environmental laws.

One contractor at a nuclear weapons plant lost 10,000 secret government documents, yet the Energy Department didn't even know they were missing until the GAO did an audit. In the words of The Heritage Foundation think tank: "These management problems and the inefficiencies that flow from them have been caused largely by DOE's continual efforts to realign itself and justify its existence."

Perhaps no project more typifies the ability of this department to throw away money than its search for a permanent nuclear

---

If that's what he calls justice...

In decision votes, all the justices of the Supreme Court are equal. But in personal perquisites, Chief Justice Warren Burger is more equal than his eight colleagues, and this apparently irks some of them. The perk in question is limousine transportation: Burger has his own limo, complete with chauffeur; the other justices have to share two Lincoln Continentals among them. Rental for the limos and a station wagon for lesser court personnel comes to $11,500 a year.

Washington Merry-Go-Round
May 30, 1980

---

waste dump. DOE bureaucrats have already spent more than $4 billion just looking at the possibility of maybe storing the waste at Yucca Mountain in Nevada. In their infinite wisdom, the bureaucrats estimate they will spend another $2.3 billion before they have finished thinking about Yucca Mountain. Construction could cost another $30 billion. But given DOE's record of mental constipation, there is no reason to fear that the project will ever reach the construction phase.

For 50 years the taxpayers have been subsidizing the production of privately sold electrical power through regional Power Marketing Administrations. These PMAs, now run by the Energy Department, sell wholesale power to electric utility co-ops. The power comes from 131 taxpayer-built dams across the country. Both the PMAs and their dams borrow money from the Treasury at below market interest rates, but their rate of paying back these loans hovers between poor-risk and deadbeat status; only 25 percent of $16 billion in loans has been repaid. Though consistently unable to repay their debt to the taxpayers, the PMAs sell their electricity well below the market price. If a big industrial user of electricity experiences a setback in business, for example, then the PMAs drop their prices. Once again, you taxpayers run a very forgiving line of credit.

This list of Energy Department throwaways rolls on: enriching uranium for private nuclear power plants; pouring $200 million into research to perfect an advanced, light-water nuclear reactor that no utility in its right mind would buy; investing millions of dollars a year in coal research when private utilities should be footing the bill; spending $250 million a year to keep the Nevada Test Site for nuclear weapons up and running; spending $430 million a year on energy conservation research that benefits private industry.

Clinton's Energy Secretary, Hazel O'Leary, added a new dimension to DOE waste—globetrotting. She spent hundreds of thousands of dollars flying first class all over the world, ostensibly to generate business for American companies, although what that has to do with the missionless Energy Department is still a puzzle. O'Leary originally claimed that her travels would be justified by $19.7 billion in new contracts coming to American companies. But the GAO did its own count and said O'Leary may have rustled up only $488 million in new business.

That hardly offsets the waste her department so often generates with the stroke of a pen on a misbegotten contract benefitting those same businesses. Nor is such corporate hustling the proper function for a Cabinet department that should never have been created.

Finding a silver lining around the pork

I will be the first to admit that there is danger in distilling these corporate welfare programs down to a few pithy anecdotes and shocking dollar amounts. There are jobs at stake along with the careers and lifework of real people with good intentions. Yet our Founding Fathers never intended for the fortunes of the U.S. economy to be so entangled with the whims of the federal government.

Nor do I mean to indulge in the popular American sport of corporate bashing. From Ralph Nader to Pat Buchanan, anti-business agitators have persuaded most Americans that contractors overcharge and defraud the government. Surveys claim that the public has turned against government contractors more now than at any time since the rebellious 1960s. People also believe corporations are banking record profits while they downsize and downgrade their work forces.

Too often, the corporate response has been defensive, evasive, arrogant and laced with business-speak that most folks don't understand. It's hard to blame the people for their hostility when corporate executives, in response to criticism, argue that their responsibility is to serve stockholders. This confirms the public impression that profits, not people, drive government contractors.

Yet, after half a century at the Washington ringside, I am obliged to report that I have found politicians and bureaucrats more at fault than contractors. Corporations that overcharge usually have no other choice. The government's ponderous processes, entangling red tape, mountainous paperwork, and infinite specifications are the worst culprits, remorselessly pushing up prices.

Most Americans realize it costs money to run the government, and they're willing to pay their share. But they believe, correctly, that the government takes too much, spends too much, and accomplishes too little. I must also confirm this much. Increasingly, corporate contractors are becoming co-conspirators.

CHAPTER SEVEN

AND THIS LITTLE PIGGY
WENT TO CONGRESS

The pious sermons on Capitol Hill about God, country and a balanced budget wouldn't have such a hollow ring if the sermonizers practiced the economy they preach. But on their home ground, they speak out of the other side of their mouths.

The spending they denounce in Washington, they praise at home—if the projects are located and the money is spent in their own backyard.

This double-speak is routine for members of Congress, who like to pose as statesmen while they engage in politics as usual. Since the inner workings of Congress are largely shielded from the public, and since no single member can be held accountable for what the whole Congress does, they can sound noble while they behave otherwise. Few legislators have the power to shape bold national policies or the authority to make great decisions. More characteristically, they bargain selfishly for patronage and pork as the price of their support for national programs.

Their favorite, if mythical, gathering place is around the "pork barrel"—an unsavory, 19th-century metaphor taken from the practice of doling meat out of a barrel to hungry field slaves who had to fight for their share. Similarly, members of Congress crowd around the money barrel, jostling to grab some. This annual scramble for pork is dressed up in solemn rules and lofty language. But, by any other name, it is still money grubbing, and the politicians' purpose is to ingratiate themselves with voters.

If a defense contract or a public boondoggle will keep a few folks back home off the unemployment rolls, it will gain the ardent support of their loyal legislators who are quick to decry boondoggles in someone else's territory. For the 50 years I've kept a watch on Washington, our politicians have been on a spending spree that they pretend to denounce, scattering our tax dollars like autumn leaves, running up deficits and camouflaging the costs.

Sadly, the taxpayers themselves are accomplices in this masquerade. Nearly $1 million spent on lowbush blueberry research in Maine may look like a boondoggle to the taxpayers in Arkansas. But the folks in Maine are just as outraged about the $4.7 million spent for a Rice Germplasm Center in Stuttgart, Arkansas. And in both Arkansas and Maine, voters will enthusiastically re-elect the members of Congress who brought home that federal bacon. Polls consistently show that voters think everyone in Congress is a profligate spender, except their own favorite legislators.

If pork didn't generate votes, the pork barrel would be replaced with something more politically productive. Voting for the representative who brings home the most pork has become democracy, American style.

The main course of any good Hawaiian is pork

In 1996 pork barrel spending amounted to an average of $5.96 going to "benefit" every man woman and child in the country, but in reality the money was not equally distributed. The big winners were Hawaiians whose state won $55.44 per capita in pork projects. That figure prompted Citizens Against Government Waste to pick Hawaii's Senator Daniel Inouye as the winner of the "Lifetime Achievement Award" in the pursuit of pork. He snagged $67 million of pork projects in 1996 for a grand total of $610 million since 1991.

This game of political poker, using multimillion-dollar chips, costs the taxpayers billions of dollars every time members of Congress sit down to play it. Some of the pork barrel projects aren't worth the paper the appropriations bills are printed on. Few are justified at a time of runaway deficits. Members of Congress doggone well know this. That's why the pork is hung out to cure behind closed doors.

I subscribe to the definition of pork suggested by Citizens Against Government Waste. Under that criteria, pork is anything that:

— is requested by only one chamber of Congress;
— is not specifically authorized;
— is not competitively awarded;
— is not requested by the president;
— greatly exceeds the president's budget request or the previous year's funding;
— is not the subject of congressional hearings;
— serves only a local or special interest.

In this time of crippling national debt, it should be appalling to the taxpayers that money would be spent on anything fitting those criteria.

Learning the four R's:
reading, 'riting, 'rithmatic and rip-offs

An accomplished veteran of the pigpen can always find money for his or her pet projects, even if the authorizing committees reject the expenditures. One of the most slippery tactics is called "academic earmarking"—appropriating money to a specific university, funneled through a given federal agency.

Representative George Brown of California got a lesson in academic earmarking from his colleagues in 1993. He was chairman of the House Science, Space and Technology Committee where the academic giveaways originate. Brown was outraged when a House subcommittee on energy and water development decided to hand out $95 million in academic grants. He angrily took to the House floor and forced a vote on the projects. They were decisively struck out of the budget bill.

But two weeks later the same grants cropped up again in a defense appropriations bill, like an alley cat with extra lives. Unfortunately, that time the House rules prevented Brown from forcing another vote. Those rules constantly shift at the whim of the House Rules Committee, which can decide how a bill will be handled, whether amendments will be allowed, and whether debate will be permitted on those amendments.

Under these rules of convenience, a $1 million appropriation for studying Brown Tree Snakes popped up in the 1996 defense appropriations bill. Incidentally, the Brown Tree Snake is found only in Guam and can't survive in North America.

How to make money
in the calendar business

Congress began its annual spending binge this year with a traditional boondoggle. The lawmakers mailed out 1.1 million calendars to the taxpayers who wind up paying the freight. Each congressman gets 2,500 of the special calendars annually and gets some free publicity with the voters by having his name stamped on them. The cost of preparing the calendars was about $600,000, but that doesn't include the money spent for envelopes and postage fees. Last year, the venture cost the Treasury $2 million.

Washington Merry-Go-Round
March 3, 1980

The wondrous rules also resulted in a 1996 agriculture budget with only 7 percent of the research grants for the Cooperative State Research programs actually requested by the Agriculture Department.

The practice of earmarking has become the favorite way to bypass the congressional process. This shortcut requires a friend who is one of the 13 chairmen of the House Appropriations subcommittees—called the "College of Cardinals." If the Cardinals look fondly on the project, they dip into the pork barrel for you. Not coincidentally, the term "earmark" comes from the practice of nicking the ears of pigs to mark ownership.

All hail the King

The King of Pork, crowned by Citizens Against Government Waste, is West Virginia's venerable senator, Robert Byrd. No other contenders came close to challenging him for the title. In 1989 he threw himself on the sacrificial altar for his state: He gave up the Senate leadership to take the helm of the Senate Appropriations Committee. It appeared to his startled colleagues to be a step down. But it was a giant leap for West Virginia. "I want to be West Virginia's billion-dollar industry," he said. He reached the goal in three years.

Senator Byrd started out as a youngster to pursue his goals on someone else's dime. By his own account, he courted his schoolboy sweetheart, Erma James, by giving her free candy that a friend had given him. The moral, boasted the senator, is "to court your girl on another boy's bubblegum." He has used the same technique to court West Virginia voters—with generous handouts of the taxpayers' money.

There is scarcely a town in West Virginia that doesn't boast some federal bauble that Byrd negotiated, manipulated or outright abducted for his state. In return, his grateful constituents have emblazoned "Robert C. Byrd" on just about everything that will hold still. In Beckley, the town fathers decided to erect a statue of Byrd, with hand outstretched, in a minipark where Robert C. Byrd Drive meets Rural Acres Drive. It is the outstretched hand, with the golden palm, that West Virginians honor.

The acquisitive Byrd won't hesitate to uproot whole chunks of the bureaucracy, such as the FBI's fingerprint bureau, and move them lock, stock and pork barrel to West Virginia.

With appropriate stealth, Byrd tried to move the entire CIA headquarters from the Washington area to Charles Town, West Virginia, in 1991. He bypassed all the usual channels and went straight to President George Bush and CIA Director William Webster. By some miracle of horse trading, he got them to put Charles Town on the top of the list of possible new sites for the CIA headquarters. No one bothered to notify the House Intelligence Committee, which has jurisdiction over the CIA, nor its chairman, David McCurdy, who was startled to learn that his charge was about to be removed from under his nose.

The indignant McCurdy convened a rare open meeting of the Intelligence Committee and raked Webster over the coals. Thus Byrd, whose manipulations were usually kept quiet by gentlemen's agreement, was caught in the glare of the spotlight.

When Webster began to falter, Byrd met privately with McCurdy. First Byrd cajoled, but the flattery failed. Then he played his trump card: He threatened to cut off McCurdy's home state of Oklahoma from the pork pipeline that ran through Byrd's committee. Incredibly, McCurdy made history that day in the backrooms of the Senate; he refused to budge. Byrd was dealt a rare defeat in the game of pressure politics.

Undeterred, he connived in 1994 to waste nearly $140 million moving 200 employees at NASA's Earth Observing System from White Sands, New Mexico, to Fairmont, West Virginia. Yet, in a debate over funding for the Space Station, he complained that "things on Earth need a little attention sooner than those things in outer space." Nobody tends to things on Earth better than Robert Byrd.

In 1984 the House voted overwhelmingly against the $200 million Stonewall Jackson Dam in West Virginia. Even the local congressman, Bob Wise, admitted it was boondoggle. But Byrd placed more than 120 calls to House members who were considering a motion to kill the project. His power of persuasion convinced them to authorize $26 million to begin the project.

What is the secret of Byrd's success in redistributing the national wealth to West Virginia? As appropriations chairman under the Democrats, he could control the outward flow of tax revenue. And he's still a master of the Senate rules which enables him to pull obscure rules out of the hat to confound his opponents. He's also as relentless as he is remorseless. He doesn't hesitate to use his power to deprive opponents of appropriations for their own pet projects. He has warned privately that anyone who crosses him will pay the price.

Most politicians caught with their hand in the pork barrel would be defensive, but Byrd is openly proud. He defiantly breaches the line between principle and pork. Pork barrel spending may be a dirty phrase, but Byrd lives and dies by it. In a debate over a pork-heavy transportation bill, he said, "Oh, they say [I am] trying to get everything [I] can for West Virginia. I would not be worth my salt if I did not attempt to represent the people of West Virginia . . . . They may call me provincial if they wish, I do not care."

If we didn't ask, who would care?

The federal government's curiosity is insatiable. Forms are constantly going out from Washington demanding answers to endless questions.

The Health, Education and Welfare Department, for example, requires every college and university to fill out several annual reports. One of the questionnaires, a 50-page document entitled "Degrees and other Formal Awards Conferred," was dispatched this year to every one of the nation's 3,055 institutions of higher learning.

But unfortunately, 37 of the 50 pages didn't apply to the 1,141 community colleges, which got the full, fat forms anyhow. These colleges, of course, returned the 37 pages absolutely blank. Since these forms came in triplicate, this amounted to about 120,000 pages of blank paper.

Washington Merry-Go-Round
August 28, 1976

At a tribute dinner for Byrd in 1994, President Clinton good-naturedly reminded the senator about how the two had disagreed over funding for the Space Station: "He said he couldn't do that [support the Space Station] unless I were willing to move the Capitol to West Virginia. I'm still considering it."

And the runner-up is...

When it comes to cleaning out the pork barrel, no one has attained Byrd's class. But Congressman Jamie L. Whitten was close. The good folks in his home state of Mississippi stood solidly for cutting the deficit as long it didn't interfere with Whitten's heroic efforts to bring federal money to Mississippi.

That's what kept the gentleman from Mississippi in the House for 52 years. In each re-election campaign, he bought newspaper ads with pictures of the projects American taxpayers had gifted to the state while he was chairman of the House Appropriations Committee.

In 1992 his appreciative constituents showed that they could give as well as receive, presenting their congressman with a monument to his magnanimity: the Jamie L. Whitten Historical Center outside Tupelo, Mississippi. It was an easy gesture for Mississippians to make; they didn't pay for it. Instead, the six federal agencies that Whitten most often tapped for pork largesse were compelled to ante up tens of thousands of dollars each to help build this self-congratulatory edifice.

In return, each of the agencies—the National Park Service, the Tennessee Valley Authority, the Appalachian Regional Commission (ARC), the National Aeronautics and Space Administration, the Soil Conservation Service and the Forest Service—got the right to set up an exhibit in the center, boasting about the projects Whitten had won from them over the years.

The visitor's book at the facility testifies that relatively few tourists are beating down the doors to see this ode to Jamie. The congressman himself didn't live long enough to enjoy it. He died in 1995.

The center proudly overlooks Whitten's biggest conquest, the $2 billion-plus, 234-mile Tennessee-Tombigbee Waterway—the project former Senator William Proxmire called "the federal pork barrel's greatest monument." It cost 10 times more than originally promised.

Derogatorily called "The Big Ditch" by its neighbors, the waterway was an Army engineer's dream. The corps likes nothing better than to dig and pave, and the "Tenn-Tom" represents a frenzy of cutting through mountains, building 10 locks and dams, scooping out two and a half times the amount of earth dug from the Panama Canal—a mighty effort to create a man-made Mississippi River less than 150 miles to the west. Whitten promised that the new commercial waterway would bring greater prosperity to the region. That didn't happen. Fishermen love the canal, but commercial barges still prefer to take the Mississippi River.

There were advance warnings about this horrendous boondoggle. In calculating the future use of the waterway, the Corps of Engineers used a 3.25 percent interest rate. That was during the presidency of Jimmy Carter when, as anyone who lived through that economic nightmare will testify, 3.25 percent was about 17 percentage points off the mark. And while the Corps of Engineers was cheerfully boasting the waterway would be worth $125 million a year to the economy of the region, the General Accounting Office was projecting closer to $12 million.

The Appalachian Regional Commission, Whitten's partner in this scam, went to some favorite Washington consultants and forked over $350,000 for a 448-page study that concluded, ridiculously, that by the year 2000, the Tenn-Tom would generate 134,600 new jobs and $1.4 billion in personal income.

When doubts were raised about continuing the funding, as frequently happened during the construction, Whitten didn't bother to seek new money from Congress. He simply dipped into leftover construction money from other Army Corps of Engineers projects.

Appalachian Regional Commission Federal Co-Chairman Winifred Pizzano flew down for the May 30, 1985, dedication of the Tenn-Tom and offered obsequious homage to Whitten. She praised him for "never wavering, even in the face of fierce pressure from a president [Carter] of his own party" who tried to stop the project. "This project is clearly a credit to everyone who helped in any way," said Pizzano.

And then, to prove that pork begets pork, she announced that ARC would spend millions more to build six ports to take advantage of what turned out to be a nonexistent traffic jam on the river.

When it came to public works projects, Whitten was a master of political engineering. He confided this political trade secret to the man who succeeded him as House Appropriations Committee chair, Bill Natcher. "If we want this [Tenn-Tom] project to succeed," Whitten told Natcher, "we must see that we start at the upper end of the project, that we start in the middle, and that we start at the tail end of it. That is the way to bring Tombigbee along. If we start in one place in the beginning at the upper end of it, we will never carry it through."

Just what we need, a machine to sit around on its butt in federal offices

Uncle Sam spent four years and $75,000 building a contraption to test the durability of sofas for federal offices. The machine whacks the sofas a couple of hundred thousand times. If the couch survives, then it is certified durable enough for bureaucratic behinds.

Washington Merry-Go-Round
February 23, 1981

In other words, move the project so far along, in a patchwork fashion; then there's no turning back. It is a cardinal rule of pork that once a project is rolling, it will pick up more money like a snowball until it reaches the point of no return—when it will cost more to stop the madness than continue.

Where there's an appropriations committee there's a way

Members of Congress who decry wasteful pork barrel spending when they address their constituents frequently drop those pretensions on Capitol Hill. In one House hearing, Representative Tom Bevill of Alabama recounted with admiration how another Alabaman squeezed some pork out of President Franklin Roosevelt: The smooth talker, who then headed the University of Alabama, met with FDR and pressed for federal funding for a new university library. As Bevill recounted the meeting:

"President Roosevelt said, 'Well, Dr. Denny, you know, it would take all the gold in Fort Knox to build a library on every university campus in this country, and if I build one for you, I would have to build one for everybody. Besides, I don't have any authority to do it anyway. What possible authority could I have?'

"And Dr. Denny said, 'Well, Mr. President, we had a library until you Yankees came through and burned it.' Then he added, 'You can build it under the War Claims Act.'"

Pork barreler Bevill finished his laudatory story by noting that President Roosevelt in fact did build it under that irrelevant law. "So I thought I might make that point here. This is the South still recovering from [the Civil War]."

On hearing pork justified as war reparations, Congressman John T. Myers of Indiana retorted: "I have heard it called a lot of things, but never foreign aid before. That's a new excuse."

Unruffled, Bevill replied playfully, "I have been trying to get foreign aid [for Alabama] ever since I have been here to recover for those war damages!"

When Democrats ruled the roost, Bevill was chairman of the House Appropriations subcommittee on water projects. He proved himself to be an unabashed consumer of pork. The head of that committee holds life and death power over more pork barrel projects than any other member. His nod of approval can mean a dam or a dredging project in the district of a colleague who needs help for re-election.

So when Bevill laid down a law for pork barrel supplicants to follow, they obeyed it, period. All except the rule maker himself. Traditionally, a dam or bridge or other pork project is first authorized by the appropriate committee—usually Public Works. Then, after hearings and debate, the Appropriations Committee must agree to put up the money to pay for it.

But in the mid-1980s, Appropriations got highhanded, drafting money bills that also wrote legislation, much to the disgruntlement of the authorizing committees. Tom Bevill to the rescue.

In a noble sacrifice of his own power as chair of an appropriations subcommittee, Bevill passed the word that no amendments would be introduced in the committee that could be construed as "authorizing legislation." His subcommittee would take the high road and adhere to its mandate, putting up the money only after the actual construction projects had been okayed by the authorizing committees.

But lo and behold, while the other subcommittee members obediently restrained themselves, Bevill inserted an amendment directing that a $9.5 million Army Corps of Engineers school be built on the campus of the University of Alabama at Huntsville. The money would come from a "revolving fund" of corps' money that had been approved earlier and not yet spent.

There were other rules Bevill ignored, like the little requirement that competitive bids be taken from other universities and the prohibition against building federal facilities on nonfederal land without the approval of Congress. Those were small hurdles for a porkmaster.

Once the pork barrel bill—with its Bevill amendment—reached the floor of the House, there was no chance that it could be challenged. It was protected by a special rule forbidding challenges to amendments. This is the traditional procedure used to protect pork projects from being excised.

Another hero
in the mighty pork brigade

Senator Quentin Burdick left a trail of pork that will not be easily forgotten, and to make sure, his proud staff put it all on paper. Burdick died in 1992 at age 84 after a career in which he left his mark as a low-profile but high-powered soldier for his home state of North Dakota. He was known for his iron handshake, his spry wit, and his ability to siphon federal funds into North Dakota.

Burdick's obscure status for a man who had been in the Senate since 1960 seems inconsistent with a list his staff assembled of all the federal projects and grants he helped acquire for his state from his vantage point on the Senate Appropriations Committee. The list filled two single-spaced, legal-size pages. It added up to nearly half a billion dollars.

Yet Burdick himself left the bows for others. A 1990 study by Southern Illinois University counted the number of mentions that senators got on network news broadcasts, and Burdick was never mentioned once in four years. His response was, "I don't make a nuisance of myself trying to get on TV just to get on there. I'm not running for president."

Burdick's brush with national notoriety—and some infamy—came after he procured a $500,000 federal grant in 1990 to help build a German-Russian museum in Strasburg, North Dakota, the birthplace of Lawrence Welk. Before it was finally withdrawn, the grant became a national symbol of wasteful, constituent-driven spending.

Burdick had a refreshing in-your-face rejoinder: "I'll get everything North Dakota is entitled to now." Even those who disagree with the principle of putting parochial interests before national ones must admire Burdick's lack of guile and deep-seated devotion to his constituents.

Upon Burdick's death, President Bush issued a statement saying that the senator had "served his country with great distinction." But Burdick was not all that popular with Bush who had Burdick in mind during a blistering attack on congressional spending during the State of the Union address in 1992. "I call upon Congress to adopt a measure that will help put an end to the annual ritual of filling the budget with pork barrel appropriations," Bush thundered. "Every year the press has a field day making fun of outrageous examples—a Lawrence Welk museum, a research grant for Belgian endive."

Pork is always on the menu

Here's food for thought that taxpayers might want to chew on as they read about congressional budget-cutting activities: The public picks up part of the tab for our legislators' meals in the dining rooms and cafeterias on Capitol Hill. Last year, for example, government auditors found that Senate dining facilities alone required $760,930 in subsidies to defray the cost of salaries and miscellaneous expenses. Even with that help, the operation wound up in the red by almost $80,000. The eateries—which are supposed to be self-sustaining—are for senators, members of their staffs and any stray taxpayers who happen to find out about them.

Washington Merry-Go-Round
May 29, 1980

These broadsides were welcomed by Burdick as confirmation of his campaign literature. So many federal dollars were steered North Dakota's way that in 1991 the state ranked third in the amount received per person.

Burdick's "Golden Mile" in Fargo, North Dakota, is perhaps pork's best example of tidying up the loose ends. The mile began as a gravel road through a sunflower field on the west side of the North Dakota State University campus. Along Burdick's mile are pieces of pork that the senator brought home—Agriculture Department research labs on the campus. Burdick looked at his accomplishments along that gravel road and decided the road needed to be paved. Of course, he wanted the federal government to pay the bill. Federal workers needed proper access to their agriculture labs, Burdick said.

The unspoken truth: It was North Dakota State football fans who needed proper access to their new 17,000-seat football stadium. And taxpayers all across the country paid for it.

Something smells fishy

Members of Congress will champion ridiculous causes to win favor at home. In 1987 Mississippi Congressman Mike Espy proposed something fishy: "National Catfish Day." The rest of Congress preferred to let this silly bill slip off the hook, but by some skillful angling, Espy saved it.

His original resolution designated April 4 as the day to give the catfish national recognition. But that date came and went while the catfish waited and the resolution wallowed in committee. Then, upon the advice of more seasoned members, Espy changed the date of National Catfish Day to June 25 and embarked on an all-out lobbying campaign.

He phoned colleagues. He buttonholed them in the corridors. He explained to anyone who would listen that his district—third poorest in the nation—was the number-one producer of catfish. He pointed out that 17 percent of his constituents were out of work, and publicity for the catfish industry would boost sales and get people off the unemployment rolls. "National Catfish Day means jobs," he pleaded.

Before long, Espy signed up 220 co-sponsors, more than enough to raise the bill on the House floor where it passed swimmingly.

In a further effort to lift the catfish from its primordial slime and elevate it to the status of a gourmet delicacy, Espy staged a catfish fry for 120 guests, among them the secretary of the Army and some Pentagon procurement big shots. In the three months before the fish fry, the Army had purchased 90,000 pounds of catfish—a culinary choice Espy wanted to encourage. He intended to see to it that the bottom-dwelling fish remained on top of the Army menu.

When the Republicans gained control of the House in 1995, they banned commemorative legislation outright. If the ban sticks, there will be no more "National Whatever" days.

Why should Americans enjoy all the pork?

Some members of Congress have developed such an appetite for pork that they can't resist laying out a spread even for people who can't vote for them. In 1989, for example, New York Congressman Stephen Solarz junketed around the South Pacific, stopping at the Solomon Islands to schmooze with the government leaders. The locals were embarrassed because they had to receive a lord high congressman in an old World War II Quonset hut which served as their parliament building.

Not to worry. Solarz arrived with the idea in his head of having the federal government give the island people a monument in memory of the American soldiers who died in the battle of Guadalcanal. Why not give the islands a parliament building instead of a plaque?

That is how the 1991 Defense Appropriations Bill ended up with $5 million for the new building. How a simple war memorial turns into a parliament building and ends up in a defense spending bill with no questions asked is a puzzle that can only be understood on Capitol Hill where it isn't considered odd at all.

The only odd thing was that Solarz didn't try to install the building in his home state.

There is harsh retribution for rocking the pork boat

In the annals of congressional history, a few bad members have gone against the tide of self-serving appropriations. They have been beaten back with such viciousness as to teach a lesson to anyone who might try again.

In 1993 the lesson was impressed on Minnesota Congressman Timothy Penny. The Democrat had joined with Ohio Republican Representative John Kasich to sponsor a $90 billion package of proposed budget cuts. It was a modest proposal by Washington standards, spread out over five years. But the Penny-Kasich bill didn't track with President Clinton's own budget agenda. First lady Hillary Rodham Clinton told the Democratic leadership, "I want Penny-Kasich dead in two days."

Penny's account of what happened next is enough to raise the hair on the back of the neck of anyone who doesn't understand business-as-usual in Washington. First the organized special interest groups were rallied to scream about the grief the Penny-Kasich bill would cause them. Senior citizens and teachers allied with liberal spenders of all stripes and generated a blizzard of mail that hit Capitol Hill. Clinton aides and Cabinet members led the chorus of howls about the suffering that would be inflicted by the cuts.

Then the Clinton congressmen unleashed the ultimate weapon, pork. From the bulwarks of the House Appropriations Committee, they fired off letters to members of Congress, warning that their home-state pet projects would be in jeopardy if they voted for the Penny-Kasich bill. The letters were personalized and itemized for each recipient, holding as hostage the pork projects they held dear. Some newer members of Congress were shocked. The veterans were nonplussed.

Oklahoma Congressman Dave McCurdy noticed his letter was signed by Tom Bevill, so he sent a reply, reminding Bevill pointedly that one of his own pork projects was pending in the committee that McCurdy chaired. And so the crossfire of mail shot back and forth with threats and counterthreats. In the end, the Penny-Kasich package lost by four votes.

First-term Congressman Thomas Andrews of Maine had a similar misadventure in 1992. He dared to challenge his fellow Democrats to reject the B-2 Stealth Bomber when it appeared in the 1993 defense bill. The party had already brokered a deal with the White House to approve 20 planes, and House Democrats invited Andrews to shut up.

But Andrews wouldn't. He couldn't understand why 20 doomsday bombers were needed to support a Cold War that had already been won. You probably guessed it; Andrews lost this budget battle. Several colleagues extended their private sympathies but explained that a vote against the B-2 would jeopardize defense contracts in their home states.

To discipline Andrews, the House Appropriations subcommittee on defense punished him by removing from the budget one of four destroyers that was scheduled to be built in his home state of Maine. The money was diverted instead to build an amphibious ship in the district of—who else?—Jamie Whitten.

Andrews had been warned. When he first stepped onto the House floor to introduce his amendment, one prominent

---

Ho-Ho-Ho

Christmas comes in September for federal agencies. The end of that month is also the end of the fiscal year, when leftover money must either be spent or turned back to the Treasury.

To prevent that bureaucratic horror of horrors, department heads authorize orgies of spending to justify the inflated budget they wangled out of Congress the year before. Useless purchases, unnecessary overtime, pointless projects—the whole mighty arsenal of federal boondoggles is drawn on to wipe out the embarrassing surplus.

One of the more colorful examples occurred in the Federal Highway Administration's Denver office last Sept. 15, when officials okayed the purchase of 120 live plants for $7,000. The plants won't be delivered until spring, but the purchase was chalked up to last year's budget. While they were at it, the highway officials signed a six-year, $21,000 maintenance contract for the greenery.

Washington Merry-Go-Round
February 15, 1979

Democrat (whom Andrews won't name) hissed, "If you keep this up, all the defense money going to your district will be under further review."

What happens when your constituents don't want any more pork?

So obsessed are your elected representatives with raiding the pork barrel that they sometimes bring home a project the voters don't need or want. That happened in Lock Haven, Pennsylvania, when Congressman William Clinger and Senator Arlen Specter proudly announced they had snagged an $86 million dike-levee flood-control project for the town.

No thanks, was the response. The town didn't like the fact that 200 buildings, half a dozen businesses, a stand of century-old trees, a Native American burial ground, and a chunk of the local economy would have to be sacrificed to make way for the levees and dikes. But try as they did, the good people of Lock Haven couldn't get Uncle Sam to take the money back. The town voted out of office all members of the city council who supported the project, but the outgoing council, as parting business, voted away nearly all the city's rights to oversee the project. And Clinger and Specter refused to back down. Lock Haven had the bacon rammed down its throat.

When the earth shakes in California, money comes out of the ground in New York

A natural disaster is always a busy time at the pork barrel. Hurricanes and floods mean hurried spending on disaster relief with very few questions asked. That may explain why a 1993 relief measure after the Mississippi River floods bequeathed little to help clean up the mess but lots ($50 million) for a vocational training program for teenagers. The earthquake relief bill for Los Angeles in 1994 included millions for potato farmers in Maine, remodeling of Penn Station in New York, and a maritime museum in South Carolina. That quake registered a 10 on the fiscal Richter Scale.

Don't be tempted to think that pork barrel spending is a victimless crime. As a sad example of the victims, consider the Chief Leschi School for Puyallup Indian children in Tacoma, Washington. In 1991 I reported that it was a death trap—an unstable mishmash of concrete, rubble, tile, plaster and bricks. The Bureau of Indian Affairs had been warned that the five-story building could collapse in a high wind and that large sections of brick could fall off at any time. Yet the BIA couldn't afford to put a fence around the building to protect the children from falling debris.

After I exposed this danger, the BIA closed the school and moved the children to temporary buildings until $26 million could be scrounged to build them a new school. Three years later I revisited the story, naively expecting that the children of the Puyallup tribe would have their new school. They were still in the makeshift buildings, still standing in line in the rain to use porta-potties. Yet that same year, Congress scraped the pork barrel and found more than $34 million to spend on "screwworm research" despite the fact that the screwworm had already been eradicated from U.S. soil.

Some pork is lighter than air

Occasionally, a pork barrel project becomes such a high-profile symbol of greed and waste that Congress can be shamed into canceling it. One such program which has finally run out of gas is the Helium Field Operations Project started in 1925 by President Calvin Coolidge.

Its purpose? To keep enough helium in a federal stockpile to operate a national fleet of blimps in time of war. In 1960, long after any rational person could have concluded that the Pentagon was not going to launch an airborne attack with blimps, the national helium reserves program was canceled. But it was hastily revived when NASA found a use for helium as a coolant. So you, the taxpayers, borrowed $258 million and bought the entire supply of helium in the country.

You now own 32 billion cubic feet of helium, enough to supply the United States for 80 years or the whole world for a decade. Who needs helium anyway with all the available hot air that's generated on Capitol Hill?

Defenders of the helium reserves, notably the people of Amarillo, Texas, where 200 people work on the project, claimed the program should have been continued because it turned a profit of several million dollars a year. But that was a profit on paper only—a sale from one government agency to another. The seller, the Interior Department, set the price too high, and the buyers, NASA and the Defense Department, could satisfy their limited needs cheaper on the open market.

After years of making fun of the helium reserves program, I had high hopes that we had seen the last of it when the Clinton administration pledged to "reinvent" government. The word around Washington was that Vice President Al Gore and his National Performance Review were prepared to stick pins in the national helium balloon.

But those hopes faded when Clinton desperately needed another vote for his 1993 budget plan. All eyes were on Congressman Bill Sarpalius of Amarillo. On the day of the budget vote, he spoke to the president on the phone four times. Surprise, surprise. Sarpalius voted to support the budget package which passed the House by one vote. Surprise, surprise. The National Performance Review retained the helium reserves.

When Sarpalius was voted out of office in 1994, Clinton revived his opposition to the helium stockpile. Congress voted to phase it out of existence. But given helium's history, it is too early to tell whether this piece of bloated pork will rise again.

A good place to trim waste

It costs the public a handsome sum to keep members of Congress looking handsome. The House maintains two barbershops for the use of members, their staffs and the few outsiders who know about them. A haircut costs only $3.50, which is a bargain, but the taxpayers get trimmed $150,000 a year to subsidize the operation.

Washington Merry-Go-Round
May 27, 1980

Another pocket of pork, highway demonstration projects, were boldly eliminated by the reformers in the 104th Congress. The projects had served for years as a slippery way for members to stick the federal government for parochial road work. Let's say that Senator So-and-So wanted the road between Nowhere and Resume Speed repaved, but he didn't want the locals to pay for it. If federal highway planners refused to put this pet project on their to-do list, the senator would simply have the road designated as a "demonstration project." Then a new kind of asphalt would be tried or fancy mile markers would be tested for their wind resistant properties. Presto, the highway would be funded outside the normal stream of highway money.

Bill Clinton's call to reinvent government in 1994 included a suggestion that the highway demonstration projects be eliminated. The House version of the highway bill that year was 176 pages long and included 900 requests for funds totaling more than $30 billion. It betrayed a feeding frenzy at the pork barrel, tinged with fear that highway pork was about to disappear. The oft-ridiculed demonstration projects were euphemistically renamed "high-priority congressional projects" in the hope they might appear respectable. But in the end, Congress bit the bullet. It eliminated the wasteful practice of earmarking highway funds for demonstration projects.

Business as usual

Despite this triumph and a few other shining moments, the 104th Congress and its idealistic Republican freshmen who had vowed to clean up the town sadly proved to be little different from the Democrats. The Republicans sneered at President Clinton because his budget proposal in 1996 didn't cut enough waste. Then they larded up the appropriations bills with $12.5 billion in pork barrel projects. Pork, it seems, is a bipartisan meat.

With Republicans in the driver's seat, the appropriations committees allotted $19.6 million to the International Fund for Ireland (a sentimental gift of pork started by then-House Speaker

Tip O'Neill to fund job creation in Ireland). The GOP also approved $9.8 million for construction at Fort Indiantown Gap military base which is slated to be closed. The "reformers" threw good money after bad—$3.75 million on top of $35 million that had already been spent on "wood utilization" research. And $20 million was inserted in the Federal Aviation Administration budget for radios the FAA said it didn't want.

Voter-rich California was showered with millions of dollars in last-minute pork for which the Republicans loudly took credit. It was an election year. They couldn't help themselves.

During the budget process in 1996, House Speaker Newt Gingrich reminded all the Republican appropriations chairmen that their first duty was to get themselves and their GOP peers re-elected. He sent a letter to the subcommittee chairmen and asked them to keep something in mind when they drafted their spending bills: "Are there any Republican members who could be severely hurt by the bill or who need a specific district item in the bill?"

Those legislators loitering around the pork barrel just before the election were also haunted by a new reality: Beginning in 1997, the president will have line-item veto power to excise pork with precision. But this is unlikely to end the feeding frenzy at the pork barrel. It has simply moved the trough to the Oval Office.

Senator Ernest "Fritz" Hollings will long be remembered as the co-author of the Gramm-Rudman-Hollings deficit reduction act, but he exempted himself from the law's lofty language. In the years following the deficit-cutting measure, Hollings presented his home state of South Carolina with tens of millions of dollars in pork barrel projects. The most outrageous was a $705,000 grant to create a national historic site out of a farm thought once to be owned by Charles Pinckney, a delegate to the Constitutional Convention of 1787. There was only one problem. Pinckney died before the house was built.

During a 1995 debate over a balanced budget amendment to the Constitution, Oregon Senator Mark Hatfield voted his conscience and opposed the amendment. He was piously attacked by self-appointed savings messiah Senator Trent Lott of Mississippi. At the same time, Lott denigrated Democrats for not making "tough choices" for "our children's future."

But behind the scenes, Lott was angling to snitch some pork that would have wasted $850 million. His scheme was to move NASA's space shuttle nozzle production facility from Utah to Mississippi. The costly notion came at a time when NASA was practically running on fumes. NASA protested the move as a waste of money. When my office tried to get a comment out of Lott about how he could reconcile his budget-cutting rhetoric with an outright abduction of NASA, Lott's spokeswoman said, "What do you want him to be, a purist?"

That would be refreshing.

CHAPTER EIGHT

COMIN' 'ROUND THE MOUNTAIN ABOARD THE GRAVY TRAIN

The story is told and retold in the Appalachian Mountains: It seems one of Washington's do-gooders got lost in the mountains of Kentucky. Well-dressed and driving a fancy car, he pulled up beside a mountain man and asked directions. The curious highlander asked what brought the stranger to Kentucky. "I'm with the War on Poverty," the young man chirped. The mountaineer looked him up and down. "Looks like you won," he observed.

The federal tax money spent in Appalachia in the past three decades would have bought several fancy cars and Sunday-best clothes for every man, woman and child in the mountains. But it didn't. In the grand tradition of federal welfare programs, Congress turned a good idea into a pile of pork, doled out by the lawmakers with the most clout and spent on projects more designed to guarantee re-election for the givers than economic prosperity for the receivers.

The focus of this misplaced generosity has been the Appalachian Regional Commission (ARC), just one flank of the War on Poverty that began April 24, 1964. President Lyndon B. Johnson declared that war while sitting on the front porch of a sagging, tarpaper shack in Inez, Kentucky. It was a publicity stunt that used the humble home of unemployed coal miner Tom Fletcher as its stage.

"I will not forget the man whose home I visited on the banks of Rock Castle Creek," Johnson wrote in his autobiography. "He regretted more than anything else that his two oldest children had already dropped out of school, and he was worried that the same fate would overtake the others. So was I. The tragic inevitability of the endless cycle of poverty was summed up in that man's fear: poverty forcing children out of school and destroying their best chance to escape the poverty of their fathers. 'I want you to keep those kids in school,' I said to Mr. Fletcher when I left him. But I knew he couldn't do it alone. He had to have help, and I resolved to see that he got it."

But Tom Fletcher didn't.

The 13 states that make up Congress's contorted map of Appalachia have since received more than $6 billion in federal largesse from ARC. The window dressing of public works projects is evident everywhere in Appalachia—new roads, water and sewer projects. But economic prosperity did not follow. Tom Fletcher is the embarrassing example. Now in his 70s, he still lives in the same shack, surviving on $284-a-month Social Security checks. Often out of work since LBJ's visit, Fletcher has made only slight improvements to his house. Outside, an indiscriminate trail of trash is flung out the back door, down the slope to the creek. To one side of the house, a doghouse sits on the otherwise barren plot. On the other side is a school bus, its wheels knocked off, converted to a makeshift hovel which some of the Fletcher brood inhabit.

These are not the best of Tom Fletcher's times, if he ever had any. His first wife, who was also his first cousin, died of breast cancer in 1983. None of the eight children, who received the presidential pat on the head and advice to stay in school, ever finished high school, with only one getting as far as the eighth grade. One son was shot to death by his own wife. Another went to prison on a burglary conviction.

In 1983, at the age of 60, Fletcher married 19-year-old Mary Porter. In January 1992 their 18-month-old baby, Ella Rose, who had a history of epileptic seizures, died and was buried in the back yard. The next month, her four-year-old brother, Tommy Jr., became seriously ill while attending the federal Head Start program. A hospital examination revealed 100 times the normal adult dosage of the painkiller propoxyphene in his system. The sheriff ordered exhumation of Ella Rose, and an autopsy showed she had been poisoned as well. Tom and Mary Fletcher were charged with murder. The charges against Tom were later dropped when his wife confessed to killing her daughter and attempting the same on her son for the $5,000 burial insurance policy the Fletchers had on each.

From the back woods to a handshake, the pipeline stays open

The tragic tale of Tom Fletcher, though more bizarre than most in Appalachia, illustrates a failed effort by the agency charged with lifting the area out of despair, illiteracy and poverty. ARC was supposed to win the war and withdraw its troops by 1971. Indeed, the first ARC chairman had forewarned in congressional testimony: "Mr. Chairman, if this organization is here in six years, it will be an embarrassment to Lyndon Johnson."

ARC continues to exist partly because it follows the first rule of the bureaucracy: Never work yourself out of a job by solving the original problem. The law that created the ARC included a proviso which called for its termination on July 1, 1971. The combined political pressures of senators from the states garnering the most money from ARC caused Richard Nixon to capitulate and allow an extension—until 1975. President Ford, though not supportive of the program, took even less persuasion to allow a four-year lease on life to September 30, 1979. The same political weight bore down on President Jimmy Carter, who wanted to kill the commission. Carter wrote, "In general, I consider the regional commission to be a waste of time and money . . . ." But, to pacify Congress, Carter kept the ARC going.

ARC won a serious fight for its life in 1981 and 1982 when the conservative wave that put Ronald Reagan in office called for an end to wasteful, pork barrel institutions. ARC called in every chit it had, which was a formidable number. Thousands of politicians and bureaucrats on the ARC gravy train generated a letter and phone campaign that amounted to more than 100,000 communications pleading with Reagan not to abolish the program. Reagan stuck to his principles and called for the termination of ARC in his budget proposal. For the next eight years, the battle was joined. President Reagan would kill ARC, and Congress would resurrect it annually, though never at more than two-thirds of its previous funding.

Where do the deer and the antelope play?

The antelope are leaving New Mexico and the taxpayers are going to pay through the nose to find out why.

The state was the home where thousands of antelope roamed, but now there are only a few hundred left. They are not in danger of extinction, but the federal government wants to know why they don't like New Mexico.

So $311,000 in public funds will be spent for a four-year study of the foods antelope eat and the types of fences they manage to pass through. The scientific community already knows, of course, that antelope like broad-leafed plants and would prefer, if given their druthers, to negotiate woven wire fences rather than the barbed kind.

But there has never been a long-term antelope-in-New Mexico study. Four years from now, that vacuum will be filled.

Washington Merry-Go-Round
May 28, 1979

George Bush was a pushover for ARC. Immediately after Bush's inauguration, Senators Robert Byrd and John D. Rockefeller IV of West Virginia had lunch with Bush for the sole purpose of pitching the dubious merits of ARC. They left encouraged enough to prepare a bill calling for another five-year extension. Bush's first budget proposal showed $50 million for ARC—an open barn door that Congress pushed to $200 million-plus a year.

In 1996, with the Republican-controlled Congress boasting that it would cut the fat out of government, ARC sustained its first real blow in 30 years. Congress cut the commission's budget by 40 percent. That put a mere $170 million in the barrel to use for ARC projects compared to the $282 million spent the year before. But given the durability of this money-sucking vampire, there is reason to fear that ARC will rise again.

The senator from Alaska has proclaimed his state as part of Appalachia

The coal counties of four states—eastern Kentucky, eastern Tennessee, southern West Virginia and southwestern Virginia—were the reason for ARC's creation. But the smell of pork lured so many other states, all demanding a piece of the change originally intended to go only to Central Appalachia, that the congressional version of Appalachia eventually put 13 states on the ARC dole. Congressional Appalachia covers 20.5 million people in 399 counties. So ARC doles out money to a region running in a diagonal swath up from delta-flat Marshall County, Mississippi, to Schoharie County, New York, near Albany.

Congressional Appalachia has a mind-boggling political lobby that protects its pork—26 U.S. senators, 60 members of the House, and 13 governors of both parties. When the Democrats controlled Congress, ARC provided a slush-fund for two pashas of pork, the chairmen of the House and Senate Appropriations Committees—Jamie Whitten of Mississippi and Robert Byrd of West Virginia. Rounding out the trio at the trough was Congressman Tom Bevill of Alabama. Since 1985, half of ARC's highway money (the biggest portion of its budget) has gone to those three states.

Without such heavyweights in Congress, the other states have not fared as well. One Eastern Kentuckian observed that "if you were to strip away food stamps, we would be back exactly where we were in 1964. Food stamps are the one major difference." And they didn't come from ARC.

It's all about connections

Only one Kentucky county, Pike, made it into the top 10 counties receiving the most ARC money. The story of Pike County in the last 30 years is a classic example of where ARC went awry. One man pulled it off, a P.T. Barnum of pork, a doctor of grantsmanship without equal among small-town mayors.

Dr. William Hambley, 79, was mayor of Pikeville from 1960 to 1990. He'd been born and raised in this city of 5,700. As a boy, he didn't like having a river running through the city because it occasionally flooded. And he resented the railroad tracks he had to cross on the way to Pikeville College up the hill and the coal trains that dirtied up the town. "And I just decided I was going to change it. I knew the only way I could do it was to get the river out of town. If I got the river out, I'd fill that in—which we've done—then I could get rid of all the filth and dirt in the town."

The dream became better than fantasy when Dr. Hambley attended several medical schools in Chicago and befriended an up-and-coming politician, Everett Dirksen. By the time Dr. Hambley finished his extended medical training in several disciplines and came back to be mayor of Pikeville, his Chicago friend was the powerful Senator Dirksen. Hambley said the senator gave him whatever he wanted. "Anytime I had anything that I wanted done, I just gave it to the Senate page and he'd take it to Mr. Dirksen. Mr. Dirksen would give it to [Kentucky Senator John Sherman Cooper], and Mr. Cooper would present the bill, and they'd pass it. And they'd send it back to me. Of course, over in the House, I took it to Carl Perkins [of Kentucky]. Carl and I were good friends;

my daughter worked for him. So Carl would pass it through the House. So I'd take the bill then, and take it over to the president's office and just leave it for his signature, you know."

Dr. Hambley exclaimed: "We got everything that the federal government put out for anything. We qualified for every damn thing! We qualified for aid to rivers, harbors, mountains, coal—everything."

His biggest project, the $100 million Pikeville Cut, was completed in the late 1980s. The Army Corps of Engineers moved Peach Orchard Mountain, gouging chunks as big as those excavated during the Panama Canal project, moving more than 16 billion cubic yards of earth—the volume required to build the Grand Coulee Dam. The Big Sandy River was detoured so it no longer flowed through Pikeville, making the city virtually flood-proof. A new highway was also built away from the city.

But the piece of the job that justified the tens of millions of dollars ARC put into this project was the creation of 300 new acres of flatland in Pikeville. Industry would be attracted, population would increase, more jobs would be created for outlying regions. That's not what happened. Instead, a privately built commercial mall went up five miles north of Pikeville, outside the city limits, on land that was already flat. Pikeville today is a professional center made up of bankers, doctors and lawyers for the local, county, state and federal courts there. The poor of Pikeville couldn't afford to stay.

So what happened to the 300 acres of flatland that the federal taxpayers created for Pikeville? "Mostly parking," Dr. Hambley replied, unapologetically. Mostly parking on those golden 300 acres? "Yeah . . . I drew plans for a three-story mall and stuff like that— but there was no way I could make it more economical than the shopping mall just outside the city limits on a thousand acres of level land."

Federal officials, particularly at the ARC, knew the Pikeville Cut wasn't the best use of federal funds. At one point, some calculated that it would have been cheaper to move the entire city out of the flood plain than to divert the river.

Deep down inside, aren't we all poor Appalachian coal miners?

The political gerrymandering that went into the creation of today's 13-state "Appalachia" covered by ARC insured the survival of the entity while guaranteeing the defeat of its initial primary objective—to create a diversified, self-sustaining economy in Central Appalachia.

When the whole rigmarole began, the "Appalachian problem" spread through the coal-producing parts of three states—eastern Kentucky, southwest Virginia, eastern Tennessee—and all of West Virginia. The tarpaper shacks, the outhouses, the muddy hollows, right down to the barefoot, malnourished children—the poster children of this War on Poverty—came from these four states. Over the years, when the violins have played for continuation of the ARC pork barrel, the sad conditions in these four states have been cited to draw sympathy. But once the money is turned loose, much of it is siphoned off to the other nine states, some of which never considered themselves part of Appalachia and still don't consider themselves to be particularly poor.

Three Maryland counties thrown into the mix were surprised to find themselves suddenly declared poor by Congress. A contemporary Maryland analysis prepared for ARC confessed that the region "never has been afflicted with the severe social and economic problems of hard-core Appalachian areas." At the time they were put on the ARC charity list, the three counties boasted an unemployment rate of slightly over 4 percent—close to the definition of full employment. Maryland managed to transcend its embarrassment and, over the years, has collected millions of dollars intended for the Appalachian poor.

Other counties and states didn't want to be painted with the Appalachian brush either. For instance, the area around Roanoke, Virginia, specifically asked to be excluded from the region. On a bigger scale, then-Ohio Governor Jim Rhodes, a critic of the federal approach to fighting poverty in Appalachia, fought inclusion of southeastern Ohio into ARC. But even he had to bow to pressure from Congress and his own beneficiaries in the region. (He eventually lent his name to the four-lane highway that ARC built through southern Ohio.)

The final state to be drawn into ARC—Mississippi—is a bald display of pork barrel at its unabashed best. President Johnson's own Cabinet official for Health, Education and Welfare had testified during the bill's hearings that Mississippi could not be included in Appalachia because it wasn't by any stretch of the imagination part of the region and did not have the same problems as the Central Appalachian states. But Mississippi Senator John Stennis knew a gravy train when he saw one roll by. He had his state added in 1967.

I'll take your money but call me poor

No sensible observer would disagree that the misguided dispersal of funds from New York to Mississippi seriously diffused the help intended for poor coal counties. Tom Gish, editor of the Mountain Eagle, smack in the center of Central Appalachia in Whitesburg, Kentucky, says, "The ARC money was targeted away from us. The whole PR [public relations] push—to be brutal about it—came from here to get something done. And it was based upon the fact that, damn it, we knew people were starving to death. But almost immediately, instead of putting it in where the need is, they started siphoning it off into Knoxville and into Pittsburg and into anywhere and everywhere. We were the reason for it. We were the PR for it, and everybody else took the money."

The truth of this embarrasses even ARC staffers when simple calculations reveal that the state receiving the most money per capita from the ARC trough was Maryland. If the money were handed out to people instead of projects, Maryland's "Appalachian" residents would have received an average $1,049 per person in ARC grants. Compare that to a mere $60 per person in West Virginia's McDowell County, whose residents were the subjects of the recruitment posters for the War on Poverty.

To add insult to the Kentuckians who are truly in need, the Marylanders were perfectly ready to accept the cash but not the association. At one point in the early 1980s, a simple road sign was erected at the eastern entrance of Interstate 70 leading to Washington County, Maryland. The sign read: "Bill Pate Portal to Appalachia." Pate was an ARC official from Maryland who helped net millions of dollars for the building of that very interstate.

The Maryland state senator who represented the county, Victor Cushwa, led a campaign in 1982 to remove the sign. The Democrat said his group didn't object to honoring Pate, "but they really object to the word 'Appalachia.'" The business community felt it was a negative word that would scare away industry. Cushwa pressed his case unrelentingly for three years. "The whole business community and everyone else resented the sign that said 'Appalachia,'" he reiterated in 1985. "It sounds like you're entering the land of log cabins and hound dogs and moonshine." Now on the road built with federal taxpayer money earmarked for the poor, the new sign reads: "WELCOME TO Scenic Western Maryland."

If Dr. Frankenstein were a politician, he would chair the ARC

ARC is a unique attempt at a federal-state partnership—a quasi-federal organization separate and apart from line agencies of the executive branch. One observer called it "a wondrously temperamental bastard, sired by state politicians, born out of the federal bureaucracy, and nursed by congressional prima donnas. It is a hybrid, part federal, part state, part something that neither of its parents can recognize." Former ARC Executive Director Al Arnett called it "an institutional hermaphrodite. It was neither federal nor state. It just didn't quite know its place. No one should be a eunuch or a hermaphrodite for too terribly long."

Critics are less circumspect, labeling ARC, in the words of one report, "the bastard child of an unholy political alliance between 13 states and the federal government that has deliberately given the most help to areas of Appalachia that least need it while throwing crumbs to the worst poverty pockets in central Appalachia."

Dr. Ronald D. Eller, head of the Appalachian Center at the University of Kentucky and a longtime ARC critic, says, "ARC has to be understood as a political animal. It cannot be understood as an apolitical thing. ARC was a vehicle through which individuals in political power at the local and state level leveraged resources from the federal government for the construction of infrastructure facilities which are going to be located primarily in their area of interest. It was more politically attractive to build roads and sewer systems."

Throughout ARC's history, too many staff slots have been filled as high-salaried political patronage positions, people who were often expected to work for the re-election campaign of the president rather than the people of Appalachia. Cronyism was particularly evident during the Carter years. The federal co-chairman was tapped for the job as a consolation prize when President Carter passed him over for other positions. One staffer found his ARC job quite a step up from his previous one as a Georgia landscape gardener who, nevertheless, had been smart enough to hitch on to the Carter bandwagon early. Another was transferred over from the National Security Council with the dubious qualifications, according to his résumé, of aiding in the "return of the Crown of St. Stephen to Hungary" and "the visit of the Romanian president [Nicolae Ceausescu] to the U.S." He worked on a book about the Romanian Communist Party while with the ARC.

ARC staffers are based in Washington, taking occasional field trips to the region like gawking bus tourists. Somehow it's not quite enough that the executive director sits behind a roundtable desk made of wonderful Kentucky walnut by a genuine Appalachian cabinetmaker.

Postage due

Inmates of the federal prisons are allowed free mailing privileges, and last year this cost the taxpayers $1.2 million. One prisoner took advantage of the system to dispatch letters to all 535 members of the House and Senate; another used his free mailing privileges to solicit contributions for his presidential campaign.

Washington Merry-Go-Round
July 2, 1979

The ARC staffers pride themselves on being able to keep their mouths shut about inequities in the system. Occasionally, a staffer will break from the ranks before being put in his or her place again. One of the deputy directors of ARC, Howard Bray, once made the mistake of candor with an Associated Press reporter, calling the commission's impact "damn small, damn modest." Bray recalled that when the quote was read by the godfather and political shepherd of ARC, Senator Jennings Randolph of West Virginia, "he exploded like methane gas in a coal mine."

A penchant for self-justification has permeated all that ARC does, from its slick quarterly, Appalachia magazine, to a $21,500 oral history project of the commission's glorious past, to dozens of studies intended to prove the ARC has made a difference. It also meant some nice trips—not to the region, however. For example, in 1977 the commission spent $20,000 to send four of its staffers to Japan, ostensibly to entice foreign investment to Appalachia. In 1987 ARC Federal Co-Chairman Winifred Pizzano took an all-expenses-paid ARC trip to the French Riviera. She delivered a paper at an international meeting on rural economic development in Nice.

For sheer chutzpa, though, the 20-year birthday bash the commission had in 1985 wins hands down. The agency set up to fight rural poverty sent engraved invitations to 750 guests. Not one of the poor was invited. The guest list included governors and former governors, members of Congress past and present, ARC staff and former staff—in short, those who had kept the pork barrel rolling. Some 2,200 gold, silver and bronze commemorative medallions were struck by the Franklin Mint for the guests at a cost of $22,000. The 14 gold medals went to the most important ARC saviors, including Congressmen Jamie Whitten and Tom Bevill. The orgy of self-congratulation reached its peak with the airing of a 22-minute film, "More Than a Promise: Appalachia 20 Years Later," commissioned at a cost of $65,000.

If the previous evidence was not enough for Central Appalachians, the consistent ARC reliance on Washington "beltway bandit" experts to conduct research studies is final proof of the distance and irrelevance of the commission.

For example, in 1975 Congress amended the Appalachian act to require "a study of physical hazards which are constraints on land use in the Appalachian region and the risks associated with such hazards." Did the commission go to the people in the region who lived with these hazards daily? No. They hired a Washington, D.C., firm that labored over the problem and produced a report identifying the hazards as—surprise, surprise—flooding, landslides and coal mine subsidence. For this, the beltway bandits soaked the federal taxpayers for $225,398.

Humorist Loyal Jones of Kentucky tells a joke that betrays the Appalachian disdain for outside consultants:

"A little town had a high birth rate that had attracted the attention of the sociologists at the state university. They wrote a grant proposal, got a huge chunk of money, hired a few additional sociologists, an anthropologist, a family-planning and birth control specialist, moved to town, rented offices, set up their computers, got squared away, and began designing their questionnaires and such. While the staff was busy getting ready for their big research effort, the project director decided to go to the local drugstore for a cup of coffee. He sat down at the counter, ordered his coffee, and while he was drinking it, he told the druggist what his purpose was in town, then asked him if he had any idea why the birthrate was so high. 'Sure,' said the druggist. 'Every morning the six o'clock train comes through here and blows for the crossing. It wakes everybody up, and well, it's too late to go back to sleep, and it's too early to get up.'"

For political reasons, the bulk of the money spent by ARC has gone to big population centers, leaving those without resources and voter clout still in poverty. Take the case of Owsley County, Kentucky, which ranked as 391 in the pecking order of funds received from the ARC.

If ever a county was deserving of War on Poverty funds, Owsley is that county. It is the poorest county in Kentucky, one of the 10 poorest in the U.S. Yet, over 28 years, it was only considered worthy of $473,500 from the Appalachian Regional Commission. It was not considered an important growth center, so it was one of ARC's unstated sacrifice areas—a place with no future for which long-range investment was deemed foolish. The folks there didn't even deserve a decent road. The per capita income of Owsley County is $4,513, and more than half the residents live below federal poverty levels. Eighty-six percent of the elementary school students qualify for free breakfast and lunch.

The biggest nongovernmental employers are a nursing home that provides 77 jobs and a grocery store that employs 18. The shopping district in Booneville, the county seat, has nine businesses, two of which sell used clothing. The only new industry that has been attracted to the county is America's easy cash crop—marijuana—grown by the kind of men who once distilled moonshine.

It is in Owsley County that ARC's accidental agenda of moving people out of the mountains is working like a charm. Desperate citizens have fled the poverty, leaving their ancestral homes for urban ghettoes in Ohio and elsewhere, decreasing the county's population by more than 10 percent in the last decade.

Fair-weather friend

When ARC was created in 1965, it was not supposed to be just another welfare program. It was charged with diversifying the region's economy to make it self-sustaining. That meant breaking the shackles of coal. Kentuckian Harry Caudill's indictment of what coal had done to the mountains, in his eloquent "Night Comes to the Cumberlands," had inspired the ARC: "Coal has always cursed the land in which it lies. When men begin to wrest it from the earth it leaves a legacy of foul streams, hideous slag heaps and polluted air. It peoples this transformed land with blind and crippled men and with widows and orphans. It is an extractive industry which takes all away and restores nothing. It mars but never beautifies. It corrupts but never purifies."

So ARC had a serious conflict of interest from the beginning which thwarted its most important chartered goal. State officials who proposed programs and the congressmen who funded them were beholden to the coal industry. Senator Jennings Randolph of

West Virginia, who more than any other senator was responsible for ARC and its perpetuation, was also coal's greatest booster.

ARC hid its face when Appalachian citizens rose up to fight the coal companies on black lung benefits and to stop the operators from strip mining in a way that left an environmental wasteland. ARC would not buck the campaign-contributing coal operators by siding with the people it was created to help. Few incidents proved this more powerfully or emotionally to Appalachians than the ARC response—or lack of it—to the 1972 Buffalo Creek Flood.

At 8 a.m. on February 26, an improperly and illegally constructed coal-waste dam at the head of a hollow in Logan County, West Virginia, collapsed during a rainstorm. Without warning, it sent a 50-foot-high wall of water through the narrow 17-mile-long valley. In all, 132 million gallons of water and a million tons of sludge poured through 14 mining camps, killing 125 people and leaving 4,000 homeless.

Incredibly, with an insensitivity only the politically protected would dare display, one official of the Pittston Company, which owned the dam, made this public statement: "We're investigating the damage which was caused by the flood, which we believe, of course, was an act of God. The dam was simply incapable of holding the water God poured into it." The flurry of reporting that followed such a brazen declaration established that company officials had been concerned about the dam breaking hours before it did but failed to warn residents, and that it had received previous warnings from the U.S. Interior Department to stabilize the dam. At one point, the company had turned down a project that cost as little as $50,000 which would have rebuilt the dam properly.

But the coal company stuck to the claim it was not responsible, backed by the governor in West Virginia, Arch Moore. Early on, Moore said it was easy to criticize Pittston and say the dam shouldn't have been there, but it had been there for 25 years, so how could they be blamed? At another time, Governor Moore demonstrated total disregard for the human lives lost, the women and children drowned in the water and buried in the sludge, when he said: "The only real sad part is that the state of West Virginia has taken a terrible beating which far overshadowed the beating which the individuals that lost their lives took, and I consider this an even greater tragedy than the flood itself."

Many Appalachians were obviously outraged at the arrogance of Governor Moore and the Pittston conglomerate. And where was the agency that had been federally funded to watch over the Appalachians? Where was ARC, which had been born out of concern for the rampant human misery in the Appalachians? Cowering in Washington, effectively silenced by the same Governor Moore who invoked gubernatorial privilege under the ARC law and forbade them from stepping foot in Logan County to help out.

An organization that would kowtow to demagogues and ignore such obvious injustice was unlikely to do anything to upset the entrenched interests. ARC should have diversified the mountain economy away from coal. Yet for years the word "coal" wasn't mentioned at ARC for fear of offending coal operators or their congressmen.

Then came the coal bust of the 1980s, with disastrous effect on Central Appalachia. Increasing mechanization in the mines and increasing global competition drastically reduced the number of miners needed. In a decade, employment was halved while production remained the same. It was a time when ARC resources

---

You can get a green thumb if you pass out enough money

A few months ago, we reported that officials in a little-known government agency had turned on the tax-dollar tap to water the plants in their offices. The agency had doled out thousands of dollars to a private plant-care firm. Recently Sen. James Sasser, D-Tenn., decided to find out how much other government agencies are paying for the greening of their offices. During a three-year period, the senator found, 26 agencies spent more than $850,000 on the care and feeding of their plants.

Washington Merry-Go-Round
August 13, 1979

---

should have been pouring into alternative industries. But the coal companies needed help. So ARC, which was supposed to wean the Central Appalachians from King Coal, supported projects to expand coal's power in the region.

In truth, ARC was caught by surprise when coal employment went belly up in the 1980s. All of ARC's high-priced experts and consultants, who were paid to predict and plan for the future of the region, couldn't figure out how to put the region back together again.

Education, jobs or clean lawns?

ARC staffers have always been hampered by the whim of Congress. Take the case of the junk car eradication effort that was added to ARC's funding by Congress and had nothing to do with what the states wanted.

When Walter Cronkite did his standup in 1963 for a special report, "Depressed Area, U.S.A.," he showed graphic video of the roadside unsightliness, intoning: "Here machines die by the thousands and lie like beer cans where they fall."

In the 1970s ARC funded studies of junk cars with the idea of removing them in six states. A Tennessee demonstration project cost a flat $300,000 "to test the feasibility of two different multi-county junk car removal programs with varying collection and disposal components." The South Carolina project, for a mere $181,446, "located and mapped over 20,000 derelict cars in a six-county region," according to its final report. A one-month pilot project focused on the small community of Pacolet "and considerable media attention was directed toward it. This had positive and negative effects since, in several cases, there were confrontations with owners who had no interest in surrendering their vehicles based on an unknown state law." South Carolinians were sensitive about just what was being called junk and what was a treasured old car. The project coordinators had to persuade local politicians, after several other attempts at blitz car removals, that there were "limited, if any, adverse political consequences to junk car collection." The expensive program, the authors conceded, "was obviously less than successful."

The Georgia project was the cheapest—only $27,200. For that money the officials removed and recycled 1,300 abandoned vehicles. They proudly reported to ARC that the total revenue from the sale of the vehicles was $9,510 or an average $7.32 per unit. Considering it cost the federal taxpayer $27,200 for Pickens County to earn $9,510, the report neglected to point out this was not a cost-effective deal. Former ARC Executive Director Ralph Widner recalled the moment when the junk car fiasco began:

"Each time we went up to testify on changes in the program . . . [before] . . . an appropriations hearing, we'd have a very carefully made case for why to do this or that. We sort of prided ourselves on the quality of the work we put into it. But you could never predict what would happen.

"I'll never forget once when we got up before the committee and spelled out the need for the housing program, maybe some education innovations. Finally, Congressman Bob Jones of Alabama says, 'What are you going to do about junk cars?' Well, we'd never even thought about junk cars. He says, 'We got junk cars in every crick [creek]. I want to find out what we can do about them. Well, what do you think it'd take to smash them down so we can put them on trucks and go out and melt them down? To get them out of the cricks so the cricks can be cleaned up?'

"Well, we walked out of that room with a $5 million junk car program. If you'd told me to sit down and design a development program for Appalachia, it's the last thing I ever would have thought of! So much for planning!"

Why was Congress allowed to get away with such shenanigans? Because, in the words of former ARC staffer James Branscome, "There was never anyone at the commission who would tell a Congressman to go to hell."

Hiding waste out in the open

In 1991 Stephen Moore of the Cato Institute think tank told the House Appropriations Committee to its face that ARC had become "one of the most grandiose pork barrel projects around." He charged that "the distribution of grants is dictated by political considerations, such as who sits on the right committees, rather than using any objective standard of economic need. In other words, it has become a purely pork barrel giveaway program."

James Branscome confirmed this from his personal experience: "It was, in every way, a frustrating situation at the commission because you had to put up with the whims of Congress. ARC was fairly well protected there, but the staff had to spend a lot of time fending off the more traditional public works type. I can remember getting calls from [Kentucky congressman] Carl Perkins' staff saying, 'We want this funded.' As time passed, this became more frequent."

Close examination of the conference reports of the last several years reveals who are ARC's biggest pork barrelers. These reports cover money earmarked by Congress; neither ARC nor the states have any discretion on

A $50,000 bench

The General Services Administration recently "stepped up" its efforts to spend the taxpayers' money. It commissioned a $50,000 sculpture depicting a set of concrete steps to be placed in front of a new federal office building in Norfolk, Va. GSA officials insist the artistic steps serve a useful purpose: People can use them to sit on.

Washington Merry-Go-Round
March 21, 1980

this matter. This puts the lie to ARC's boasts about complicated spending formulas and amicable trade-offs between the states to divvy up the money. Only three states—Alabama, Mississippi and West Virginia—have gotten earmarked monies. The three amigos of ARC pork turned out to be the usual suspects—Robert Byrd, Tom Bevill and Jamie Whitten.

By Byrd's standards, the ARC money he grabs is small potatoes. Between Senator Byrd and ARC's godfather before him, Jennings Randolph, West Virginia has received at least 17 percent of ARC's total expenditures while having just 8.6 percent of the population of congressional Appalachia. That's according to the official ARC calculation. But the true figure is about 30 percent once the earmarked money is factored in. Unlike the other big beneficiaries, Alabama and Mississippi, at least some of West Virginia is located in the Central Appalachian region originally intended to be helped by the program. Unfortunately, the coal-mining counties got little of the pork. Most went to the growth centers of Charles Town, Huntington, Beckley and other cities.

For years ARC had a lock on the House Appropriations Committee as well in the person of Chairman Whitten. He liked to say that Mississippi is "in the foothills" of Appalachia. With the help of Whitten and Senator John Stennis before him, Mississippi became the third highest "Appalachian" money recipient per capita in ARC history—bringing $583.60 to every man, woman and child in northeastern Mississippi districts.

ARC didn't whimper when it was dunned, along with five other federal agencies Whitten squeezed for pork, to build and fill with exhibits the Jamie L. Whitten Historical Center outside Tupelo, Mississippi.

When Whitten began to slow down and his age cost him the chairmanship of the House Appropriations Committee, Tom Bevill assumed the role of ARC's political shepherd. Bevill was in a position to call the shots as chairman of the House Appropriations Subcommittee on Energy and Water Development—the boys who fund the big water projects for the Army Corps of Engineers.

Bevill's subcommittee also appropriated ARC's annual budget. He was no piker when it came to taking a piece for his constituents. Among ARC's gifts to Alabama was the Tom Bevill Community Center in Rainsville. Bevill even squeezed money out of ARC for a save-the-owls project at a natural history museum in his home state.

A highway to Nowheresville

The supreme pork barrel coup by both Whitten and Bevill was the $2 billion Tennessee-Tombigbee Waterway, partially funded by ARC. Whitten and Bevill were so proud of their part that the Whitten Historical Center was located on the Tenn-Tom, as was the Tom Bevill Visitor Center in Carrollton, Alabama. The latter is operated by the grateful Army Corps of Engineers that Bevill's subcommittee funded each year.

There is a great, albeit hidden, lesson within the political engineering aspect of the Tenn-Tom—which also applies to ARC road construction and may have been the guiding principle all along. The General Accounting Office once criticized ARC for planning a large road system and then building it in patchwork fashion so many sections are still not connected or finished. But the GAO missed Whitten's trade secret—to begin a project at both ends and in the middle so that canceling it becomes more painful than finishing it.

The same saving principle has worked well for ARC. Roads have not been built logically from one end to the other. After 30 years of construction, the ARC system is a patchwork of often unconnected highway fragments. The piecemeal construction has kept ARC alive.

Highway construction is the cornerstone of ARC's work. Its logo features a highway going off into the distance. Two-thirds of its total funding has gone into highways. ARC may have drawn its inspiration from Lyndon Johnson who promised to "put this region out on the bright highway of hope."

The premise was flawed, of course. It takes more than accessibility to attract industries to a region, but roads were the most politically acceptable solution. All the states agreed that roads were what they wanted most from the federal taxpayers. And members of Congress were happy to comply. After all, roads get politicians elected.

The roads that the ARC states wanted first were the ones that connected their major cities; never mind the poor folks in the hollows. Nor did the states want money spent connecting themselves with other states. The highway projects most often put on the back burner have been small segments connecting the corridors at 21 different state boundaries. Harold Gouthrie, an Ohio expert who studied the ARC road program for three years, concluded: "The rich areas got richer and the poor areas did not change."

The original highway plan in the Appalachian Regional Development Act of 1965 directed ARC to build 2,350 miles by

1971 at an authorized cost of $850 million. ARC now estimates that the 26-highway corridor system will cost approximately $9 billion and will take a bit longer to complete—2060. Two-thirds of the system has been completed, and the average cost is now about $11 million a mile.

ARC has a raft of excuses for this 1,060 percent increase in cost, plus the extra 89 years added to the construction schedule. Congress, for its part, added four more states to its definition of Appalachia and authorized another 675 miles to build. Construction costs have inflated; design, safety and environmental standards have increased; Appalachian terrain is difficult to cut through. But the truth is the original estimate was deliberately lowballed.

It's part of the pork barrel principle of getting the project rolling. Government programs are harder to kill than Dracula. Congressmen as a group rarely seem to have the will to drive a wooden stake through the heart of their colleague's pet projects, no matter how much blood they drain from increasingly anemic federal taxpayers.

Maybe the generals' wives would like the job

Pentagon brass hats are notorious for their apparently incurable penchant for going first-class. This prodigality of the most pampered agency of our government extends to the smallest items in the military budget.

Just one glaring example turned up by Rep. Norman Dicks, D-Wash.: Leafing through a Pentagon spare parts catalog, Dicks was astounded to see that a small aluminum bracket used in A-7 attack aircraft was listed at $235. So he sent a staff aide out to shop around.

Sure enough, the identical part, fabricated in a local machine shop, cost $2.15. But of course you can't expect a general or an admiral to go out shopping just to save the taxpayers some money.

Washington Merry-Go-Round
October 5, 1979

Bridging the gap between your pocket and Congress's

Bridges add a quantum leap to costs, but Bobby Byrd, the Pontiff of Pork, wants them for his folks. West Virginians do have strong feelings about bridges, even more so than roads. Roads don't have to be paved, but rivers have to be crossed. Back in the

1960s, David Brinkley did his War on Poverty television turn in Wayne, West Virginia. Standing on a one-lane wooden bridge, he called for the government to keep its promises to the impoverished people of the region. The grateful Wayne citizens erected a sign over it: "The David Brinkley Bridge." But, alas, the sign crashed into the river with the bridge when an overloaded truck crossed it. In 1977 when another local bridge collapsed in the small burg of Vulcan, West Virginia, the town's self-anointed mayor wrote the Soviet Embassy in Washington asking for help to rebuild it. A Soviet journalist was sent to cover this unusual appeal for foreign aid while the local radio station was besieged with threats to bomb any bridge the "commies" built. State officials quickly came up with $1.3 million for Vulcan's bridge.

ARC has paid tens of millions of dollars for other bridges in West Virginia, including the spectacular New River Gorge Bridge near small Fayetteville. ARC kicked in $26.3 million to help the state erect it—the world's longest arch steel-span bridge and, at 876 feet above the river, America's second-highest bridge. But it hasn't exactly fueled major industrial development or created jobs nearby. There is one consolation: It has become a favorite of bungee jumpers and skydivers. What this has to do with helping the impoverished citizens of coal counties only a politician can tell you.

New highways make it easier to drive past the poverty

The whole point of the roads and bridges is to encourage economic development in these isolated regions. ARC rolls out figures, toting up tens of thousands of new jobs created near highways, but this doesn't tell the real story. The real story is that many of the jobs might have developed anyway without gold-plated super-highways; that these jobs are primarily in the minimum-wage service sector like fast food restaurants at highway interchanges instead of higher-paying manufacturing jobs; and that despite the new jobs, Central Appalachia continues to fall further behind the rest of America.

The ARC road building offers another clue as to who was pulling the strings all along. Aside from the local, state and federal politicians re-elected by this federal taxpayer pork, the biggest beneficiaries were the coal barons. Appalachian highways amounted to another taxpayer-funded subsidy for the industry. Now those ARC roads are taking such a pounding from overweight coal trucks that it will probably cost more to repair and rebuild them in the next decade than ARC paid in the first place.

A final down side to the roads is that most of ARC's fancy four-lanes bypassed the poor. Impoverished Calhoun County, West Virginia, had to mount a major campaign to get one freeway access ramp to the new expressway ARC had built to open up that part of the state.

One doesn't have to stray far off a four-lane highway in Central Appalachia to find the poverty that persists. It has just been pushed a little farther up the hollows, away from the people traveling the proud highways.

There's an old riddle in Appalachia about roads: "What are the three R's hillbillies learn in grade school?" The answer: "Readin', 'Ritin' and Route 23," or the "Road to" Akron, Dayton or other cities to which Appalachians fled for jobs. The new version of the joke credits ARC's spanking new highways: "They're wonderful. They're progress. They've given us a faster way out of here!"

A single wise man among an army of fools

The increasing Appalachian addiction to the dole as a result of ARC's misplaced good will is a shock to old-timers in the region. Septuagenarian Alice Schaller of Linden, West Virginia, was the youngest daughter of Anderson Boggs, a Christian Advent Church preacher who died in 1961. Her father became ill early in his career and had a hard time keeping a job. Her mother suffered from diabetes. But mother and children, all 13 of them, would work on the farm, pick fruit, dry apples, harvest crops, do whatever was necessary to put food on the table and clothes on their backs. Several times local officials came around saying the family was well qualified for public assistance. But Preacher Boggs would have none of it. "That kind of aid will not help people," he would shout. "It pulls them down. They will have no desire to work or provide for themselves." He never changed his mind, remarking a few years before his death: "When I die, write on a stone and place at my head, 'Here lies the pauper who lived and died without the United States' dole.'"

Mrs. Schaller says proudly, "We never got a dime from public assistance. Poppy said it would ruin the country. And you know what? I think it is."

CHAPTER NINE

THE WAR WE LOST

When I was 11 years old, my father bought a big, beautiful house for our family in an affluent Salt Lake City suburb. Then, almost immediately, he announced that the Andersons could not afford to live in such lavish accommodations, so he moved us into the basement and rented the rest of the house to a family of more means. All the bathrooms were upstairs, so we used an outdoor privy, rain or shine, summer or winter. My family did not move upstairs until I was almost old enough to leave home.

Those years in the basement, slinking to the privy that was a neighborhood eyesore, taught me a frustrating lesson about thrift. At the time I thought my father was an old skinflint without the serendipity to enjoy the bounties of life. Now that I am well beyond the age he was when he bought that house, I see his point. He was willing to live beneath our house rather than live beyond our means.

I relate this story by way of full disclosure. Yes, I am a child of the Great Depression who grew up believing that you didn't spend more than you had; that if a person wanted work, he or she would find it; that any job is better than no job; that adults must take responsibility for their own choices; and that getting something for nothing erodes a person's spirit. I make no apologies for my philosophy, even as I acknowledge that it has fallen on hard times in the late 20th Century.

Before we moved to the big house and ended up in the basement, our modest home was filled with a seemingly endless stream of out-of-work men my father would meet on the street and bring home for a meal. One of them stayed for a year and sold my mother's homemade cookies door-to-door to help earn his room and board. From those men I learned that one can be poor in pocket without being poor in spirit.

Today the federal government tells us that being poor means making less than about $14,500 a year to support a family of four. Indeed, that doesn't sound like much. But I have known people who lived on less and didn't consider themselves to be poor. I have also known people with much more who were still impoverished by bad choices and calamitous circumstances.

The look of poverty

In 1965, when President Lyndon Johnson declared his War on Poverty, he announced, "The days of the dole are numbered." But he failed to specify what number.

Since then, the United States has spent $5.4 trillion trying to achieve an illusive goal—to eradicate poverty as defined by a ratio of wage to family size. In the process, our nation has become so impoverished in spirit as to threaten the very fabric of our civilization.

Children we sought to save are gunned down on the streets by other children we also sought to save. Daughters aspire to be just like mommy and collect more welfare for each child born out of wedlock. Sons aspire to be just like the thugs on the street because there is no Daddy around for a role model. Before preschoolers understand ABC, they know WIC and AFDC and SSI.

America's picture of poverty is not the sunken-faced children of Ethiopia or the rag-clad beggars of Calcutta. In many ways that picture of poverty would have been easier to eradicate given $5.4 trillion and three decades to work with. Our picture of poverty is more complex.

It is the angry, sullen look of a young man loitering on a street corner. He is the great-grandson of the generation of men my father brought home to our basement. He has no job, no skills and no frame of reference he can use to change his circumstances. He is not hungry or naked or homeless because we spent $5.4 trillion to keep him fed, clothed and marginally housed. He can read the "help wanted" ads in the newspaper because we sent him to school. Yet all of our money has not been able to change the fact that he is poor.

Perhaps it is time to change the definition. The Heritage Foundation, a Washington think tank, has offered a definition of "behavioral poverty" that coincides with my own thoughts on the subject. It is "a cluster of severe social pathologies, including eroded work ethic and dependency, lack of educational aspiration and achievement, inability or unwillingness to control one's children, increased single parenthood and illegitimacy, criminal activity, and drug and alcohol abuse."

Wherever we find such behavior, whether or not it is linked as yet with material poverty, financial decline will soon follow. This financial distress is caused by the burden imposed on taxpayers to pay the terrible cost of moral decay. It's not the deprived and the dispossessed who threaten to bankrupt America; it's those other poor—the poor in spirit, the poor in morals, the poor in values, and the poor in character.

Giving them food stamps, job training, rental assistance and medical care simply has not worked. I don't deny that the basic needs of life must be met for all Americans. A nation as prosperous as our own would be shamed if many people should starve or freeze to death on our streets. I have seen that kind of poverty, but not in America. It happens here only in isolated cases when someone, usually because of severe mental illness, manages to elude the $5.4 trillion safety net we have thrown out.

Our safety net has provided the basic needs for the vast majority of poor Americans, yet they are still poor. Not only has the War on Poverty failed to reduce financial poverty it has fomented moral poverty.

Those caught in the benevolent toils of the government have also become apathetic; public programs tend to produce more whiners than doers. Tenants of public housing, for instance, may well be the descendants of those who cleared the wilderness. Yet they're apt to complain listlessly that weeks have passed, and no one has come around from the Housing Authority to fix the toilet or scrape off the flaking paint that is poisoning their children.

What's $770,000 between neighbors?

The Navy was overcharged $770,000 for aircraft engines because no one at the Pentagon bothered to keep up with international currency exchange rates. A Canadian subcontractor miscalculated the U.S.-Canadian exchange rate on its share of a $60 million contract given to Pratt and Whitney Corp. of West Virginia, resulting in the $770,000 overcharge. The Navy has yet to attempt recovery.

Washington Merry-Go-Round
August 20, 1979

Everywhere in America, people are grappling with the federal octopus. Many become entangled in its tender embrace. Its undulating tentacles simultaneously caress these docile citizens and restrict their movements. Unable to outmaneuver the many tentacles, these people become the pampered captives of the octopus.

The bureaucrats in their federal cubicles have gained a mastery of the regulations books with which they confound the real world. They threaten the fundamental spirit of the American system—innovative enterprise. A new idea involves change and risk. The tendency of most bureaucrats is to resist—a tendency that is hardened into an obstacle course of rules.

Our political leaders, for their part, practice yesterday's politics at the expense of tomorrow. In a global economy, their focus is parochial. In the technological age, many still protect smokestack industries and champion archaic labor unions. In the name of getting the most for their constituents, many seek government subsidies for obsolete factories and oppose funds for future research. Admirably, they have assigned high priority to social progress. But to achieve social equality, they have lowered standards, leveled the masses, and de-emphasized excellence.

We have taken it as a law of nature that each American generation will do better than the one before. At least, we believed that the next generation certainly would not slide backwards. Yet, for the majority of Americans, the 20th Century will end with a generation of sliding backwards. We are slowly awakening to the awful recognition that this may not be just a temporary reverse; it's beginning to look like a permanent fall never contemplated in the American promise.

The great irony is that the federal benevolence, which was intended to provide a better life for the next generation, is the principal cause of the backward slide. By sucking up 22.3 percent of the gross domestic product—in other words, by squandering money that would be better used for private purposes—the federal government is blithely picking your pockets.

As chairman of Citizens Against Government Waste, I have learned that the most inefficient way to achieve an objective is to assign the federal government to do it. The government routinely robs people to pay bureaucrats. CAGW found that excessive government spending reduced your paycheck to 13 percent lower than it could have been had Uncle Sam been more prudent. That's 13 percent less that you have to keep your own family from becoming a poverty statistic.

We reap what we sow

Here is the report from the front lines of the War on Poverty, as far as it can be defined by numbers, 30 years after LBJ deployed the cash:

Until President Clinton signed the Welfare Reform Bill in 1996, Uncle Sam operated 67 different welfare programs costing $240 billion a year and serving about 13 million people. The money that was sunk in welfare amounts to 5 percent of the gross domestic product. That's a measure of how much has been spent on food stamps, rent, child care, school lunches, foster homes, health care, preschools, utility bills, job training and economic stimulus programs in depressed areas.

Yet today the poverty rate is higher than it was in 1965. Instead of lifting people up, the anti-poverty programs seem to have pushed people down. One out of every seven children is now being raised in a home that lives on the monthly AFDC check (Aid to Families with Dependent Children). That's 4.7 million families. They will get AFDC handouts for an average of 13 years. This AFDC payroll costs the taxpayers $25 billion a year. For all the talk of family values in America, one third of our children are born to single mothers, setting up the mother and the child for a lifetime of living on the margin and living on the dole.

Our good intentions have had bad results. How bad?

Research at Stanford University in the 1980s showed that an increase of 10 percent in welfare benefits can cause a 6 percent increase in the birthrate of unmarried women. A University of Washington study found that a $200 increase in the monthly welfare check for a family resulted in a 150 percent increase in the illegitimate birth rate.

June O'Neill, director of the Congressional Budget Office, collected alarming statistics while conducting academic studies with colleagues before she joined the CBO. If AFDC payments and food stamps are increased by 50 percent a month in a state, the rate of illegitimate births in that state will rise 43 percent and the number of mothers jumping on the AFDC bandwagon will go up

75 percent. So will the number of years the average person spends on welfare. Even more disturbing, O'Neill found that the IQs of young children who have spent at least part of their life on welfare will slip, on the average, to 20 percent below the IQs of children from non-welfare families of the same race and income level.

In the 1970s the Office of Economic Opportunity traced welfare recipients in Seattle and Denver to determine how their long-term earnings had been affected by increases in welfare benefits. Those who advocated throwing money at the problem had argued that more money would buy better results. But the researchers found that for every $1 of extra benefits, the workers' labor and earnings went down 80 cents. The more they were given, the less they worked and the less they earned.

A University of Michigan study revealed that young men who grew up on welfare will make less money as adults than their peers who came from working families of the same income level.

> ### And the gold metal in waste goes to...
>
> In 1972 Congress created the Annual Assay Commission to make sure that U.S. coins contained the proper amount of gold or silver. More than a decade ago, the government stopped putting either gold or silver in its coins—but the commission continues to hold its annual luncheon meeting. Solemnly, the commissioners measure the amounts of non-precious metals in U.S. coins, and strike a medal to commemorate their meeting. This useless exercise costs the taxpayers about $20,000 a year.
>
> *Washington Merry-Go-Round*
> *August 20, 1979*

In study after study, children raised on welfare are also shown to be more likely to drop out of high school. Other research compared single mothers on welfare—those raised on welfare when they were children and those raised without government assistance but in the same income bracket—and found that the girls raised by working families will get off the dole faster than the girls raised on AFDC.

In plain terms, a hand up is more effective than a hand-out. The family that gets something for nothing in some psychological way hobbles its children. No matter how you multiply it, nothing times nothing equals zero.

It takes a man to raise a man

If the studies and statistics are correct, single parenting is the greatest cause of the social disintegration that afflicts America. More than 15 million American children live in homes without fathers. The structure of our welfare programs encourages this massive flight of fathers—which causes suffering rather than alleviating it. The absence of fathers in the lives of impressionable young boys has turned our cities into armed camps. Not race, not income level. The problem is fatherless families.

When June O'Neill examined data from a nationwide survey of youth, she found that young black men raised by a single parent were twice as likely to embark on a life of crime as were black men raised by two parents—all other things being equal, including the income and education of their parents and the neighborhood environment in which they were raised. Other studies have reached the same conclusion about inner cities dominated increasingly by unwed mothers and haphazardly raised children.

When you take responsible, caring men out of the lives of boys, the results are tragic. Uncle Sam will pay a teenage mother welfare benefits because she's single and then take away the money if she marries the father of her child. Our national rhetoric glorifies the family. Our national Treasury sends a different message with every welfare check. Maybe Uncle Sam should put his money where his mouth is.

President Franklin Roosevelt, who launched a few welfare programs in his time, sounded a warning about the public dole. More than 60 years ago he said, "The lessons of history, confirmed by the evidence immediately before me, show conclusively that continued dependence upon relief induces a spiritual and moral disintegration fundamentally destructive to the national fiber. To dole out relief in this way is to administer a narcotic, a subtle destroyer of the human spirit."

Liberal Democrats have taken most of the heat for the welfare state, but the record shows that both major parties have taken the easy way out—shoveling money at people instead of helping them achieve self-sufficiency. During the Reagan and Bush presidencies, welfare recipients increased from 10.6 million to 14.1 million people. The numbers slipped in the three years after Clinton took office to just under 13 million. When Clinton took credit for reducing the welfare rolls, Republicans countered that the number of people on the dole was still "20 percent higher than the historical average." They failed to mention that the historical average was skewed by Reagan and Bush.

Poisoning people with kindness

As happens with everything that Uncle Sam touches, the welfare rolls are loaded with opportunists getting more than is their due and bureaucrats mismanaging the pot of money. Food stamps are sold and traded for drugs and guns. The waste and mis-use of food stamps alone, by some estimates, may cost taxpayers as much as $2 billion a year. People behind bars continue to get their welfare checks because the bureaucracy doesn't bother to keep up with their change of status, although it doesn't have any trouble processing their change of address. Drug addicts and alcoholics can continue to collect aid on the condition they stay in recovery programs, with the money going to third parties. One investigation revealed that the responsible third party for a group of 40 alcoholics was the owner of a liquor store who was using their welfare money to run a $160,000-a-year tab for them.

That doesn't hold a candle to what Uncle Sam himself did in the name of charity. The Social Security Administration spent $32 million trying to recruit more people to join the Supplemental Security Income (SSI) rolls. That's the account that pays welfare to the disabled and elderly poor and to children who don't perform at "age-appropriate levels."

Starting in 1990, the Social Security Administration began paying local recruiters to drum up more SSI customers. These bounties were euphemistically called grants and the hunt was called an "Outreach Demonstration Project." The recruiters spent your money on billboards, booths at state fairs, door-to-door canvassing and even an SSI rap song to get out the message: Uncle Sam wants you to take his money.

The recruiters signed up ineligible Indians on the reservation just because these softies didn't want Uncle Sam to disappoint the Indians one more time. The recruiters drove through East St. Louis with bullhorns begging for people to join the welfare generation. They had a little trouble in New Orleans where two of the recruiters were shot by the needy souls they wanted to help. Also in New Orleans, they were slowed down by a Hatfields-and-McCoys dispute between the residents of two rival housing projects. One university received an outreach grant for $175,000 but signed up only four new people for the dole, which gives rise to questions about the economy of scale. A more direct approach might have been to commission welfare recipients as their own recruiters, offering them cash and cutting out the middlemen.

It is reassuring to note that the recruiters found that their biggest stumbling block was pride. Many of the people they tried to hustle onto the SSI rolls didn't buy the argument that it wasn't really welfare. Others told the recruiters to go away, saying that the disabilities that qualified them for SSI were temporary personal setbacks and none of the government's business. Happily, Uncle Sam's misguided charitable efforts haven't succeeded in wiping away all of our national pride.

Presidential waste doesn't amount to peanuts

Jimmy Carter promised voters he would ferret out government waste and improper use of taxpayers' money. But in his search for misused funds, our millionaire chief executive failed to look in the handiest hiding place of all—his own pocket.

During his first two years in office, Carter spent only one-seventh of his $50,000 annual expense allowance. But instead of turning the two-year total of $85,727 left over back to the Treasury, Carter put the money in his personal bank account.

There's nothing illegal about a president pocketing unused expense money. The practice has been sanctified by tradition in the 30 years of presidential walking-around money. Carter's predecessors in the White House didn't turn back their leftover allowance, either.

Washington Merry-Go-Round
July 10, 1979

How much job training does it take to work at a quicky-mart?

The problem is that members of Congress, and we the people who elect them, can't figure out how to break this vicious cycle of poverty. The popular method has been to offer various job-training programs in the hope that people can eventually grab their bootstraps and pull themselves up.

So the government now trains people for jobs rather than putting them to work. President Roosevelt crafted the New Deal to bring America out of the Depression. His notion of welfare was to create jobs by establishing agencies to provide work, such as the Civilian Conservation Corps and the Works Progress Administration. The success of those jobs programs apparently was geared to the peculiar notion that people should work for their keep. And even if those jobs were provided largely by the federal government, they were still jobs that required people to work for the check they got from Uncle Sam.

Not so now. The jobs programs of the late 20th Century have focused on training and education instead of putting people to work. Now our welfare programs cycle people through redundant, often worthless, courses, workshops and pep talks. The end result is frequently a minimum wage job the worker keeps for a few weeks and then walks away from out of boredom, laziness or frustration. The system is also ripe for the pickings by con artists who set up diploma mills; the faculty's best-honed skill usually is sending tuition bills to the Treasury.

These scams do not just drain the Treasury. Worse, they drain the enthusiasm and waste the time of deprived people who genuinely want to work. Too many people who spend years living out of the taxpayers' pockets hop from low-wage job to low-wage job, working long hours but still not seeing enough money to pay child care and afford bus tokens to get to the job.

I'd like to believe the axiom that if you give a man a fish you feed him for a day, but if you teach him how to fish, you feed him for a lifetime. I'm afraid the axiom needs some reworking in the 1990s. If you give an unwed teenage mother a hamburger, you feed her for one meal. But if you teach her how to flip hamburgers, you must also subsidize her child care, rent and doctor bills because a single mom cannot support herself and her children on a minimum wage.

That unwed mother needs what it is already too late to give her—two parents as role models and a few years to get an education and a moral foundation before she had that first child. She could also use a husband to bring a second income into the family. I'm not referring to rich and clever Murphy Brown having a baby. I mean the half of all welfare mothers who rank in the bottom 20 percent of women in math and verbal skills and who, because of the cycle of poverty in which they and their parents and grandparents drift, are doomed to failure in even the most basic of job-training classes.

Federal job-training programs have fallen out of favor as taxpayers have become more aware of the results. Taxpayers not on welfare resent having to pay not only their own way but the tuition of others to attend vocational training and then compete with them for jobs.

The crackdown

Our national dialogue over how to reform welfare has been suspended while Americans await the impact of the reform legislation approved by Congress in 1996. The Republican-controlled 104th Congress had sent Bill Clinton two other remakes of welfare which he vetoed. The third time, Clinton signed the bill over the vigorous protest of his own party, his activist friends in high places, and some members of his Cabinet.

The new law abolishes AFDC and turns cash assistance programs over to the states. No longer will Uncle Sam be funding an open tap of cash flowing out to AFDC families. Instead, states will get a fixed grant from the federal Treasury and they must decide how to spend it locally. Lest any state be too generous with its federal appropriation, the law limits the time anyone can stay on federally funded welfare to five years. And after the first two years, the person on welfare must be working, too, or the benefits will stop. States also are required to get half of their current adult welfare population off the dole and into jobs by 2002.

Welfare benefits for legal immigrants who don't become U.S. citizens will be curtailed under the new law. Adults without children will have their food stamps cut off after three months. Anyone convicted of a drug felony will see no more food stamps, period. Unmarried teenagers who have babies will get welfare only if they stay in school and continue to live with their families.

Some of this is the meat-ax approach that plays well at the polls. Some of it is promising reform which nevertheless will cause much pain and sacrifice before we see the benefits of it. Those who wish to avoid all pain will be the stumbling blocks who will resist carrying out these reforms.

Welcome to the future

Defenders of the old welfare system have been successful in maintaining the status quo for 30 years because they honed name calling to a science. Try to cut welfare and you are a "racist." Stereotype welfare recipients and you are "bigoted." Question the value of a program and you "endanger children." I have listened sincerely to their arguments for years and searched my own soul.

I think my record allows me to speak up without shame. My syndicated column, the "Washington Merry-Go-Round," was founded in 1932 by my mentor, Drew Pearson, to defend the downtrodden, to be a voice of the voiceless, and to expose the tyranny of government over its people and the tyranny of the majority over the minority. In countless stories, I have come to the aid of the deprived and disadvantaged when their government sought to marginalize or dismiss them.

Perhaps I can now come to their aid in a larger way—by invoking whatever influence I may have and by citing whatever credentials old age and experience may have invested in me. That experience—50 years of Washington combat, of shooting and being shot at, of exposing villainies and being despised for it—has convinced me that we cannot continue to degrade and debase people in the name of charity.

I have seen the future, and I don't want it to happen to the America I love. My offices are located in Washington, D.C., which is a 10-square-mile model of the future. This is what all America will be like if we continue to depend on government solutions.

The nation's capital has become a microcosm of the utopia that awaits us on federal planning boards—a welfare state micromanaged by bureaucrats for the benefit of mankind. Every conceivable program with a multibillion-dollar price tag has been dumped on Washington. It is a city overflowing with good intentions and bad results.

Unhappily, the Washington model has turned out to be not the paradise that was once promised, but more like perdition. What is life like in Welfare City? No state or major city has higher income taxes. No state or major city has higher property taxes. None has spent more public money, per capita, on education, housing, health care, welfare and corrections facilities.

Yet the results have been catastrophic. Per capita, the District of Columbia has the most murders, the most robberies, the worst schools, the most abortions, the highest illegitimacy, the most one-parent families, the highest infant mortality, the most adults behind bars and the most people on welfare.

We can thank the dreamers and schemers who inhabit Washington's ivory towers for this dream that has turned into a nightmare. They have federalized poverty, fomented violence and bankrupted the city treasury. Children are fed with food stamps and starved of initiative. The federal hand on their shoulders doesn't lift them up but pushes them down.

Plainly and simply, benevolent bureaucrats have transformed the nation's capital into a disaster area. Their voracious appetite for greenbacks has depleted the coffers and sent taxpaying citizens fleeing the city. Apparently, it didn't occur to the city fathers and mothers that taxpayers don't have to stay in Washington to be plucked like chickens.

What money is available, as the bureaucrats' first priority, goes for their own care and feeding. Little has been left to fill the potholes, repair school buildings, and police the streets. It is taking a transfusion from the national treasury to finance the city's recovery.

But if Washington's fate spreads all across the land, who will provide the transfusion?

CHAPTER TEN

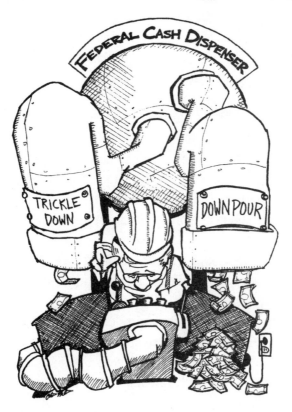

DOWN THE MOTHER OF ALL DRAINS

An accomplished hustler's favorite larceny, petty or grand, is picking Uncle Sam's pockets. But the mother of all heists occurred on a quiet Sunday morning in 1994 in faraway Somalia. Someone broke into a United Nations cashier's office and made off with $3.9 million in stacks of neatly wrapped $100 bills fresh out of the U.S. Treasury.

Jesse James never had it so easy. The money was not locked in a strongbox but stacked in an old carton that once held water bottles. The carton was not kept in a safe but in a filing cabinet drawer. The filing cabinet was not shut in a vault but stored in a storage room. It could be entered through a door that could be jimmied with a credit card. The existence of the stash was common knowledge to dozens of U.N. employees who were regularly paid from the drawer.

Somalia had no banks, so the U.N. stockpiled cash to run its peacekeeping operations. Officials passed out our greenbacks with careless abandon—altogether typical of how the U.N. has squandered the money and good will of American taxpayers. Nothing short of a major revamping of its bloated bureaucracy can help the U.N.

In this instance, American taxpayers can proudly boast they are deadbeats; they owe the United Nations $1.3 billion in unpaid dues and special assessments. It is money well saved. It has been withheld as a protest against the U.N.'s 50-year accumulation of booty.

Congress appropriated only $304 million for the U.N. in 1996—just a small dent in the total debt—and the dispute over the U.N.'s money management is far from settled. Take the peacekeeping budget. Republican legislators don't think the United States should have to pay 31 percent of all peacekeeping operations, which is what the U.N. assesses Washington. So they rammed a bill through Congress unilaterally ratcheting it down to 25 percent.

The U.N. is UN-concerned with waste

One-quarter of the U.N.'s $10 billion annual budget is supposed to come out of Uncle Sam's deep pockets. Here are some examples of what the U.N. does with that money:

• The Asian bloc insisted on having their own state-of-the-art conference facility in Bangkok. They were grateful enough for all that was being spent on the needy and neglected in Asia, but what they really wanted was a new building. The U.N. General Assembly obliged and authorized the building—at a cost of $44 million.

It was finished in 1993, except for two oversights. First, somebody forgot to install telephone conduits before the building was completed. Another $5 million was appropriated to install the telephone lines. Second, the U.N. has no regular use for the building, so it's rented out for weddings and socials.

• In December 1984, when the world was wrenched by photos of starving Ethiopian children, the General Assembly voted $73.5 million to build a conference center in Ethiopia. On the same day the vote was taken, the hat was passed among employees and diplomats in the U.N. basement to solicit contributions for the dying famine victims. Today the cost of the conference center has escalated to $107 million. When done, it will be of little use to the U.N.

• Much of the annual $30 million that the U.N. Children's Fund (UNICEF) spent in Somalia slipped through Somali fingers. One man who was hired to direct the digging of hundreds of wells hired relatives. If any of them ever dug a well, there's no record of it. An auditor from New York headquarters found rampant skullduggery. But the miscreants had the last word. When the auditor finished his work in Mogadishu, he left the office for lunch. He returned to find his report, all the data, and his computer stolen. Yet the outside door was still locked, indicating it was an inside job.

• The U.N. has invested millions in a system to solve one of its most pesky problems. On any given day, the U.N. doesn't know how many people are on its payroll, how much they're paid, or what positions they hold.

When a U.S. senator requested a simple list of all "supernumeraries," employees who are paid but have no position, it took the U.N. more than a year to produce a list of three dozen—and even then couldn't assure the senator it was a complete list. Some supernumeraries were drawing more than $100,000 a year while sitting at home for months waiting for another posting.

• The average cost to produce a U.N. document is mind-boggling. According to one U.N. estimate, it costs a minimum of $830 a page for documents in New York and $1,100 in Geneva. This doesn't include the cost of preparing or drafting the papers.

Are U.N. documents engraved in gold? No, but they are printed in six official languages—English, French, Spanish, Russian, Chinese and Arabic. Arabic was added in the 1970s at the behest of oil-rich Arab nations, which promised to pay for the interpretation and translation. The Arabic versions continue, but the payments stopped more than a decade ago. A routine three-hour U.N. meeting costs $5,000 for just the interpreters. Since the U.N. has about 12,000 meetings a year, this means the cost for simultaneous oral translation is $60 million. Then it takes a larger battery of translators to convert the printed word into six languages. For decades, this has been done by dictating to a third set of employees, the 500 typists.

The U.N.'s printing press is the second largest in the world; only the Government Printing Office in Washington has one larger. Under the U.N.'s leisurely management, its print shop expended up to 40 percent more money to produce a document than it would have cost at a commercial print shop. The wages were also 40 percent higher and the workers took five times as many sick days, double the vacation days, and double the coffee breaks of private American print shop employees.

A 1992 environmental summit in Brazil, convened in the name of the U.N., churned out an estimated 30 million pieces of paper. It took 220 garbagemen to haul away seven tons of nonrecyclable trash—an ecological nightmare—from the convention center.

The only good news: Some U.N. reports don't consume any paper at all—because they're never completed. The U.N. spent $2.5 million in 1991 on a study of the Chernobyl nuclear disaster but failed to produce a report. Instead, the Secretariat asked delegates to authorize another $2.5 million for a report to explain what happened to the first report.

From noble cause to cause for alarm

Countless similar cases of fraud, waste and abuse have created a new legacy for the United Nations—an institution that was founded to help others now more often helps itself. In 1945 it got along on a budget of less than $20 million, with a staff of only 1,500. Today the U.N. spends $10 billion a year, most of it to maintain a permanent staff of 51,600, and an additional 80,000 in peacekeeping forces.

The U.N. evokes powerful images of noble causes, brave peacekeepers and the best hopes of mankind.

The reality is that at age 50, the U.N. is the world's biggest pork barrel which has become a massive drain on the U.S. budget. It is mismanaged, often redundant and endemically corrupt. For every success story, there are a dozen tales of unfettered greed, badly conceived activities, and jerry-built bureaucracies decimated by petty politics and turf battles. Most votes in the General Assembly concerning the budget are created by nations that pay less than 2 percent of the budget.

The most persistent U.N. critic, South Dakota Senator Larry Pressler, complains that the U.N. is a Third World system: "Most countries in the U.N. are not democracies. Most countries, in fact, are kleptocracies, as defined by our own State Department, where the leaders of the countries are dictators and they steal from their own people. In their countries, frequently government service is a chance to get rich. So once these types get on the U.N. payroll, they are frequently out to enrich themselves."

We need a guide on how to use a pink slip at the Treasury

The Treasury Department has had a hard time convincing the American public to use the new Susan B. Anthony dollar coins. So now the U.S. Mint has issued a special guide for consumers on how to use the dollar. Almost a million copies of the glossy leaflet, extolling the virtues of the coin, were printed at a cost to the taxpayers of 23,897 shiny dollars. The guide has an entire section devoted to the benefits of the dollar coin; it explains among other things that the coin is easy to distinguish from other coins because there's the picture of a woman on it.

Washington Merry-Go-Round
April 14, 1980

When the U.N. rattles the tin cup, large donor nations like the United States have the same concern as tourists besieged by panhandlers. Any charity, it's suspected, will go for alcohol or drugs instead of food.

In the U.N.'s case, the fear is that top officials and staff assistants will divert the donations into their own pockets, leaving little to trickle down to the needy. The fear is real: A whopping 79 percent of the regular budget for the U.N. goes to the staff in the form of corpulent salaries and benefits.

The impression of industriousness is promoted through speeches, conferences and publications. But for the most part, this is much ado about nothing—which makes the budget decisions all the more repugnant. When the U.N. is forced to tighten its belt, it cuts programs that serve, and unnecessary staff personnel hang on. An old joke at the U.N. goes: "How many people work at the U.N.?" Answer: "About half."

One reason for the problem is that so many of the staffers are patronage appointees who come from countries where the work ethic is a truly foreign concept. The U.N. has become the favorite international pork barrel for the pigs of the world—a wallowing place for hacks from 185 countries.

The United Nation's generous compensations

The elite U.N. bureaucrats are compensated as if they work for a royal court. The operating guideline is the "Noblemaire Principle," named after the head of the 1921 League of Nations committee, which decreed that international civil servants should be paid more than their highest salaried counterparts in national governments. The rationale was that only exorbitant salaries could induce a highly skilled civil servant to leave his or her country to work as an expatriate.

At a minimum, the current U.N. base salary is generally at least 15 percent higher than those in comparable positions in the U.S. government. Here's a look at part of the lucrative benefits package (let me remind you again, U.S. taxpayers pay for 25 percent of these benefits):

• U.N. staffers work 35 hours or less each week. This laid-back schedule was the real reason they scrapped a $938,000 security system at headquarters that was installed but never activated. Their union held up activation of the turnstile entrance that would read electronic I.D. cards, claiming fear of health hazards from radio waves. They were worried about a far greater threat: The cards and turnstiles had a clocking system that would record the exact time employees arrived and departed.

• From the day a person is hired by the U.N., he/she is entitled to six weeks of paid vacation per year. Free travel is provided to their homelands every two years, not only for the workers but for their families.

• Yearly allowances are paid for dependent spouses, plus $1,270 for each child up to 18 years old. Employees also receive grants for their children to attend private schools and universities. Those grants cost $62.1 million a year. Little documentation is required to claim the money, which has turned this benefit into a gold mine for dishonest U.N. employees. One staffer submitted false documentation on her four children, building a $41,207 nest egg before she was caught.

• Housing allowances are added to the salaries of those not serving in their home countries. There has been no audit of this huge subsidy, nor any criticism of U.N. officials who always seem to live in high-rent districts. Secretary General Boutros Boutros Ghali lived at 3 Sutton Place in New York, the Georgian estate overlooking the East River which was built for billionaire J.P. Morgan's daughter.

• A language allowance is given to staffers who are proficient in a second of the six official languages of the U.N., even if that second language isn't needed for their job.

• Generous overtime payments make it possible for security guards, for example, to make more than $100,000 a year.

Conference-room messengers, who relay phone messages and paper-work to delegates, make upwards of $80,000 a year with overtime.

• U.N. staffers not only live well; they also leave well. Early retirement is possible at 55, and pensions are one-third better than the U.S. civil service offers. Only the Russians have cause to complain about their pensions. Former Secretary General of the U.N. Kurt Waldheim unconscionably handed over the pension funds for the Soviet staff (in hard currency) to the Kremlin, which promised to pay the Russians in rubles at the official rate when they retired. Now the rubles are worthless, and the Russian retirees are howling for relief. That could mean U.S. taxpayers will be dunned a second time for the same Russian pensions.

• All U.N. salaries are tax-free. The IRS grants no leniency, but the employees simply get reimbursed by the U.N. for taxes paid. These paybacks average $40 million and are a direct contribution by the U.S. government.

Economies on scale

How many taxpayers' dollars will fit on the slide of a bureaucrat's microscope? About 100,000, apparently. The General Services Administration recently decided to brighten the lives of workers in a federal office building in Idaho by commissioning an artist to sculpt a totem pole outside the entrance. The GSA art buffs were so pleased with the result that they're planning to grace nine other government buildings around the country with similar poles. The artifacts fetch some $10,000 a copy, but a GSA official dismissed the cost as "microscopic."

Washington Merry-Go-Round
March 12, 1980

The system is wide open for fraud because the U.N. and the IRS won't compare notes. The last time the system was audited in the 1980s, widespread fraud was discovered. It's easy to cheat this system; the culprits simply submit a claim for more taxes than were actually paid.

Serving at New York headquarters can hardly be called hard-ship duty, yet New York-based staffers claim additional perks beyond those noted above. The U.N. building features subsidized conveniences and merchandise for which there is no sales tax: a gourmet restaurant; a well-appointed bar (once 20 deep on election day when it was the only one open in Manhattan); gift shops on a par with airport duty-free stores; a spacious staff cafeteria fronting on the East River and offering meals for low prices.

But no perk is more jealously guarded than parking. U.N. officials use diplomatic immunity to park illegally, though the U.N. parking garage is an adequate legal shelter, with spaces that are either free or cheap. But the number of spaces is limited.

Taking candy from a starving baby

Sadly, the most blatant waste at the U.N. is found in a place where the waste costs lives—the office of the U.N. High Commissioner For Refugees (UNHCR). Founded in 1949, this Geneva-based institution tries to care for and feed more than 15 million refugees around the world with a staff of 2,000 and an annual $673 million appropriations. The efforts of UNHCR have twice won it a Nobel Prize.

But while many dedicated individuals still carry on, UNHCR's effectiveness and reputation have plummeted since the last Nobel was awarded in 1981. During the past decade, reports of widespread corruption and mismanagement, even in the commissioner's office, have tarnished the agency.

UNHCR's most shameful debacle occurred during the early stages of the Somali refugee crisis after the fall of Mohamed Siad Barre in January 1991. Thousands of refugees died unnecessarily while UNHCR fiddled. At the Dolo refugee camp in southern Ethiopia, 50 refugees a day died from January to April in 1991 while UNHCR food aid was diverted to private markets and sold for profit.

At the Liboi refugee camp in northern Kenya, the killer was lack of water. A well with a pump, which could have been installed in two days, would have saved many lives at the camp. But arguments between the Nairobi office of UNHCR and the local contractor delayed construction for months. Meanwhile, at least 15 died at the Liboi camp each day.

When UNHCR finally shows up at the scene with food, it routinely brings more than is needed, for UNHCR has become the world's worst head counter. Refugee populations are too often overestimated, so food is wasted. Or worse, it is sold to line the pockets of local scalawags or U.N. employees.

If the U.N. Food and Agriculture Organization (FAO) had done its job with the $10 billion it swallowed in the name of the starving, less refugee help might have been needed over the years. More than half of FAO's $650 million annual budget is absorbed by the staff who work in a six-story marble building and annex near the Colosseum in Rome.

Some FAO projects make sense. But surely there were other priorities in Iraq after the Gulf War, for instance, than trying to control their honeybee diseases ($77,000). Did the starving North Koreans need help for goose breeding ($20,000)? Does the ultra-rich United Arab Emirates really need $15,000 to improve the reproductive efficiency of the dromedary camel? And what reasonable explanation is there for making Saudi Arabia one of FAO's biggest beneficiaries, to the tune of tens of millions of dollars?

Promoting economic development— their own

The U.N. Development Program (UNDP) has as its mandate to promote faster economic development and higher living standards in the poorest countries of the world. It has failed miserably, though not for lack of money and manpower.

UNDP pays for more than 5,000 projects which cost an estimated $5.6 billion. It has opened a network of offices in 115 developing countries with a staff of nearly 7,000. Half of UNDP's income is spent on this sprawling staff, whose voice is louder inside the U.N. than the cries of the poor around the earth.

For instance, back in 1971, UNDP self-servingly concluded that the single most important factor needed more urgently than anything else was good housing for staffers. So, abracadabra! The UNDP now owns or rents 790 properties in 41 countries for its pampered staff. It's considerably more than they need. A 1993 review found that 165 of the properties—or 21 percent—were vacant.

Some UNDP projects are heartening, considering the areas and people served. But many others simply make no sense: $66,000 in Brazil to train diplomats in negotiation techniques; $177,000 for a museum at the Institute of Ethiopian Studies; $3,000 to build a memorial for air-crash victims in Tanzania.

The most curious UNDP aid projects were bestowed upon rich countries that can afford to fund their own aid. Among the more egregious examples are genetic preservation of Arabian horses in Saudi Arabia and translation of great literary works in Japan. The two richest countries on earth, per capita—Kuwait and Brunei—got UNDP grants for health care projects. American taxpayers provide 10 percent of UNDP's grab bag.

If a vote were taken, would Americans condone the allotment of $164 million a year to terrorist-sponsoring nations? According to 1991 figures, Iraq, though at war with a U.N.-sanctioned military force, was consigned $58 million in development aid by UNDP. Other rogue nations receiving U.N. development money are Iran, Libya, Syria, North Korea and Cuba—all autocratic countries that spend a prodigious amount of their own wherewithal on repressive militaries.

Finally, one of the most pernicious practices afflicting U.N. humanitarian agencies is the rampant bribing in countries whose people they are trying to help. The amount has been spiraling upward, raising the cost of helping the indigent in impoverished nations.

How to make easy money while still in college

Government scholarships are supposed to be awarded to those who cannot afford an education. But on American Samoa, scholarships are granted to critics of the government to shut them up.

The daughter of Samoa's House Speaker, for example, received a scholarship after a promised government job fell through. Presumably, this soothed the feelings of both the daughter and the Speaker. A lawyer involved in litigation against the island's attorney general received another scholarship. A third grant went to the man who was supposed to become president of the Samoan Community College but was rejected by the Samoan governor. The scholarship was a consolation prize, which kept him mollified. The three scholarships cost the taxpayers a total of $150,000.

Washington Merry-Go-Round
October 23, 1978

UNICEF, in its internal audits, doesn't call bribery by its true name. They call it, quite neatly, "salary supplements and other incentives to government employees working on projects assisted by UNICEF." An internal audit turned up nearly $6 million in such incentives in 1991 and 1992.

The U.N. Educational, Scientific and Cultural Organization (UNESCO) became so mired in corruption that the U.S., Britain and Singapore all withdrew their support in 1985. An incredible 76 percent of the budget still goes to its own 2,600-person staff. To prepare and perpetuate the staff for the future, they spent $200,000 to bring 21 leading intellectuals to Paris in 1993 to discuss "the problems of the next century." There was no conclusion after two days, except that they should meet again (at UNESCO expense, of course).

What price peace?

The public perceives the U.N. to be an organization that promotes peace. That was certainly the intention of the founders five decades ago. Unfortunately, the U.N. has not had much success as a peacemaker. There have been more than 300 regional and civil wars, consuming 20 million lives, in the last 50 years. The U.N. appeared helpless to stop genocides in Cambodia, East Pakistan (Bengal), Bosnia and Rwanda. U.N. peacekeeping forces obligingly stepped aside so Egypt's Gamal Abdel Nasser could invade Israel (1967) and Israel could invade Lebanon (1982). The U.N. was simply ignored when the Soviet Union invaded Hungary (1956), Czechoslovakia (1968) and Afghanistan (1979).

U.N. peacekeepers had been mostly just a thin, blue-helmeted line trying to keep belligerents at bay—until the Cold War thawed out. Then the U.N. became the global 911, the world's police force. The Security Council approved operations faster than they could be funded—sometimes in places where there was no peace to keep. Missions proliferated at a dizzying pace with acronymic names that sound like brands of sleeping pills (UNOSOM), dental floss (UNAMIC), cold remedies (UNTAC, UNIFIL), or creatures from a Japanese horror film (ONUMOZ).

Under the Willy Sutton doctrine (that criminals rob banks because that is where the money is), peacekeeping operations represent the U.N.'s biggest opportunity for plunder—because that's where the money is.

They can speak six languages but can't balance a checkbook

The problem is compounded by the U.N.'s ineptness at keeping its books straight. Inventory counts are practically unheard of; there hasn't been one at U.N. headquarters since 1987. If there ever is, the auditors would find millions of dollars in unused computer equipment had been thrown away because it was incompatible with other U.N. systems. One headquarters committee ordered $30,000 worth of invitation cards, gold-edged with white envelopes; but by the time they arrived no one could remember why.

As for cash, the U.N. keeps its reserves in bank accounts that pay a paltry interest. And there's little hope that the U.N. might cash in on wiser investments. Half of its $500,000 Nobel Peace Prize for peacekeeping was squandered on a bad investment.

Add to those endemic problems the multibillion-dollar peace-keeping budget, and you have a recipe for financial havoc. At a minimum, a wise manager would employ more auditors to watch for inevitable theft and fraud. The U.N. doesn't bother. It bud-geted a mere $70,000 for auditing the billion-dollar budget for the peacekeeping effort in the former Yugoslavia while it was spending $10,000 a month to rent a villa in Zahgreb for the head of the operations.

The U.N. paid $1.7 billion for an election in Cambodia, reserv-ing a bare $120,000 for auditing. In contrast, $1.2 million was spent on laundry and barber services for the Cambodian mission.

When oversight is so devalued and money is being thrown around like confetti, the U.N. can count its blessings that it lost only tens of millions of dollars (so far as is known) in fraud, waste and abuse on its top three peacekeeping missions in Bosnia, Cambodia and Somalia.

The U.S. Congress has raised its collective voice in a squawk for U.N. reform, using the lever of reduced U.S. contributions. Congress would get more for its money if it concentrated on one single task—to pressure the U.N. to produce clear, simple budgets in time for the member states to consider them. The U.N. uses so many tricks in drafting its budget that nobody can figure out what to look for when the obtuse documents are delivered.

It's a running joke around U.N. headquarters that no other organization in the world can make this boast about its work: "Printed in six languages and read in none." But the joke is on you, the American taxpayers.

CHAPTER ELEVEN

TODAY'S
SERMON:
THE MEEK
SHALL INHERIT
THE DEFICIT

ROBBING THE YOUNG
TO BENEFIT THE ELDERLY

The late Soviet leader Nikita Khrushchev once issued a warning about nuclear war that, when paraphrased, could apply to the outcome of the 1996 election: "The living will envy the dead." Those who had the good fortune to lose election to

Congress can sit back in comfort and watch the winners slowly roast in the fire of public wrath over a crisis that can no longer be ignored—Social Security.

Look around at your fellow Americans and understand that 43 million of them are currently collecting Social Security from a pot of money that equals almost half of all the retirement benefits, public and private, paid out this year in America. Social Security amounts to 4 percent of our gross domestic product.

Social Security is also one of the cars on a runaway train of entitlements. Two other cars are Medicare and Medicaid. Together, they eat up 38 percent of the federal budget. If you add a caboose—federal employee retirement benefits—and put the train on an undeviating course, it will crash in 2030. That is the year when those entitlements will completely consume the entire federal budget if no one applies the brakes.

I do not use the word entitlement lightly. Those who follow this debate know that entitlement is a fighting word. But I won't play the games of semantics that make seniors feel better about the money they are siphoning from their children and grandchildren. I prefer an even stronger term. Welfare.

What would you call it if all the money you put into your pension plan over your working life was paid out to you in the first four years of your retirement, and the taxpayers had to continue sending you support checks for the rest of your life?

Collection orders collecting dust

The Justice Department made a big show recently out of forcing Watergate conspirator G. Gordon Liddy to pay off the remaining $23,000 of his $40,000 criminal fine, imposed in 1973.

Unfortunately, the department hasn't been nearly so enthusiastic about collecting millions of dollars in fines slapped on convicted Mafia figures and drug dealers. Though many of these crooks are still raking in big bucks, they have successfully thumbed their noses at the government's collection agents.

In fact, the government's own ledgers show that of the nearly $5 million in fines levied in more than 800 criminal tax evasion cases since 1970, only $1.8 million had been paid off by September of last year.

Washington Merry-Go-Round
December 10, 1982

What would you call an insurance plan that allowed everyone who paid premiums to collect many times the value of those premiums? Yet many Americans feel more comfortable when they think of Social Security as an insurance plan.

Would you call Social Security your "right" if your adult children mailed 12.4 percent of their salaries to you every month instead of funneling the payments through Uncle Sam? Having an intermediary like the federal government makes it easier to justify your right to your children's money. Social Security was supposed to lift a great burden from the back of our children. Sixty years ago, before we had Social Security, aging people had to rely on their kids for support.

So whom are they relying on today? Yep—their children! The difference between then and now is that Social Security fulfilled its purpose of easing what Senator Daniel Patrick Moynihan has called "the great terror of life"—aging without anyone to care for you. Now, instead of relying on the whims of their offspring, seniors have a promise from the federal government, written in concrete, that they will be taken care of by their offspring.

Surveys of senior citizens show they continue to live the fantasy that Social Security is a pension plan and that they are entitled to take out what they put in. In reality it is a pay-as-you-go system; working people are taxed to fund the pensions of retired people.

The writing was on the walls

Social Security was established by President Franklin Roosevelt in 1935 on a safe bet: If you lived to be 65, Uncle Sam would take care of you in your golden years. At the time, life expectancy was less than 60. But right away, the logic went awry. The first person ever to get a Social Security check, Ida Mae Fuller of Ludlow, Vermont, put a grand total of $22 into the system. Against all odds, she lived to be 99. Before she died she had collected more than $20,000 in Social Security. That wasn't supposed to happen.

The ABCs of FICA

Here, in short form, is how Social Security works today:

You and your employer together pay a Social Security tax which amounts to 12.4 percent of the first $62,700 of your annual salary (6.2 percent taken out of your paycheck and 6.2 percent contributed by your employer.) Your pay stub calls it FICA, taken from the Federal Insurance Contributions Act. The money goes into two accounts: Old Age and Survivors Insurance, and Disability Insurance. The first, OASI, is your basic retirement account. The second, DI, is the welfare money that goes to people regardless of age who, because of a mental or physical disability, cannot work.

When everyone who is entitled to a share of your FICA money has been paid, there will still be about $65 billion left unspent this year. Add that to the $400 billion already in surplus which is earning you more than $30 billion a year in interest. This is good news, right? Yes and no. The surplus goes into a trust fund for future retirees like yourself, but don't picture a bank vault where the money is piling up for you. Picture instead a drawer full of IOUs. The unspent Social Security taxes and the interest go directly to the federal Treasury to be squandered at the whim of Congress for everything from B-2 bombers to research on the mating habits of cockroaches. Don't worry, Uncle Sam promises he will return the money when you need it. He'll just borrow from somebody else to pay you back.

When are you a bad credit risk to yourself?

Technically, because the Treasury pays interest on the money, you have achieved the equivalent of buying a government Treasury bond. In more stark terms, your Social Security taxes become part of the national debt. You have borrowed your own money and are paying yourself interest. That's so Congress can have $65 billion more a year to play with.

Congress decided in 1990 to come clean with this cash-swapping scheme. It passed a law to remove Social Security from the general budget for the purposes of bookkeeping. The Treasury still gets your money, but at least it shows up on the books as a loan—deficit spending, pure and simple. No one could ever calculate it in any other terms, but before the law was changed, politicians could always play fast and loose with the bottom line of debt and deficit. The ruse dates from 1968 when President Lyndon Johnson needed a bookkeeping gimmick to hide the fact that the Vietnam War and his Great Society welfare programs were driving up the national debt. Johnson simply lumped Social Security Trust Fund holdings in with general revenues, and voila! The next year the Treasury ran a $3.2 billion "surplus." That was the last time we saw the budget in the black. Deficit spending continued at such a crippling pace that even the Social Security Trust Funds couldn't make it look better.

Now it looks like a debt and quacks like a debt, so Congress must call it a debt—although old habits have proved hard to break. In most cases, when you hear a politician or bureaucrat quote the current annual deficit, they have not included in the bottom line the amount borrowed from the Social Security Trust Fund. For example, the 1996 deficit is most frequently pegged at $146 billion. There was another $97 billion on top of that borrowed from trust funds.

> ### It ain't the Chattanooga choo-choo
>
> Thanks to the beneficence of the federal taxpayers, Miami has a new elevated rapid-transit system. It cost $1 billion to build. It would have been cheaper to give each rider cash to purchase and maintain a new car. Now Los Angeles wants a transit system just like it.
>
> *Washington Merry-Go-Round*
> *July 2, 1985*

On the books the money is recorded as a loan. Your lawmakers decided on this bit of accounting candor not out of a sense of shame at the deception but out of a need to protect Social Security from budget cuts that came with deficit reduction mandates. This protective attitude is rooted not so much in fond regard for the elderly but in fonder regard for re-election.

The big grey machine

Social Security has long been the "third rail" of American politics—the rail that carries the electrical current. You touch it and you die. In fact, the entire senior citizen agenda has become the third rail. A lawmaker who is foolish enough to touch the entitlements that seniors hold dear will not only be shocked but will be run over by millions of outraged senior citizens and their well-greased lobby in Washington, the American Association of Retired Persons. When the history is written of special interest lobbies in the 20th Century, AARP will go down as the most ingenious and most insidious.

Millions of people join AARP for the cheap dues and senior citizen discounts. They may not share a common ideal, but by allying themselves with this behemoth, the hands-out/palms-up attitude of the lobbyists in Washington becomes the agenda for all seniors, like it or not. On any given debate, AARP can rally hundreds of thousands of seniors to make phone calls and write letters that scare the socks off of Congress. The theme is always the same—no matter who else gets hurt, Congress must not mess with the benefits of senior citizens.

Senator Alan Simpson is no friend of AARP, which he once described thusly: "These guys are just a group of human beings, 33 million people pay eight buck dues, bound together by a common love of airline discounts . . . "

AARP literature about Social Security abounds with words such as "generous" and "fair" and "successful." When an AARP publication made the mistake of using the words "entitlement program" in a story on Social Security, hundreds of seniors wrote letters of protest. AARP officials cast about for another phrase to use and came up with "contributory program." It has a nice ring to it.

In informational brochures, AARP steers its members away from the idea that they would have been better off had they put their FICA taxes into private investments. Social Security is and always will be their best bet, according to AARP.

Spending set on autopilot

Older Americans are as much in favor of balancing the budget as younger Americans, but not if it means cutting Social Security. Some surveys show that support for balancing the budget runs high among the overall population—80 percent—but plunges to 32 percent if balancing means touching Social Security.

The seniors are in the best position to push their agenda because cutting Social Security is not as easy as cutting, say, the budget for the Head Start program. Social Security and its sister program, Medicare, are entitlements, and that means a certain class of people are entitled to get those benefits whether or not money exists to pay them. With other programs, Congress can say each year that it will spend a fixed amount and no more: "Here's $25 billion for education programs. Don't spend it all in one place." That's called "budget authority" or permission to spend.

But with entitlements, the tail wags the dog. Once the program is set up, as Social Security was six decades ago, and once the qualifications for eligibility are set, the money pours out uncontrollably. The only way Congress can reduce the amount of money it spends is to change the rules about who is entitled to this money and how much. Most members of Congress would rather have a root canal.

Instead, politicians tiptoe around the elderly like cave dwellers trying not to wake a sleeping bear. In 1972, when Richard Nixon was running for re-election, he courted the senior vote by introducing "Project Find"—which incredibly was designed to seek out older Americans who were not getting all that was due to them from the federal dole. The program gratefully faded away after Nixon was elected.

Nixon also sent letters to 28 million Social Security recipients taking credit for an increase in their checks when, in truth, Congress had approved the increase over Nixon's objections. Then Nixon ordered six government agencies to mail out millions of pamphlets touting the contributions the president had made to Social Security. The mailing cost $250,000.

As their idea of reforming Social Security, timid lawmakers have raised the benefits and have increased taxes to pacify seniors. But real reforms cannot be put off indefinitely because of the eventual retirement of the baby boom generation—all 76 million of them born between 1946 and 1964.

It's like taking the savings from a baby

Today, there are five workers paying into Social Security for every one retiree taking money out. But by 2030, there will be only three workers for every one pensioner. The first wave of baby boomers will hit age 65 in 2011. That year the Social Security Trust Fund will stop growing and begin its plunge down the charts.

The average annual benefit in 1990 was $8,648. In 30 years it will be our equivalent of $12,700. Total benefits paid out will double every decade. By the year 2050, when my grandchildren begin to retire, the payout will reach $20 trillion a year. The number crunchers at the Social Security Administration calmly assure us that the money will still be there—at least until 2030. And that's so far away, why worry now?

Yet, like most government projections, that's a Pollyanna scenario. The Social Security Administration assumes wages will grow 1 percent a year, generating enough taxes to keep Social Security afloat until 2030. That's nearly two times the rate wages have increased in the last two decades.

More people believe in UFOs, polls show, than believe in Social Security. They fear they are paying into a system that will be drained dry before it's their turn to collect. Do you know something? Unless the system is drastically overhauled, they'll be right.

Consider the inequities: An average wage earner who retired at the age of 65 in 1980 drew everything out of Social Security in just four years that he/she paid into it over a lifetime. After the four-year payback, that retiree lived off the mandatory charity of people still working.

Yet a person who turns 65 in 2030 after earning an average wage all his/her working life won't be so lucky. He or she will have to live 26 years after retirement to get back their "investment."

These statistics flatly dispute any notion that Social Security is an annuity. The public debate should not be driven by people who irrationally insist they're getting back only what they put in. In point of fact, the elderly get what the young put in.

That isn't necessarily a bad concept; the young and fit ought to take care of the aging. What has gone amiss is that Social Security takes care of those who don't need it. It is a welfare program that pays the rich and the poor the same amount. It sends a check to the poor widow with no private pension and to the millionaire with an IRA, a 401-K, a golden parachute and a fat corporate pension.

How much is enough?

Is it fair for the older generation to charge their high living standards to the younger generation? Whenever Social Security has faced a fiscal crisis, Congress has gladly raised the FICA taxes to make sure the system does not default and the elderly are not deprived. Yet today's senior citizens, on the average, have a net worth of more than $80,000. The average senior is also drawing $10,000 in government aid each year. That's 10 times more than is spent on the average child, even though the child is six times more likely than the senior to be trapped in poverty. What accounts for the difference? Poor children can't complain when Congress cuts their health programs or food stamps or nutrition programs.

Around 20 percent of all American children live in households that fall below the poverty line. Yet their parents pay FICA taxes to support grandparents who are usually better off. The poverty rate for seniors is only 3 percent. That's not to say that seniors are rolling in money. But at least one million people who collect Social Security benefits receive more than $100,000 from other sources. The Social Security Administration estimates it could save $6.3 billion a year by cutting off benefits to the affluent elderly. And it could save $25 billion more by lowering the eligibility to those who make less than $50,000 a year.

In his 1992 election campaign, President Clinton claimed that restricting full benefits to only the poor would net "very modest revenues." Look again. The wealthiest third of Social Security recipients suck more than $98 billion a year from your paychecks.

At age 70, a millionaire can pocket $1,120 in loose change each month from Social Security, plus another $560 for the lady of the house.

These inconvenient facts compel me to say what my wife refuses to listen to and no one of my generation wants to hear: To stave off a national crisis, those of us who have adequate means must agree to give up our Social Security payments.

Means testing, or dispensing Social Security only to those who need it, would shake the foundations of the system. To keep that from happening, senior citizens have formed a political juggernaut which terrorizes Capital Hill. The key to their power is semantics. If Social Security were called by its real name, welfare, it would be difficult to defend. It would become as vulnerable to partisan politics, say, as are food stamps and homeless shelters. As AARP officials tried to argue, "It would hardly be fair to deny benefits completely to people who are better off. That would undermine the whole earned-right concept on which Social Security is based."

Flag waving and whistle blowing

The six members of the International Trade Commission (ITC) are supposed to advise the President and the Congress on tariff matters. They appear to spend most of their time, however, in the pursuit of unique and ingenious ways to waste the taxpayers' money.

Recently, for example, the ITC discovered a budget surplus of $20,000. Instead of returning the funds to the Treasury, the ITC went on a shopping spree for new office furniture.

Earlier this year, the ITC ordered up $5,000 worth of official Commission flags. Ten of the handsome, hand-woven banners were delivered to Commission offices along with decorative official ITC seals.

Only one meager voice, that of Commissioner Daniel Minchew, was raised in protest. "Since I was able to perform my duties for eighteen months without the benefit of a Commission flag and seal in my office," fumed Minchew in a memo to his colleagues, "I can manage now without them."

Washington Merry-Go-Round
November 12, 1976

Defusing the bomb

How do we fix the system before it blows up in our faces? Congress has chosen, up to this point, to raise taxes and to bleed money from one generation to give to another. This could kindle class warfare as fiscal stringencies cause the young to revolt against tax support of the old.

It should be obvious that some pain will have to be inflicted on some people. Some benefits will have to be cut or at least stunted. This will mean readjusting retirement ages, lowering the benefits formula, or eliminating automatic cost-of-living increases. The standard for these COLAs is the Consumer Price Index, which overstates inflation and bloats the actual cost-of-living changes. The CPI could be reduced, but that would simply buy a few more years of solvency and delay the inevitable. A 1 percent decrease in the CPI, if you could get it past the clamorous senior lobby, would buy about 19 more years of solvency.

The decision to grant automatic COLAs to retirees, thus leaving Congress with even less authority over entitlement spending, was made during the Nixon administration. It appears to have happened almost without consideration of the consequences. Peter Peterson, who was Nixon's Commerce secretary, tells what he remembers of the decision in his book, "Facing Up."

"As far as I could tell, the White House reaction to these extravagant benefit proposals was entirely political. I do not recall any of our domestic economic staff talking of fiscal costs or future tax increases. I do recall Richard Nixon's chief of staff, Bob Haldeman, walking into a morning staff meeting with a yellow legal pad of notes from his regular meeting with the President. For starters, he asked what we would think of putting the American flag on the generous new benefit checks (The American flag was then the code symbol of the Republican Party.) He then wanted to know what we thought about the President sending out personally signed notices with all the checks, which were to be mailed just after the 20 percent benefit hike and before the 1972 election."

Peterson says that Nixon later told him the COLA decision was "probably his most serious economic and fiscal mistake." We can either choose to continue to live with that mistake or correct it. Some have suggested at least a cosmetic change—tweaking the elderly by putting an account balance on each Social Security check, indicating the amount that person paid into the system and the amount they have taken out. That might help to put to rest the entitlement argument, but it would not save the fund from bankruptcy.

At the very least, Social Security recipients could be taxed on the amount they receive above the amount they have paid, plus interest on that amount. That would make about 80 percent of today's Social Security checks taxable. In 1983 Congress figured the beneficiaries rightly should pay taxes on the half that employers contribute toward the FICA payments. But today's Social Security recipients collect much more untaxed income beyond what they and their employers pay into the fund.

If we're going to call a duck a duck, why not treat Social Security like any other income tax? It seems only fair that people who earn more should pay more. People now pay a FICA tax on the first $62,700 only of their annual income. That means a person who earns $62,700 will pay into the system the same tax as a person who earns millions of dollars a year. The end result is that working stiffs pay a higher proportion of their salaries to run the government than do fat cats. (Keep in mind, the taxes that are funneled through FICA go not into the Social Security system to fund retirement checks but into the Treasury to fund government operations.)

No able person, whatever his or her age, should be discouraged from working. But that is exactly what Social Security does when it scales down benefits for people who continue to work past 65. If the elderly are going to be penalized for making more money, then why not adopt an outright means test? People who don't need Social Security shouldn't get it.

One solution: Give them what they think they have

The most radical reform may be the most promising of all—privatizing the Social Security system.

President Clinton appointed a Social Security Advisory Council to test the waters of reform. In 1996 the panel ventured a suggestion: Why not invest excess Social Security funds in the stock market instead of entrusting them to a slippery-fingered Congress? But 1996 was an election year; no politician with any hope of re-election wanted to get near the third rail.

Now that the votes are counted, it may be safe to renew the suggestion. Privatization could take a number of forms. In one scenario, only part of the worker's payroll contribution would go into the Social Security Trust Fund. The rest would be deposited in a Social Security Individual Retirement Account, which would be invested in stocks and bonds instead of in government notes—sort of a mandatory IRA. That money, plus earned interest, would be returned to the retiree directly. Everyone would get an equal share of basic Social Security taxes, but the individual accounts would be privately invested and therefore would vary in their return to the elderly. This plan, ironically, would give seniors what many of them think they already have—an account somewhere with their name on it, containing money they contributed, which is paid back to them after they retire.

This system would be great for savvy investors in higher income brackets. In fact, they'd gladly opt out of Social Security completely if Congress would let them keep all their invested money. Mandatory IRAs wouldn't work for those who lacked the time or skill to follow the market or for women whose lifetime income is lower because of wage discrimination and time taken out of the work force to raise children.

This plan would also cut retirement payments to the disabled and deprived elderly. Their contributions to their mandatory IRAs would be lower during their working years, thus their return would be lower. Since higher-income workers would leave only half of their retirement money in the Social Security Trust Fund, the amount to share with the poor would be smaller.

An alternative plan would keep the 6.2 percent contribution in the general pool, but add an extra tax of 1.6 percent as a mandatory contribution to an IRA. Others think the whole pot should be invested in the stock market instead of loaned to the federal Treasury. There are dangers in that idea too—not the least of which is watching the nation's pension fund ride up and down on the roller coaster of the stock market.

Dumping the Social Security billions into the stock market would be a multibillion-dollar infusion of capital into private business. If the Social Security till is depleted, Uncle Sam couldn't spend it. He'd be obliged to borrow money from private investors. Every penny those investors put into government Treasury bonds would be a penny they didn't put into the stock market. The Social Security pot would become richer because the stock market would probably bring a greater return on the investment. But there would be no new savings generated in the country.

Yet, despite the drawbacks, I believe privatization of Social Security would benefit everyone in the long run—if the investment options were carefully crafted to assist those who aren't stock market wizards.

Stretch limos
but no stretched dollars

Last March we reported that the Capitol Hill elite claimed to be exempt from President Carter's crackdown on oversize limousines. Shortly thereafter, Speaker Thomas "Tip" O'Neill gave up his comfortable Cadillac for a Mercury. More modest cars were ordered for Democratic leader James Wright and Republican leader John Rhodes. On the Senate side, eight new Marquis were ordered to replace four Cadillacs and four Lincolns. House Sergeant-at-Arms Kenneth Harding, while settling for a Marquis, ordered one with a flashy moon roof at an extra cost to the taxpayers of $50. "But," he assured our reporter, "I buy my own gas and oil."

Washington Merry-Go-Round
July 25, 1977

Those who favor privatization of Social Security went looking for an example of how it could succeed. They found a pay-as-you-go retirement plan in Chile that was paying-as-it-went right into the poor house until 1981—the year the system went private.

Chilean workers now can choose to put up to 20 percent of their income into any one of 20 private investment plans. Their rate of return is averaging 13 percent. Anyone who had worked under the old system was welcome to keep their money in it. They will collect a standard pension until, one by one, they pass on. Then the old system will be canceled.

The stakes are high

Still, changes should be made cautiously. When the system runs amuck, the people who most deserve help are the first to be hurt. I will never forget a story I first heard in 1981 about a woman who fell through a gaping hole in the Social Security system's safety net, with tragic consequences. Evelyn Mattson lived in Phoenix with her daughter Nancy. She was disabled, but the Social Security Administration didn't believe her. Chronic dizziness had forced Mattson to leave her job less than two years before she would have been eligible for retirement benefits. Despairing that she would ever win her battle for a Social Security check, Mattson took a lethal dose of a painkiller. Two days later an appeals court ruled that she was indeed eligible for Social Security after all.

Her daughter found a note pinned to the bathroom door: "Nancy don't come in. Please do not open this door as I don't know what you will find . . . . I can't figure another way. . . . Don't feel bad for me. I never wanted to get old and not be able to care for myself and I can see it coming. I'm sure now I won't get my disability. . . . "

There is still a terror that comes with aging, a fear that we won't be able to care for ourselves. Many seniors need to be taken care of by the government because they have nowhere else to go. The sooner we begin to treat Social Security as a fallback position for the needy, funded by the fortunate, the sooner we can make the system work for those who otherwise would suffer.

The obstacles ahead must not deter us from making changes. This will require tough choices and political courage—two qualities often missing in today's elected officials. Both the young and the elderly must serve notice on their representatives that they're willing to try other options. This must be done soon. Otherwise, the D-Day generation we all revere for saving the world will also be held responsible for burdening future generations with bills beyond their ability to pay.

CHAPTER TWELVE

MEDICARE, HEAL THYSELF

President Lyndon Johnson signed Medicare into law in 1965 with a grand promise: "No longer will older Americans be denied the healing miracle of modern medicine. No longer will illness crush and destroy the savings that they have so carefully put away over a lifetime."

The promise has been fulfilled. Older Americans now enjoy all the benefits of the "healing miracle of modern medicine" without any crushing cost. Instead, taxpayers of all ages are feeling the crush, laying out $196 billion a year for LBJ's miracles for the elderly.

Medicare and Medicaid fuel the third largest cash outlay in the federal budget, after Social Security and defense spending, and medical bills are rapidly overtaking military expenditures. At present growth rates, the double M's (Medicare and Medicaid) will be causing the greatest drain on the Treasury by 2000. In 2002 the federal government is expected to pay $329 billion for Medicare, plus another $167 billion for Medicaid. Medicaid is the sister program administered by the states; it funds health care for the poor of all ages and nursing home care for the poor elderly.

Once considered just loose change for doctors and hospitals, Medicare now pays more than half the hospital bills and one-third of the doctor bills in the country (not counting obstetric and pediatric care.) Indeed, Medicare money accounts for 2.3 percent of the gross domestic product.

The high cost of war

The War on Poverty, conceived by Lyndon Johnson, gave the elderly carte blanche at the doctor's office and stuck the taxpayers with the bill. From its inception, Medicare had two parts: Part A is the Hospital Insurance Trust Fund which draws money from a payroll tax—1.45 percent each from the workers and their employers. Part B covers doctor visits and outpatient care. To finance this, Medicare beneficiaries pay premiums, deductibles and prescription costs as they would for private insurance. But unlike other insurance plans, the premiums and deductibles for Medicare come nowhere near covering the cost of treatment. Patients pay only 25 percent of the total amount billed by Medicare doctors. The federal Treasury—that's you—pays the balance.

Lyndon Johnson's oversized heart was in the right place. Who could argue that the elderly, with their reduced incomes and their failing health, didn't need care? In times past, they suffered in silence rather than seek costly treatment. When their money ran out, there was nothing left to do but die. The time had come for the federal government to come to the aid of a vulnerable part of the population. In those days of fiscal security, politicians had the luxury of favoring welfare payments over means testing.

Johnson was building his Great Society; it seemed to him that the U.S. colossus generated enough wealth to wipe out poverty and suffering.

But the legislative patchwork that came out of Congress in 1965 became the seeds of Medicare's inevitable failure. It's a story of big-money politics, with the American Medical Association pulling the purse strings. Fearing the government's proclivity to regulate everything it touches, doctors fought to keep the federal nose out of their profession, mounting a fierce campaign to sabotage Medicare. They had nightmares—premature, as it turned out—of the feds restricting doctors' fees and poking into their bank accounts.

During the 1964 congressional campaign, the medical fraternity invested heavily in a last great stand against Medicare. They passed out a large amount of money to anti-Medicare candidates and organized a letter-writing campaign against pro-Medicare candidates, calling the latter "enemies of private enterprise" and "advocates of socialism." This attempt by the doctors' lobby to kill Medicare coincided with the more altruistic efforts of other doctors to expose cigarettes as a health hazard. I was engaged, in my capacity as a hell raiser, in their anti-smoking crusade. My investigative instincts led me to a story so bizarre that I could hardly believe my own reporting, so incredible that the AMA prefers to pretend it didn't happen. But I assure you that it did happen.

The AMA, in response to the ruckus we were stirring up over the cigarette hazard, began investigating the effects of smoking on health. We also got the attention of the Surgeon General, who started an official tobacco study. Accordingly, the AMA abruptly canceled its study on the grounds that the Surgeon General's investigation would make it unnecessary.

The tobacco crows, in anticipation of the Surgeon General's findings, prepared to counteract it. Their strategy: They offered to finance a <u>new</u> AMA study of smoking. This might have created the impression that the government report wasn't conclusive and, therefore, smokers didn't need to kick the habit until the AMA results came in at some indefinite date.

By this time, the AMA had become so obsessed over Medicare that its doctors entered into a peculiar alliance with the cigarette makers. The AMA secretly agreed to revive the canceled cigarette study; and in return, the tobacco lobby promised to use its influence in Congress to block the Medicare bill. The doctors were more concerned about Medicare, which they fancied to be a threat to their fees, than about the threat to the nation's lungs. So it happened that those who cause and those who cure illness lay down together in millennial bliss.

The AMA suddenly approved a brand new cigarette study December 4, 1963, on the eve of the great struggle over Medicare. To finance this study, the AMA accepted a magnanimous $10 million grant for tobacco research from six cigarette companies. That happened on February 7, 1964. Three weeks later, the AMA astounded government doctors (and not a few of its own members) by agreeing with the tobacco industry, in effect, that cigarettes should not be labeled as a health hazard.

The AMA delivered a letter to the Federal Trade Commission that sounded almost as if it had been written by tobacco lobbyists instead of medical scholars. Contended the AMA: "The economic lives of tobacco growers, professors and merchants are entwined in the industry; and local, state and federal governments are the recipients of and dependent upon many millions of dollars of tax revenue." Thus, by official declaration of the AMA, the doctors put the economic welfare of tobacco people ahead of the health of the American people.

My sources claimed the AMA's curious attitude toward cigarettes was part of a deal to get tobacco-state legislators to vote against Medicare. Though the AMA issued an indignant denial, the

If at first you don't succeed, pour money on the problem

In Egypt, land of the pyramids, lavish construction projects are certainly nothing new. But the U.S. government's extravagant 20-year effort to provide a suitably posh residence for the American ambassador would make a pharaoh blush.

So far the boondoggle has swallowed $6 million of taxpayers' money like so much dishwater poured onto the sands of the Sahara—and with about as much effect. There is still no residence.

Washington Merry-Go-Round
June 13, 1986

doctors' lobby and the cigarette lobby continued for a time to blow smoke rings together on Capitol Hill.

As Medicare worked its way through Congress, the AMA quietly withdrew its roadblocks and concentrated its efforts instead on the bill itself. The AMA added its loving touches to the final legislation that was to make Medicare a financial blessing for doctors. The compromises ensured that doctors would accept Medicare patients, all right, on condition that the federal government couldn't dictate how much they could charge or what services they could perform.

Lawmakers were so blinded by their vision of medical care for senior citizens (and winning the elderly's gratitude in the form of an outpouring of votes) that they didn't realize they had entrusted the henhouse keys to a lair of foxes. So for the first 18 years of Medicare's existence, physicians happily billed the federal Treasury for a whole array of new medical services, and Uncle Sam paid those bills with few questions asked.

Not until 1983 was Congress jerked awake by the warring Medicare members. Alarmed, the members started to apply brakes, limiting what hospitals could bill to Medicare. Still, it took another 10 years for Congress to impose the same fee restrictions on individual doctors for outpatient services, restricting them to only 59 percent of what private insurance companies would pay. The howling reverberated round the country, but the doctors piped down when they discovered they could make up some of their losses by charging non-Medicare patients extra. This is called "cost shifting"—which, along with advances in technology, are largely responsible for the spiraling increases in your insurance premiums and out-of-pocket medical bills. By one estimate, cost shifting is to blame for half of the premium increases that cannot be attributed directly to inflation.

You can also credit Medicare for some of the technological advances that now cost you so much. It gave doctors and hospitals a blank check for so many years, with little reason for patients to worry about their medical bills because Uncle Sam paid them. Thus, the government provided a happy breeding ground for unnecessary procedures and overuse of medical wizardry, plus a demand for more of everything. This fertile environment has helped Medicare expenses to grow at twice the rate of inflation and twice the rate of national income. Since 1966, Medicare payments have gone up an average of 15 percent a year.

No surgical process can remove the thought of re-election from a politician's mind

Inevitably, the pressure to balance the budget in recent years has focused on this sinkhole. But as Senator Bob Kerrey once said of Medicare and Social Security, "In Washington, the only force more compelling than mathematics is politics." Thus, any attempt to reform these systems, no matter how the numbers exploded, has inevitably been sacrificed on the altar of re-election. The freshmen Republicans, who arrived on Capitol Hill in 1994 with a great clanking of the crusaders' armor, learned this lesson. They held high the "Contract with America" until they realized they had to cut Medicare to balance the budget. Then they stopped short.

Democrats are fond of taking credit for establishing Medicare, and they have rushed to its defense. So when Republicans arrived with their shearing scissors, the Democrats rallied seniors for the battle. The Republicans promised to balance the budget; then they cast around for some way to cut billions of dollars. This led, inevitably, to Medicare, not through any masochistic desire to take on the senior juggernaut, but because there was no other choice. If you want to save money, you must go to where the money is—entitlements.

The Republicans set their goal—a $270 million reduction in expected Medicare bills over the next seven years—but the plan was shy on details about how that goal would be reached. Republicans swore it wasn't a cut, but merely a slowdown of Medicare's growth. But however delicately the GOP tried to trim, it still looked like butchery—which would result in reduced services, higher premiums and fewer choices.

President Clinton, who was gung ho about using money carved out of Medicare to pay for his own universal health care program, was less eager to cut Medicare to fund the GOP vision.

Republicans scheduled hasty hearings and pushed through their agenda without full disclosure of where they would find the $270 billion, causing tempers to boil in Congress. After one hearing, Congressman Sam Gibbons, a Florida Democrat, stormed out of the room, declaring his Republican colleagues to be a "bunch of fascists!" This aroused California Congressman Bill Thomas's Republican anger. His response further provoked Gibbons, who grabbed Thomas's tie. "Don't pull my tie!" Thomas shouted, his dignity affronted.

The brawl reminded me of my early days when I was first let loose on the nation's capital. To a newcomer whose mores had been formed in an austere Mormon family, Washington caused something of a culture shock. It was not uncommon in those days for a congressman, who was cantankerous enough, to make a debating point by hauling off and punching his opponent—or the reporter whose account of the debate displeased him.

I went a round in 1947 with the dean of the Senate, the shriveled ruin of a once impressive legislator from Tennessee named Kenneth McKellar. In his younger years, he had attacked a fellow senator with a pocketknife. His temperament was not mellowed one whit by age. Consumed by a sputtering rage over some intolerable journalistic affront, he lurched at me and pummeled me with frail fists. I was startled, wounded in spirit, but above all eager

---

Whose limo is it anyway?

What did Environmental Protection Agency big shots do when the inspector general told them the agency's 11 chauffeured cars were underused? Cut down on the number of cars? Don't be silly. They just made 120 more bureaucrats eligible to be chauffeured around town, for a grand total of 150. The auditors learned that the cars were used mainly during lunch hours, and calculated that the average trip cost $45, including the drivers' salaries. The inspector general suggested phasing out most of the chauffeured cars and using taxicabs at probably $5 tops per trip. It would save the taxpayers about $300,000 a year.

Washington Merry-Go-Round
May 20, 1986

to get out of there before the old termagant expired. I fled awkwardly through the nearest exit.

So I beheld the Gibbons-Thomas imbroglio in 1996 with a sense of nostalgia.

In the end, the Republicans mustered enough votes to pass their Medicare "reforms," but they didn't have the final word. On December 6, 1995, President Clinton vetoed the GOP balanced budget package, giving as his major reason the Medicare cuts. For political effect, Clinton had the Lyndon Johnson Library in Texas send him the same pen that LBJ used to sign Medicare into law in 1965. Clinton used the pen to sign his veto.

It was grand theater, but it left taxpayers with the same insupportable burden. Because they failed to reach a compromise in 1995, lawmakers pushed the Medicare reform debate into an election year, guaranteeing that no progress would be made at least until 1997.

The sinkhole comes into focus

Meanwhile, the Medicare train is hurtling toward a brick wall; the crash will come in 2001. That is the dreaded year when the program's Hospital Trust Fund is projected to become insolvent. The fund started operating at a deficit in 1995, two years earlier than expected—to the shock of the keepers of the trust fund.

Even if Congress can put off insolvency temporarily, the baby boomers will bring down the system anyway. They will swell the Medicare rolls from 37 million today to 66 million when the baby boomers start feeding at this trough. The cost of their medical bills after age 65 will average $54,000 each.

Even if the money were well spent, which it isn't, the taxpayers couldn't afford it. About 10 percent of the money that is pumped into Medicare and Medicaid enriches charlatans and incompetents. That's nearly $50 million a day. Here's more chapter and verse:

• Nursing homes are permitted to farm out their Medicare paperwork to outside carpetbaggers. Some billing companies then dip into patient records and wreak havoc, submitting bills for procedures and medications that the patient never gets. One billing agent dunned Medicare for $211,900 in surgical dressings for a three-month period. Then, in the same three-month period of the next year, the company's bill for surgical dressings shot up to $6 million. Medicare paid without raising an eyebrow.

• One chain of some 130 hospitals billed Medicare $2.6 million in one year for administrative expenses. Medicare paid it, but the General Accounting Office disputed it. Auditors discovered that nearly half the amount was padded, including $17,755 for alcoholic beverages.

• Medicare lays out about $280 a month to rent an oxygen unit for a patient at home; the machines can be purchased outright for about $1,200. I use an oxygen machine that has been pumping air for a dozen years. The rental company could make a 1,500 percent profit in seven years.

• One anesthesiologist submitted bills to Medicare that added up to a workday of more than 24 hours. Medicare officials didn't flinch; the sleepless doctor got his money. (I should say <u>our</u> money.)

• A favorite of con artists is the "rolling lab"—moneymobiles that have sucked $1 billion in claims out of the system. Here's how the scam works: Seniors are offered a free medical screening from a mobile lab that rolls up to the senior center or the retirement home or a shopping mall. "Free" means that the company conducting the cursory exams—eyes, hearing, blood pressure, whatever is easy— will waive the co-payment for the patient, but not to Medicare. All the patient has to do is give the lab his or her Medicare number. That is the magic key health care providers need to get away with a tidy chunk of change. One investigation of rolling labs brought the indictment of 12 operators and a fine of $18 million—which, as you may have guessed, has not been paid.

• It may be macabre, but it isn't unusual for doctors to continue billing Medicare for treatments that apparently didn't succeed—since the patients died.

• One pharmaceutical salesman made a $6 million living reselling used heart pacemakers. This enterprising recycler gave doctors kickbacks or supplied them with prostitutes for implanting second-hand pacemakers in unsuspecting patients. When investigators caught up with him, they discovered he was getting his used pacemakers mostly from corpses.

How does the CIA waste money? In secret, of course

The Central Intelligence Agency has been overcharged, undercut and just plain robbed to the tune of at least $1 billion during its slovenly seven-year effort to supply weapons to the anti-Soviet guerrillas in Afghanistan.

The waste of more than one-third of the $3 billion in covert funds (half of it contributed by Saudi Arabia) is a direct result of the agency's refusal to adopt even the most elementary accounting procedures, along with a "hang-the-expense" attitude. Arms merchants, corrupt officials and even, reportedly, CIA agents have grown fat on the Afghan arms trade.

The CIA has admitted substantial losses. Behind closed doors, agency officials have acknowledged to Congress that at least 20 percent has been skimmed from the program. They shrugged this off as merely the typical cost of doing business in that part of the world.

Even if this were true, it would still amount to a whopping $600 million loss. But the CIA has boldly misled Congress. Our own conservative estimate is that the diversion of Afghan arms is around 60 percent, or $1.8 billion.

Washington Merry-Go-Round
May 1, 1987

• A California home health-care provider billed the government for legal fees, liquor, meals in expensive restaurants, even an orchestra and ballroom that he rented for a party. When Medicare caught on, he dissolved the company, formed a new one and began collecting from Medicare again. Other home health-care agencies have submitted Medicare bills for rental cars, staff Christmas parties and, in one case, private school tuition for the owner's daughter.

• With the stroke of a pen, a doctor can jack up a Medicare bill simply by "upcoding"—substituting the code for a more expensive procedure than was actually rendered. Codes are assigned by Medicare to control costs and set maximum fees. But this complex system is faulty because few patients are familiar with the codes and can't tell whether the doctor is playing a numbers game.

• For quick profits, nothing beats billing Medicare for phantom services—like the Ohio eye doctor who beamed his miniflashlight in his patients' eyes and then billed Medicare for laser treatments for glaucoma. Perhaps he would rather have performed the actual laser treatments, but his machine was broken. A Pennsylvania doctor told patients that he had his own lab for analyzing test results in his home. But no such lab existed. The samples went in the trash, and the bills went in the mail to Medicare.

• Until Congress got wise and outlawed the practice in 1990, some doctors would refer patients to their own labs for costly workups, and Medicare would cough up the payments. Not surprisingly, doctors with a financial interest in labs ordered 50 percent more tests than did doctors without labs. This scam was not limited to labs. One hospital in California was owned in part by 62 doctors who divided half the hospital's profits and were the primary source of its patients. In Colorado a group of doctors owned a medical office building. When a physical therapist opened a clinic there, he was obliged to pay not only rent, but 10 percent of his gross receipts. In return, the doctors/landlords sent patients to the physical therapist.

• An ophthalmologist in California dispatched salespeople to places where seniors congregated and offered free cataract screenings. The victims were diagnosed with phony cataracts on the spot, bused to the doctor's office, and operated on. Business was so lively that the doctor did 36 operations in one day. Before he was caught, his total take from Medicare was $15.5 million.

• The administrator of a St. Louis hospital used Medicare money to hire a belly dancer to liven up a staff meeting.

• An eye surgeon in California doing cataract surgery on his patients would deliberately sew one stitch too tight. When the patients complained of vision problems, he would then diagnose astigmatisms which he would correct by cutting the stitch. When he billed Medicare, it was for a $2,000 cornea transplant. His take in four years was $1.3 million.

• In 1996 the Health and Human Services Department filed a suit against 132 hospitals claiming they were using unapproved experimental techniques and equipment on patients, but writing up the bills to reflect traditional treatment methods. Cooperating with the investigators, an anonymous executive from the hospital industry testified before Congress wearing a bag over his head. He claimed doctors would use experimental techniques to remove plaque from arteries and then write up the bill as a balloon angioplasty. They even had a private term for angioplasty, calling it the "reimbursement balloon" because Medicare would pay for it.

• A Philadelphia dentist billed Medicare $1.3 million for more than 3,000 oral cancer exams on patients in nursing homes—exams that were never performed. Nursing home patients are easy marks for Medicare scams. Uninvited doctors work the halls of nursing homes, posing as visitors. They may take a temperature or listen to a heartbeat or do nothing at all, but Medicare still gets the bills. One psychiatrist in Minnesota engaged in small talk with nursing home patients and called it psychiatric care. Podiatrists drop in on residents, clip their toenails, and bill Medicare for foot surgery. A Minnesota speech therapist stopped at nursing homes, lunched with the nurses, and then billed Medicare for a variety of patient services, including speech therapy for a patient who was dead and flash-card drills on a patient who was blind.

• The GAO found that some oncologists arranged to meet their patients at hospitals to give them cancer treatments. The treatments could have been administered in the doctors' offices, but then Medicare reimbursement would have been lower.

• One Georgia doctor bribed his patients not to complain about his scam by paying them kickbacks. He submitted $4.5 million in bogus claims, distributing a third of the profits to his patients.

• Medicare pays for what it calls "durable medical equipment" such as hospital-style beds, crutches, canes and wheelchairs. Much of this equipment is necessary to maintain an improved quality of life for ailing seniors and allows them to care for themselves at home. But there is a booming industry in side products that puts the Home Shopping Network to shame.

Take for instance seat-lift chairs, those handy ejector recliners that eliminate the need for someone to give you a hand getting out of your easy chair. Arguably, some home-alone seniors need these. (In fact, I once exposed the story of a poor man who needed such a chair, but Medicare denied his claim because he didn't qualify. The rules said he had to have a disease of the legs to earn a seat-lift chair. As a double amputee, he was out of luck.)

The marketers of these chairs would make less money if they sold them only to people who really needed them. As any retailer knows, to earn the big bucks you must reach beyond "need" to "want." TV ads and door-to-door hawkers can easily talk a senior into badgering his or her doctor for a medical voucher prescribing the equipment so Medicare will pay the bill—especially if the seller waives any co-payment by the senior.

> ### Flying the very friendly skies
>
> When Adm. John Hayes, commandant of the U.S. Coast Guard, wants to fly out of Washington on official business, he doesn't have to check airline schedules like lesser mortals. He simply has his driver take him to an inconspicuous white hangar at the north end of National Airport and hops aboard a Coast Guard plane kept there for his convenience.
>
> When Federal Aviation Administrator J. Lynn Helms wants to take a trip, he uses his agency's $800-an-hour Citation jet, and generally takes his wife along for the ride.
>
> The planes Hayes and Helms commandeer for their trips are just two of the 650 aircraft owned by federal agencies other than the Defense Department. The planes are worth $340 million and last year cost $446 million to operate. Most of them have proper uses, such as inspections and surveillance, but many are routinely abused by high officials with an inflated sense of their own importance.
>
> *Washington Merry-Go-Round*
> *November 11, 1982*

When I first investigated this chair scam in 1989, I found one Medicare carrier in Texas who had trimmed the total outlays for these chairs from $7.3 million a year to $10,700 a year. He simply mailed a terse letter reminding doctors that misrepresentation of the facts on a Medicare claim is fraud. Suddenly their patients did not need as many chairs.

The buck doesn't stop there

Medicaid, like its twin, Medicare, is routinely fleeced. A New York dentist working on welfare patients drilled "cavities" in perfectly healthy teeth, took X-rays of his excavations to prove the teeth had holes in them, filled the holes, and then billed Medicaid. An enterprising New York City "blood bank" paid homeless people $10 a pint for blood to obtain their Medicaid numbers. Then it falsified blood tests on these "patients" and billed the taxpayers $31.6 million. A California doctor stole Medicaid vouchers from his patients and gave the vouchers to another Medicaid doctor as payment for a loan. A New York pediatrician gave his neighbor's dog an antibiotic and charged it to Medicaid. Kentucky officials saw a cryptic notation "Fill 25 bill MA 50" posted in one pharmacy. It turned out to be instructions to fill 25 prescriptions and bill Medicaid for 50. A nursing home administrator billed Medicaid for veterinary charges and airline tickets for his pets. Another charged the taxpayers for the wedding cake, bridal gown and flowers for his daughter's wedding, plus the stable bills for his horses.

Those who shake down the taxpayers don't go completely unnoticed. Many outraged taxpayers have tried to complain, but they frequently get the brushoff. If you see something amiss on your medical bill, the logical place to complain is at the office that's processing the bill for Medicare. Uncle Sam hires insurance companies to do the billing because they are supposed to be better at it. But not long ago, the General Accounting Office listened to 1,000 telephone calls coming in to those insurance companies to check how they handled complaints. About three-fourths of the calls indicating fraud were not investigated. In many cases, the callers were told to call Medicare directly or to put their suspicions in writing.

Undaunted by the brushoff, some callers complained to Medicare whose inspector general has only one criminal investigator for every $2.25 billion expended and one auditor for every $800 million in bills paid out.

Ruth Garnett of Weslaco, Texas, spent six years trying to get someone in authority to pay attention to her Medicare bill. In 1984 she broke her hip and wrist in a fall. When she got the hospital bill, she was shocked to discover that Medicare, in her behalf, was dunned $950 for a pacemaker and an arm splint—neither of which she received. The hospital agreed a mistake had been made and corrected the bill. But Mrs. Garnett later found out that Medicare had paid in full anyway.

Otto Twitchell made repeated phone calls to Medicare trying to persuade officials that $417 was too much to pay for a booster shot. The bureaucrats chided him for complaining when someone else was paying the bill. So Twitchell appealed to his congressman who got the charge reduced to $97.

Florence Paul of Santa Ana, California, complained to a doctor about a back problem. He examined her but couldn't diagnose the problem. Yet he billed Medicare $927. She spent three days on the phone trying to find someone in Washington who cared. Then she wrote letters. Then she gave up.

Although there are vigilantes among our seniors who watch their Medicare bills for fraud and waste, the system has hardly encouraged them to be thrifty. Not only does it routinely ignore reports from eagle-eyed seniors of fraud, by its very structure Medicare does not breed cost-consciousness in the beneficiaries. Why worry when someone else is paying the bill? Why argue if the doctor orders more lab tests or a CAT scan or an extra day in the hospital? Where does an aged, ailing, often frightened senior citizen find the courage to ask whether the procedures are absolutely necessary? If someone delivers a cozy recliner to a senior's door at no charge because Medicare paid the bill, it takes a person of exceptional character to say thanks, but no thanks.

How do we clean up this mess?

We need only look at the statistics to spot at least one way to save—simply by leveling the standards across the country. Medicare reimbursements vary wildly depending on where you live. The program pays for more than 7 million surgeries a year; but if the statistics are to be believed, seniors in Utah need three times as many hip replacements as their cousins elsewhere, and elderly southerners require more of coronary bypass surgery. Medicare pays for more mammograms, per capita, in Northern California than in Southern California. If you want a bilateral cardiac catheterization courtesy of Medicare, get out of North Carolina where the denial rate is higher. And if you think you might need ambulance services, better move to Illinois.

The insurance companies Medicare hires to process its claims operate on the same basic rules of reimbursement, but their record for paying claims varies greatly. Regional preferences and traditions affect certain medical procedures, and some companies are just better at spotting fraudulent claims. The result is yet another form of fraud—carrier shopping. Companies that overcharge Medicare and the elderly tend to funnel their bills through carriers most likely to pay them.

Because of quick-to-protest doctors and quick-to-complain patients, Medicare has hesitated to pursue the savings it could achieve by requiring that certain surgeries be performed only at experienced, high-volume hospitals. Volume and experience not only brings the price down but also lowers the risk of death. However, such policies lead smaller hospitals to complain of discrimination, which stirs their protective congressmen into action. Also, the elderly are reluctant to travel far from home for surgery.

Up until this point, members of Congress have passed the buck for cutting doctors and hospitals, who are compelled to reduce their fees. It's not complicated, and, as one hospital administrator wryly put it, "Hospitals don't vote; seniors do."

Yo Ho Ho and a barrel of pork

Some luxury-loving State Department and U.S. Information Agency employees have been taking advantage of permissive travel regulations to book passage on posh cruise ships when they take their families on home leave between assignments.

The taxpayers foot the bill for these vacations, which cost several times what the airfare would be.

Travel records of the two agencies show that in fiscal years 1982 to 1984, a total of 260 employees and dependents elected to travel by sea, as the rules allow. The cost was $556,232—more than $400,000 higher than airline tickets would have been.

Washington Merry-Go-Round
October 1, 1985

The only care may be a bitter pill

Unable to hold down the cost of medical care, Congress has focused instead on how to slow the rate of growth by capping the fees. But that won't keep the system solvent. Inevitably, our political leaders must start to think the unthinkable and do the undoable. They must . . . Ugh? . . . increase taxes or premiums. So far, Medicare beneficiaries have not been significantly inconvenienced by this battle to balance the budget—although it isn't easy to convince aging people on a fixed income when they have watched their premiums rise every year.

People over age 85 will pay an average of $3,800 a year from their own pockets for medical bills. Those older than 65 will pay about $2,500. Yet their personal outlays come nowhere near paying the total bill. A couple who retired in 1995 after living on one income all their married life will cost the taxpayers about $126,700 more than the taxes and premiums that the couple paid into Medicare.

Any reforms that would stick seniors with their own medical bills are dangerous, as Congress has learned the hard way. In 1988 Congress passed the Medicare Catastrophic Coverage Act to set up insurance coverage that would protect seniors against the cost of a medical disaster—a long-term hospital stay or a financially devastating medical condition. President Ronald Reagan was eager to court seniors, but not eager to burden the Treasury with the bills, so he agreed to sign the act if the cost would be completely covered by the premiums, which would run about $145 a month.

There were a couple of problems: The new law caught the usually alert senior lobby asleep at the controls. And the premiums for a government-run catastrophic care policy were more than twice what seniors were already paying to buy similar insurance policies on the private market. Congress endured 16 months of abuse from outraged seniors before repealing the Catastrophic Coverage Act.

The delicate problem of selling seniors on any changes in their benefits is compounded by the notion that Medicare, like Social

Security, is an earned right—a payback from years of paying Medicare taxes. But like Social Security taxes, those Medicare taxes have been a pay-as-you-go exercise, taxing the young to pay directly for the needs of the old. Medicare never was a savings account for individual contributors; it was never intended to be a medical care fund for their old age.

We MUST reform Medicare or scrap it. For example, wage earners could be given tax incentives to put some of their money in "Medi-save" accounts—IRAs for future medical bills. Not only would this funnel money into private investments, it would give people more control over their own financial welfare and thus make them more guarded about how their money is spent.

(A quick way to save Medicare billions of dollars is to wage an all-out campaign against three vices—smoking, alcoholism and drug abuse. The Columbia University Center on Addiction and Substance Abuse says Medicare will spend $1 trillion in the next 20 years treating diseases stemming from those deliberate abuses of the body. Cigarette smoking cost the Medicare budget more than any other single condition, virus or ailment. But that is a subject for another book.)

A controversial yet promising cost-saving measure: Simply issue seniors vouchers so they could shop for cheaper care through Health Maintenance Organizations. The beauty of HMOs, at least in theory, is that they can keep costs down because they have no incentive to permit unnecessary procedures. They charge a fixed fee, so the HMO saves money by minimizing care. Seniors, however, don't like HMOs because many package plans restrict a right that the elderly consider to be as American as baseball—the right to choose one's own doctor.

Seniors already have the option of using an HMO instead of Medicare, but only 9 percent have chosen that option. One way to encourage more HMO use, thereby raising revenues, would be to charge seniors an extra monthly fee if they opt for traditional Medicare instead of a cheaper HMO. If their choice costs the taxpayers more money, then perhaps they should pay for that choice.

Medicare's Part B, which pays for doctor and outpatient bills, was originally designed as a 50-50 proposition. The premiums paid by the elderly were supposed to cover half of the medical costs. But changes in the formula have dropped the beneficiaries' payments to a mere 25 percent. This current premium is $54.70 a month; had Congress kept the original formula, seniors would be paying $92.20. To cover the full cost of Part B outlays, seniors would have to pay $184.40. While that may sound like a fairly cheap insurance policy, it could cripple an older person living on Social Security or a small pension. Yet not all seniors survive on a small pension; some can afford to pay higher premiums, but they enjoy the benefits of a program that was intended to help the helpless.

Radical reconstruction necessary

The bottom line: We won't be able to help the neediest if we continue to pay the bills for everyone. Lyndon Johnson's "Great Society" will become a bankrupt society unless we change our spending habits. Public hospitals in our great cities—New York, Philadelphia, Detroit, even Washington—are already running vast deficits, facing bankruptcy, firing personnel, closing their emergency rooms and clinics. Doctors everywhere have begun to turn away patients covered by state or federal programs.

The current reaction to the cost crunch is for all parties in the chain to shift their responsibility for paying the bills to the next lower echelon—the feds to the states; the states to cities and hospitals; insurance companies to the insured through deductibles and exclusions; employers to workers through reduced benefits and higher employee contributions.

Meanwhile, the gorilla is threatening to break out of the medical closet. Some 37 million Americans have no medical insurance; another 50 million are inadequately insured; and a growing percentage of the middle class are becoming insurance-poor. Already, medical costs have become the leading cause of bankruptcy among private individuals and small business.

This medical care crisis is fueled by the spectacular cost explosion for ordinary illnesses; the mushrooming of money-draining diseases such as AIDS, drug addiction and the protracted ailments of the aged; the mass emasculations or cancellations of health insurance coverage by employers; the mounting refusal of debt-ridden hospitals—public and private alike—to treat those who cannot pay.

Each ingredient in this stewing pot will be further spoiled by what otherwise would be an unallowed blessing—breakthroughs in medical technology that will increase the price of treatments. All will combine to produce a continuing parade of pathetic spectacles, unmet needs and rising protests. The question marks will grow darker with each new spectacle: **Who will mend the broken parts? And WHO WILL PAY THE RISING COSTS?**

CHAPTER THIRTEEN

FOURTEEN WAYS TO CHEAT THE FEDERAL GOVERNMENT

The easiest way to welsh on a debt owed Uncle Sam is simply to refuse to pay. Deadbeats owe the federal government more than $250 billion, of which all but $50 billion are unpaid taxes. But be it taxes, fees, penalties, fines or royalties, the odds are good that the bureaucracy won't have the time, personnel nor inclination to catch up with America's certified deadbeats.

Those the government does manage to locate can usually sweet-talk their way out of the debt by pleading poverty. "Uncollectible" is the government's favorite rubber stamp. It's the official term for "Don't Bother Us." If all else fails, deadbeats need merely to wait. They're likely to die before Uncle Sam applies any real pressure to repay.

Government clerks in their cubicles don't like to be distracted from their paperwork. Their purpose in life is processing, studying and shuffling papers—not tracking deadbeats, assessing their ability to pay, and then seizing salaries or assets until the debt is settled. If anyone has the tools to do that, it should be the federal government. But the bureaucrats would rather not go to the trouble.

They were quite proud of themselves in 1993 because they managed to reduce the uncollected debt by $6.6 billion. But that wasn't accomplished by any method you or I would call debt collection. In fact, the $6.6 billion never reached the Treasury at all. Instead it was written off as uncollectible.

Neither a borrower nor lender be— unless you know what you're doing

How does a government overridden with accountants and auditors and tax collectors let itself get fleeced out of billions of dollars? By being the lender of last resort, throwing money away on the most risky borrowers because, well, nobody else will and because, gosh darnit, they deserve a chance. Of course, many respectable people, down on their luck, have borrowed money from their Uncle Sam for education, business development and other worthy causes and have proved their mettle by paying back those loans. But many others know a sucker when they see one.

These opportunistic deadbeats are not always the struggling poor. They are also borrowers who pay the mortgage, make car payments, finance a vacation to Disney World, and eat at fine restaurants—yet can't seem to find the spare change to repay their student loans. One California dentist owns an $817,000 house at the beach and drives a Lincoln Town Car. He's also $3.5 million in arrears to the Farmers Home Administration.

Your 14-step plan for fleecing the nation

You, too, can take advantage of Uncle Sam. Here are a few quick and dirty ways:

1—Don't pay your income taxes. Hole up in a cabin in Montana and wait for them to come for you. You'll probably wait a long time. The amount of unpaid taxes has more than tripled in the last 10 years—hitting $111 billion in 1991 and bouncing up to about $150 billion in 1996. Defunct corporations account for about 39 percent of the taxes owed the Treasury. Another 27 percent are simply unable to pay. About 8 percent have vanished from the IRS's radar scope, not counting the indebted dead—3 percent who will have to answer to a higher authority. The rest of the debt is attributable to bankruptcy or legal snarls.

In the real world, most delinquent bills are cleared up within 180 days. That's about the time it takes the IRS to begin wondering whether your check was lost in the mail.

The IRS estimates that 48 percent of those delinquent taxes will be written off. However, when the General Accounting Office reviewed cases that the IRS had closed as "currently not collectible," the auditors found 55 percent may have been collectible after all.

But let's give the tax collectors some credit. They do try to collect from delinquent taxpayers. A common reason they can't is that they were wrong in the first place. The accused didn't really owe the money.

2—Don't pay your student loans, or better yet, open a diploma mill and bill the government for your tuition. You can call it a "trade school." Even if the majority of your students drop out because your curriculum is worthless, you get to keep the money. Defaulted student loans went from $200 million in 1981 to $3.6 billion in 1991.

It's not too late for you to climb aboard this gravy train. Even if you have defaulted on a past student loan, apply for another one. It doesn't matter whether you plan to actually show up for classes. The Education Department loans money willy-nilly to people who attend schools of higher learning that don't seem to care whether their students ever come to class.

Trade schools just love Uncle Sam. About 5 percent of higher-education students are enrolled in trade schools instead of colleges or universities. But about 19 percent of the money loaned by the federal government for tuition goes to trade schools. One school employed 23 instructors, 70 loan processors and 109 salesmen. The latter made the rounds of welfare offices to drum up a student body.

There's little incentive for the Education Department to worry about this problem because no one in the department is held accountable. They simply go to the Treasury for more money to lend. No one in this process, except the taxpayers, has any interest in reversing the high default rate. The students, the schools, the lenders—they all get their money. Only taxpayers are screwed.

3—Even if you owe Uncle Sam money already or have defaulted on a prior government loan, you needn't be shy about asking for more. Many of the people on the default lists are repeat offenders.

You must have been working hard, Mr. Senator, to get such a deep tan

When Congress takes a break between sessions, some members continue working. They work on their tans. They work on their wardrobes. They work on their snorkeling skills. Anything to serve the American taxpayer. For the American taxpayer, after all, picks up the tab when members of Congress go abroad on "official business."

Funny how much official business crops up in the tropics every winter. During the recent congressional recess, dozens of lawmakers clambered aboard military jets with the spouses and staffs. Most of them headed unerringly for warmer climes.

We tracked the records of 74 members of Congress who traveled through 34 countries on "official business" in January. One would think we were negotiating world peace with Australia or New Zealand. Twenty of the members managed to include those two countries on their list of official visits in January. A staffer at the New Zealand embassy in Washington explained the attraction: "Our January is like your summer vacation."

Washington Merry-Go-Round
February 15, 1988

4—Request a loan from the Farmers Home Administration. This agency was set up to help farmers through hard times, but it has become an open wallet for farmers seeking a steady cash flow.

If you can't pay back the loans on time, no problem. You'll be no different than 70 percent of FmHA borrowers who are delinquent or who're negotiating easier terms. In one year alone, FmHA lost nearly $21 billion in bad loans. Will a bad debt with FmHA hurt your credit rating? Not with Uncle Sam it won't. FmHA is a soft touch and frequently loans more money to people who have already shafted the agency.

5—Set up an oil well on federal land. Sure, the government will assess you royalties based on the price you can get for the oil, but Uncle Sam will let you decide what that price is likely to be. Just lowball your price by about 20 percent, and the feds won't notice. In 1996 10 major oil companies drilling on federal land in California owed Uncle Sam $856 million because of their lowball estimates. This multimillion-dollar debt has been hanging over the federal establishment since the 1980s, but the feds have botched the effort to collect it. The Minerals Management Service keeps dropping the amount of money that it considers to be collectible but doesn't explain why it wants to give the oil companies a break. The $856 million is only the amount <u>suspected</u> to be owed by California companies. Auditors think the total lowball figure for oil leases, lying uncollected across the country, may be closer to $2 billion.

6—Desert from the military and continue to collect your paycheck. In one month the Army cheerfully paid $6 million to 2,269 people who no longer had any right to the checks because they were either AWOL, dead, deserters or dischargees.

7—Have your property declared a superfund site, but don't bother to pay for the cleanup costs. If you own toxic property, you're supposed to clean up the mess or pay the EPA to do it for you. By the end of 1992, after a decade of cleaning up toxic waste-land, the EPA had cleaned the taxpayers out of $7.3 billion. Of this, the EPA arbitrarily declared that $5.7 billion would never be recovered from the polluting companies. They had collected only 9 percent of what was owed.

8—Get your name on the Social Security disability rolls for some temporary physical ailment, and you will never have to go back to work again. The General Accounting Office believes as many as three out of every 10 people collecting disability checks from the government are capable of working. Six million Americans are currently collecting monthly Supplemental Security Income (SSI) checks at a cost to taxpayers of $53 billion. Less than one-half of one percent of them will ever get off this gravy train. How do they get away with it? Apparently, the folks who manage this welfare program don't bother to encourage disabled people to go back to work. The GAO says only 8 percent of people receiving disability payments are referred to rehabilitation programs that might start them working again. While the able are collecting disability, thousands of truly needy people who can't work because of an illness or injury are waiting in line for social workers to process their cases.

9—Have your child officially designated as too moody or too hyperactive to perform up to expectations. This is a ticket to SSI payments for the little tyke. SSI was established to pay adults who are unable to work, but in 1990 the Supreme Court extended this welfare to disabled children too. After the court decision cleared up misunderstandings about what children could qualify for SSI, the number of little ones enrolled skyrocketed. A study in Arkansas showed a 250 percent increase in special benefits to children during the three years following the high court's ruling.

10—Form a public housing agency in your community to house the homeless, then sit back and watch the money roll in from the Department of Housing and Urban Development. You can solicit kickbacks from contractors for sending construction business their way. You can create fictional landlords and tenants, then keep the money you get for their housing. You can let the housing you manage go to pot, yet keep collecting money. The folks at HUD are so caught up in their own bureaucratic whirl they may never figure out what you're up to.

11—Replace cash with food stamps as your primary currency. You can trade food stamps for guns, liquor, cars, even surface-to-air missiles (yes, it actually happened). And you won't have to mess with sales taxes. In Wisconsin, undercover cops bought a house with food stamps. The fraudulent traffic in food stamps may cost the taxpayers as much as $1 billion a year. You don't qualify for food stamps? Never mind. Find someone who is eligible, but who would rather have cash than groceries. Then offer them 50 cents on the dollar for their food stamps. (Prices may vary locally.)

12—Hang out your shingle as a doctor and bill Medicare for treating people who are already dead. If you can't collect the Medicare numbers of enough dead people to make this profitable, comb the streets for homeless people and drug addicts. It has been done.

13—Cut a deal for free surplus government equipment and then sell it. There are many ways to work this scam. One is to take advantage of a Forest Service program that gives surplus military cargo planes to private fire-fighting outfits. Apparently, you don't have to use your gift from the Forest Service to fight forest fires. From one giveaway of 35 planes, two of the planes ended up hauling private cargo for profit in Kuwait. Four were sold and netted

Club Fed

It's an annual rite in Washington: Every summer, the members of various committees on Capitol Hill play spin-the-globe to determine which of the world's hot spots need their personal attention during the recess.

The locations tend toward the pleasure spots. Indeed, the uninitiated might be amazed to learn how many problems are screaming for solutions in such places as Paris, London and Rome.

Tentative plans are drawn up, and staffers are dispatched to make arrangements. Air transportation has to be requisitioned from the Defense Department. Surface transportation, hotel reservations and baggage carriers have to be lined up by the State Department.

The woebegone diplomats also have to dredge up some officials of the host governments who are willing to give up a few days of their summer vacations to "confer" with the visiting dignitaries. Can't have an "official business" trip without some official business, you see.

Washington Merry-Go-Round
August 22, 1985

the seller more than $1 million. Congress considered taking back the 35 planes and then selling them, but only 24 of them could be found.

14—After you're finished mourning the death of an elderly loved one, take lots of time to notify the Social Security Administration that the dearly departed no longer needs money. Social Security pays hundreds of millions of dollars every year to dead people. You see it takes an average of 11 months for state vital statistics offices to get the word to Washington if relatives of the deceased fail to report the deaths. With nearly two million Social Security recipients dying every year, Uncle Sam has trouble keeping up with all those obituaries.

The same scam applies to other government checks besides Social Security. A coal miner collecting government benefits to compensate him for his black lung disease died. His son continued to cash the government checks, collecting $21,000 more in benefits before authorities got wise. In a variation of this theme, one woman submitted claims for her husband to collect black lung benefits and managed to bank $38,427 before the federal government figured out that her husband had never been a coal miner.

For those who may be tempted to try any of the scams I have described in this chapter, they may find themselves eligible for a final government benefit—free room and board in a federal prison.

CHAPTER FOURTEEN

PAY NOW OR PAY LATER

C an the federal government live within its means? Here is the
bottom line: The budget deficit in 1996, though $22 billion
less than the year before, was about $146 billion. In other
words, Uncle Sam paid out that much more than he took in.
Had there been no interest to pay on the federal debt in 1996
($241 billion) Uncle Sam would have had a surplus of $95 billion.

Except for one small problem. That $146 billion deficit does
not include the $97 billion borrowed from Social Security,
Medicare, federal employee pensions and other federal trust funds.
Yes, that $97 billion was tax revenue collected in 1996, but it was
supposed to be saved for the future. Instead, Uncle Sam borrowed

it and left an IOU. So the real budget deficit was $243 billion. Still, if we didn't have to pay $241 billion interest on the debt, Congress would have needed to cut only $2 billion in spending to break even in 1996.

But we can't wish away the interest on the debt, and we can't maintain our lifestyle without the money borrowed from the trust funds. If we don't begin to whittle away that debt today, our children and grandchildren won't be able to pay for their needs and pay our old debts too.

Baby boomers will soon precipitate a bust

The real pressure for reform is demographic. We can sustain the current level of borrowing for the current level of services all right. In fact, the budget deficits proposed by Congress for the coming five years are quite modest in a $1.6 trillion budget. But they don't begin to retire the accumulated debt. Nor do they provide for the future. By 2010, when the baby boomers collect their gold watches, the tax-tax, spend-spend, borrow-borrow routine will flounder, and if there is no change in policy, the system will crash.

Because the baby boom was followed by a baby bust, the ratio of workers to retirees will be thrown out of balance. The number of people over the age of 65 will double between now and 2030, but the number of working people will increase only 25 percent. Today nearly five working people pay into Social Security and Medicare for every one person taking money out. At the height of the boomers' retirement years, this ratio may slip to fewer than three working people for every one retiree. It doesn't take an economist to figure that workers will have to pay more or retirees will get less.

If we don't reduce spending now or dramatically raise taxes, we must continue borrowing to support our government in the style to which we all have become accustomed. Then our total debt will expand to more than twice the total economic output of the nation by 2030.

A call to arms

All spending cuts are not created equal. About two-thirds of government spending is mandatory. It is driven by laws already passed, promises already made and debts already incurred. Interest on the debt and entitlement programs, including Social Security and Medicare, keep mushrooming. This mandatory spending is a garden of weeds that is growing out of control.

Uncle Sam could uproot the wasteful weeds, one at a time, and save money. But it's the creeping vines—health care and Social Security—that must be curtailed. Otherwise, these high-growth areas of spending will choke the government.

The first thing we should do is eliminate the waste. Citizens Against Government Waste, which I co-founded with the late industrialist J. Peter Grace in 1984, has been slashing waste with a vengeance. During our first decade, we wiped out $433,518,000,000 in wasteful practices and procedures, redundancy and duplication, snafus and abuses. Yet this is a mere fraction of the massive waste that we located and identified.

The rest still lies stinking under the noonday sun. Its elimination, I believe, would save enough money to eradicate the deficit and stabilize the government's finances. It wouldn't be necessary to deprive the poor or shortchange the elderly or cut back legitimate benefits.

Government economists scoff at my claim. Purging the waste, they say, couldn't possibly produce enough savings to balance the budget. But a Pentagon auditor told me privately that half of our defense dollars are wasted. A doctor at the National Institutes of Health swore to me that the government's procurement practices and personnel policies triple the cost of medical research. Other insiders have calculated that sheer waste adds about 25 percent to the cost of everything the government touches.

Even Congress has now acknowledged what it had pretended for decades not to see. In late 1996 the House Committee on Government Reform and Oversight declared that "public perceptions of pervasive waste, fraud and mismanagement in the federal government are unfortunately accurate."

So I offer a challenge to the skeptics: Prove me wrong! I'll point out the waste. Let the government eliminate it, and then we'll find out how much can be saved. This will require a change in the federal routine. Members of Congress, who are caught in a budget squeeze, now mandate across-the-board reductions. They always cut numbers instead of specifics to escape blame for any particular loss. They leave it to the bureaucrats, who are forced to tighten up, to decide what to cut. These clerks in their cubicles become surly over the involuntary reductions; so they keep their wants and cut the people's needs.

Icy-hot vacations

There were plenty of congressional junketeers traveling on the taxpayers' dollar during the January recess, but the "Most Intrepid" award goes to the merry band with the mission to watch a Coast Guard cutter smash through ice near Antarctica.

But hold your admiration for these fearless travelers. You can't get there from here without passing through Australia, New Zealand and Hawaii. The trip was not without its warm days—10 to be exact—spent coming and going through the sunny South Pacific. There were three days in Antarctica.

Washington Merry-Go-Round
February 17, 1988

Over the years, the federal apparatus has become a government of the bureaucrats, by the bureaucrats and for the bureaucrats. They divert funds away from real work into paperwork. Rather than feed the poor, they study how hungry the poor are. Rather than house homeless, bureaucrats hold seminars on the problem. They inconvenience the public and pamper themselves; they produce fuddle and create fat.

It's time to whack off this bureaucratic blubber and trim down the government. This can best be done not with a meat ax, but with a scalpel to surgically remove the waste. It would be an operation that would cause minimum pain to the citizens, who own the government.

Most certainly, the architects of waste have no standing to tell senior citizens to sacrifice. Cutbacks must begin with the politicians and the bureaucrats who flagrantly waste the people's money. After the waste has been eradicated, then we will inevitably have to put a cap on entitlements.

No one is entitled to break the bank

Any change in entitlement spending should begin with a change in how we view our "right." Only about one-fourth of this mandatory spending is means tested. People with generous private pensions and personal means still collect Social Security. Medicare picks up the medical bills for the rich and the comfortable. By basing individual deductible payments on the patient's ability to pay, the wealthy would leave more money in the Medicare pot to care for the less blessed.

Social Security pays us to retire prematurely. Congress has already passed legislation to raise the retirement age gradually, but this reform needs to be speeded up. Social Security should also be privatized, in part, by giving workers the option of diverting some of their FICA taxes into private individual retirement accounts. Eventually, workers who can do better for themselves in the private market should be given the option of bailing out of Social Security altogether.

The growth in our entitlement programs can be blamed heavily on cost-of-living adjustments and other automatic increases tied to the consumer price index. This encourages generous raises. In 1997 those COLAs will account for $10 billion in increased entitlement spending automatically without Congress ever taking a vote. A new COLA formula is needed, one that doesn't break the bank.

Government spending on Medicare for the elderly has risen 10 percent in the last decade. Spending on Medicaid for the poor has jumped 15 percent. Private insurance companies have not seen the same increase in their outlays, demonstrating again that they are better custodians of the dollar than the government has proved to be. At this rate of federal largesse, the Congressional Budget Office has predicted that the amount of money spent on each Medicare or Medicaid patient will gain altitude at twice the rate of inflation in the next decade.

Time to bow out of the dance

The Byzantine budget process is also in sore need of reform. It resembles the kabuki dance, a traditional Japanese drama that can be described as an elaborate pretense. The actors wear lavish wigs and makeup. They go through ostentatious motions, singing and dancing with stylized poses and gestures.

This is exactly how our Washington ensemble performs when they prepare the federal budget. Like the kabuki dance, this annual ritual has become an art form—an elaborate performance that distorts reality. The performers hide behind false faces, draft stylized language, and go through ritualistic routines. It's all part of the great pretense.

This fiscal charade features current services budgeting, a juggling act with billions of bucks that keep multiplying before your eyes. The budget ensemble begins with a wish-list, then borrows enough money to make the wishes come true. The performers then take the last budget, add a few billion dollars for inflation, and presto! They have the next budget. This assures that, each year, the performers will juggle more billions in the air than the year before. It makes the kabuki dance, as performed in Washington, the most costly dance on earth.

I have a small suggestion that would improve the dance materially: Call upon Congress to pass a law that reverses the current services routine. Instead of adding more billions each year, require the budget troupe to subtract the billions instead. Force them to cut the budget a certain percentage each year, making the federal government leaner and meaner. If they wonder what to cut, I'll be happy to provide a list of wasteful expenditures and profligate practices in every government agency.

At the very least, every agency of government should be subjected to a five-year evaluation to determine if it should continue to exist. Today we continue to throw money at government offices that were created 50 years or more ago to solve a specific problem. They include such black holes as the National

Helium Reserves, the Export-Import Bank, the Power Marketing Administration, the Cooperative State Research Service, and the Tennessee Valley Authority.

Any agency that has failed to solve the problem is was created to correct should be scrapped. Here are some prime examples.

The Small Business Administration lives on despite its failure to do anything significant to advance the cause of small entrepreneurs. Only 0.5 percent of America's small businesses have been touched by the SBA. Its mission is lending money that never gets paid back.

Elsewhere in this book, I have argued for the elimination of the Energy and Commerce Departments. The Education Department should join them in the exodus. It spends $30 billion a year, but not a dime of that goes to the public schools where your children are educated. Those schools are funded by state and local taxes. The federal contribution to education is confined to the ivory towers, where paid thinkers study, plan, ruminate, re-evaluate and set goals. Since its creation in 1979 the Education Department has more than doubled its annual budget and proliferated its mission. It has expanded into a balkanized federal structure of 240 programs, none of which have managed to stop the decline of public education.

When Congress and President Clinton couldn't agree on a budget in 1995 and 1996, the

Nothing is taken for granted

Congress gave the Department of Energy $600 million to set up a program of grants to local governments and public institutions that want to find ways to conserve energy—but the applicants may wind up paying more than half that amount just to fill out the DOE forms.

The form worked out by DOE bureaucrats is so complicated that even the agency admits it will take about 84 hours to complete. Grant applications are routinely filled out by specialists in the arcane art of grantsmanship, and the going rate for these experts is about $30 an hour. Multiplying this by the 125,000 applicants DOE expects to get, gives an impressive $315 million for the 10.5 million hours of work filling out the forms.

Washington Merry-Go-Round
May 29, 1979

government shut down briefly. This gave us an idea of how necessary some departments are. During the shutdowns, 89 percent of the Education Department's employees were classified as nonessential and sent home—as were 98 percent of the employees at the Environmental Protection Agency. A full 100 percent of the National Labor Relations Board staff was excused, as was 90 percent of the Equal Employment Opportunity Commission staff and 98 percent of the Federal Maritime Commission staff. Granted, a few days without the services of a government agency are no indicator of how well we would survive without it over the long haul. But the brief hiatus may provide a starting point for deciding just how essential some government services are.

When it comes to cutting, the sweetest meat is next to the boneheads

If Congress wishes to prevent a financial meltdown, its members must get out the shears and start cutting—immediately! A good place to begin is on Capitol Hill. More than 37,000 federal employees are assigned to attend to the care and comfort of the members. These legislative staffs are devoted, above all else, to the re-election of their bosses.

Start with franking privileges. Each member of Congress is allowed to spend 67 cents worth of postage per address in his or her district. This official mail increases dramatically during the election season. Then the House mailroom overflows into the hallways with outgoing mail. The post office has become an $80 million-a-year incumbent-protection agency for our lawmakers. The franking privilege should be just that, a privilege; it should be limited to answering constituent mail. All else is unsolicited, taxpayer-financed junk mail. One member of Congress, Joe Early of Massachusetts, resolved to send no unsolicited mail. In one year, his office answered about 40,000 letters, spent $15,000 on postage, and returned the leftover $150,000 of his franking account to the Treasury.

There are many more perks that Congress must deny itself if it expects sacrifice from the rest of us. For example, members of Congress can keep for personal use the frequent-flier miles they chalk up on government business. Better still, they can travel on military aircraft, even if a commercial flight is available at a cheaper rate. They receive free medical and dental care from military hospitals. Though 58 percent of private-sector workers have no pension plan at all, members of Congress have bestowed upon themselves one of the most generous pension plans in existence. Lawmakers who retired in 1994 will earn an average lifetime retirement benefit of $1.9 million each. Members of Congress are entitled to car washes, tax preparation service, limousine service, swimming pools, office redecorating, haircuts, meals, showers, gyms and parking garages—all paid for outright or subsidized by the taxpayers. They get an allowance to run offices back home in their districts, another perk conceived to help re-elect incumbents. This costs taxpayers nearly $350 million year.

Losing excess fat with a pork-free diet

The pig people on Capitol Hill seem incapable of keeping their snouts out of the pork barrel. That leaves no alternative but to impose external controls. The passage of the line-item veto, giving the president the power to excise parochial budget items line by line, could help. But the chances are great that spending will go up instead of down because of his new veto power. The president will likely use that power to get what he wants out of Congress. He'll let the pork slip through if Congress will fund his pet projects. But I can promise you this much: We at Citizens Against Government Waste will monitor each line item and keep the president's feet to the fire.

Another way to control pork barrel spending would be to impose a new rule: No member of Congress should be allowed to seek an appropriation that benefits only his or her constituency, and congressional committees should be prohibited from obtaining an appropriation in a member's behalf. If special constituencies are to benefit narrowly from legislation, then Congress as a whole should make that decision.

In the case of military base closings, Congress established (1) that it doesn't have the guts to say no, but (2) that it at least has the wisdom to pass the buck to someone else. For two decades prior to the post-Cold War military downsizing, Congress had been unable to close a single obsolete military installation. So, when push came to shove in the late 1980s, Congress established an independent commission to determine which bases would be shut down. The lawmakers absolved themselves of any blame for separate closings.

**A good call
by government official**

The federal government recently set up a hotline so whistleblowers could report waste and corruption. A federal transportation official called the number to report a gripe and was advised to "tell it to Jack Anderson."

*Washington Merry-Go-Round
July 23. 1979*

With only a few glitches, it worked like magic; more than 400 facilities were slated for downswing, reorganization or complete shutdown. The beauty of it was that members of Congress could tell their constituents, "It wasn't my fault. "

If it worked for military bases, why not apply this no-fault process to all pork? Congress could appoint independent commissions to eliminate projects while the lawmakers sit safely and smugly on the political fence.

Personal incentives
for a smaller budget

In private business, a standard of competence is furnished inexorably by the profit factor. If a business branch is wasteful, loses money or suffers declining profits, a bell goes off at headquarters and that branch is either pruned or cut off. Whether a branch manager is doing a good or a bad job will be proved definitively by the bottom line.

But the government bureau, with no such automatic arbiter, can always claim that a poor result could be improved upon with a bigger staff and more money. The bureau chief is rewarded, not for efficiency which cannot be measured, but by the number of people under his or her thumb. The more bodies, the higher the boss's status.

The bureaucrats, therefore, have developed a cavalier attitude toward government appropriations. Enough is never sufficient; they must always have more. With expansion and expenditure as their motive, they are constantly maneuvering for more money which they squander with abandon.

A powerful incentive is needed to encourage the bureaucracy to save money. Why not reward bureaucrats for seeking out and eliminating unnecessary expenditures? Instead of the higher salaries they now get for padding the budget, why not give them bonuses for cutting the budget?

If the bureaucrats were offered, say, a flat 10 percent of all the money they saved, the taxpayers would save 90 percent. Thus some anonymous clerk could become an overnight millionaire by saving taxpayers hundreds of millions of dollars. The fortunate clerk would merely need to locate the waste and convince a citizens' board that the nation could do without it.

Under my plan, the bureaucrats would have more to gain by searching for ways to reduce expenditures than looking for ways to spend more money.

Following a paper towel into debt

Cutting back on the millions of hours Americans spend filling out redundant and ridiculous government forms would net a savings for the bureaucrats who waste time reading, processing and filing all that paperwork. For example, Americans spend 5.4 billion hours a year just doing their tax returns.

I once received a letter from a poor woman who lost a quarter in a government vending machine. She had tried to extract a soda from a machine at the Army's Cameron Station supply base in Alexandria, Virginia. The machine swallowed her quarter but coughed up no soda pop. So she followed the instructions on the machine and applied for a refund.

Instead of her two bits, she got a three-page questionnaire containing 20 questions that were to be answered before she could get her money back. There was an affidavit-like statement to sign at the end, attesting that "the answers given are true to the best of my knowledge."

After demanding the refund applicant's name and exact place of work, the questionnaire turned into an interrogation:

"Do you consider yourself a) a regular vending machine patron, b) an infrequent vending machine user, or c) a first time user?

"How did you insert coins? a) drop, b) snap, c) spin, or d) other (please describe).

"Did the coin make a falling sound? a) behind slot, b) into mechanism, c) into coin box, d) into coin return, or e) other (please describe).

"Following insertion of coins did you a) tap on the coin slot, b) tap the machine below the coin slot, c) kick or shake the machine, d) none of the above, or e) other (please describe)?"

Assuming total recall by the thirsty victim, the questionnaire asked if the machine was full, partially full or other. Were there any signs of machine abuse? Did anyone else manage to use the machine successfully?

This was not some wisenheimer's idea of a joke. It was real enough, and it is repeated in absurd paperwork in every corner of governance. There are savings to be realized by eliminating this kind of stupidity. Then taxpayers and bureaucrats could rejoice together, in triplicate.

There is still more that we can do

• Congress must set strict standards and establish a tradition of terminating programs. If an agency has accomplished its original mission, then put it out of business. Don't just give it something else to do. Or worse yet, don't let the bureaucrats with time on their hands run around willy-nilly, assuming and appropriating new duties to justify their existence. If the cost of doing something exceeds the benefit derived, stop doing it.

• We can charge fees for the use of federal land that reflect the value of the resource and the ability of the person to pay. Certainly we shouldn't fleece senior citizens who want to take a hike in a national park. Nor should we charge school kids for field trips at the Smithsonian Institution. But we can take a fair share from the profits of cattle grazing on our rangelands and ski resorts in our national forests. (The formula for billing ski resorts hasn't been changed in 30 years.)

• We can stop being taken to the cleaners by students and others who refuse to pay back their federal loans. A government that has the power to lift taxes from a worker's paycheck before the laborer even sees the money has no excuse for not being able to collect its debts.

• We can stop buying land that has no recreational or environmental use. Uncle Sam already owns more than one-fourth of the land in the United States. If he feels compelled to buy more property for some preservation purpose, then money for the purchase should be raised by selling land that isn't needed.

• We can award federal grants to states and cities based on need instead of the political ambitions of their representatives. Some areas are simply poorer than others. If we truly want to help the poor, instead of pleasing all of the people some of the time, we should channel our money where the need is greatest. Uncle Sam manages 600 different programs that grant money to states and cities for local needs. That allocation is rarely determined by the big picture but, more often, by the political clout of the supporters.

• We ought to eliminate any federal program that costs more to run than its benefits can justify. Take, for example, price supports for agricultural products. We are taxed to subsidize farmers so the farmers can keep their prices down, so shoppers won't have to pay as much at the supermarket. In this game of pay-me-now-or-pay-me-later, we would be better off keeping our money and making our own decisions in the marketplace. It would be cheaper to give the taxpayers their money back and let them buy the services or products they choose.

• We should cancel any program that doles out more to the bureaucrats who run it than to the intended beneficiaries. Instead of pouring money into new housing construction for the poor and salaries for paper shufflers to manage the housing, why not give rental vouchers to the poor and let them choose where to live?

• We should remake any agency that consistently overruns its cost projections and drags out its contracts. No private company would tolerate a department head who couldn't match the numbers and who kept coming back and asking for more money to finish a job. The people at the top of the offending agencies should be replaced with others who can make the trains run on time. And any contractor who is the cause of a cost overrun should pay the difference.

• We can change the eligibility so that money intended for the poor actually goes to them. In a grand but meaningless gesture, for example, President Clinton decided the taxpayers would pay for free vaccinations for all children, regardless of need. That program is now costing you more than $450 million a year to buy vaccines for rich kids with private health insurance.

They keep the title of 'President' and the perks

Much has been written about the "imperial presidency"—the sometimes-royal splendor in which our chief executives, their families and their huge staffs are pampered at the taxpayers' expense.

But few Americans realize the staggering costs of what might be called the "imperial ex-presidency"—the pensions, expenses, Secret Service protection and office-library upkeep for our former presidents. The situation becomes absurd when you realize that the three current living ex-presidents are all either millionaires or close to it, thanks largely to the opportunities that arose directly from their years in the White House.

The estimated cost of the imperial ex-presidency this year alone is $27 million. Three years ago, the bill was $18 million. And in 1955, when the single ex-president was Harry S. Truman, a man of devoutly democratic tastes, the cost was only $64,000.

In a perverse sort of way, it was the spectacle of Truman, carrying his own luggage into his home in Independence, Mo., and answering his own correspondence after he left office, that inspired Congress to provide staff and stationery expenses for former presidents.

Washington Merry-Go-Round
March 17, 1983

• The well-intentioned Child Support Enforcement Program helps divorced parents collect child support from deadbeat former spouses. You spend more than $1 billion a year helping those parents, many of whom live well above the poverty level and could afford to hire lawyers and collection agents to track down the deadbeats.

• We can continue to cut defense spending. The Cold War really is over. Why do we still have 100,000 troops in Europe? Why do we subsidize a merchant marine that the Pentagon no longer needs? Why are we still buying B-2 bombers and Seawolf Submarines and C-17 cargo planes? Why are we stockpiling nuclear weapons? These are the costly strategic accoutrements of global warfare, whose threat has diminished if not disappeared. A quick $5 billion can be cut from the defense budget without a peep out of the Pentagon: Eliminate non-defense pork barrel projects that are attached like barnacles to the Pentagon budget every year by members of Congress.

• We can stop letting unscrupulous contractors take advantage of us. If your boss discovered you were embezzling money, you would be fired and probably prosecuted. If Uncle Sam discovers a contractor has cheated on a deal, he may continue to pay that contractor and may even grant him/her more contracts in the future. In one case, a university took a $4 million federal grant to test new buses, then the "testers" submitted false payment records without doing the work. Uncle Sam has known about this rip-off since 1994 but is still debating how to respond. Delayed justice makes the federal government look like easy pickings. It is.

• We can stop letting lazy public servants take advantage of us. If your boss discovered you were taking three-hour lunches and fudging on your time card, you would be fired. If Uncle Sam discovers that a public servant is doing this, the standard procedure is to bypass the slackard or pawn him off on some other unsuspecting department. The rules for getting rid of useless federal employees are so arcane and so mired in paperwork that any supervisor is a fool to rush into the quicksand. We have what the Chinese call an "iron rice bowl"—a bowl that cannot be broken, or a paycheck that is guaranteed no matter what.

• We can stop year-end spending sprees by federal agencies trying to zero out their budgets so they can justify an equal level of spending next year. A simple fix: Just prohibit any agency from spending more than one-twelfth of its budget in September, the last month of the federal fiscal year. One year the Interior Department awarded a $145,322 contract on the last day of business to a consultant whose assignment was to advise the department how to stop awarding so many of its contracts on the last day of the fiscal year.

• We can reform the budgeting process in Congress to make it understandable to the people who pay the bills. Simplifying the process would also free legislators to legislate. The budget consumes so much of their time that it has become rare for them to debate anything else at length. Television viewers were riveted by the Congressional debates on whether the United States should enter a war against Iraq in 1991. There should be more such compelling debates on matters of national morality and foreign policy.

• The least we should do is make every federal program pass this simple test: Does it duplicate or contradict another program? (For example, 14 separate government agencies run 150 employment and training programs.) Does it compete with what private enterprise could do as well or better? Does it benefit individuals or groups who could, or should, care for themselves?

• We must NOT slice the budget to pay down the national debt, then use the savings for any other purpose. It does no good to save money in one account and spend it out of another. It's not enough to reduce the deficit. We need to reduce the debt rather than leave it for our children to pay back. Why not allow taxpayers to designate a percentage of their tax bill for repayment of the debt? This debt buy-down would have to be set in legislative cement guaranteeing that Congress could not replenish the lost revenue by borrowing more.

• We can ban, under penalty of prison, the congressional practice of adding pork barrel projects to emergency relief bills. This

costly habit has become the real
emergency. The 1994 Earthquake
Relief Bill, for example, provided
$6.2 billion to help victims of
quakes. But by the time the finished legislation progressed
through Congress, the cost had
high-jumped to $11 billion. The
lawmakers had added an appropriation here and some more
funding there—money for joint
U.S.-Russia space ventures, extra
employees at the FBI fingerprint
lab in West Virginia, a train station in New York, and high-speed
rail research.

• We can straighten out any
twist in the procurement rules
that forces bureaucrats to spend
more money than requested. For
example, the Davis-Bacon act of
1931 says all government contractors must pay the "prevailing
wage" (translation: union wage),
even if a bidder can be found
whose employees are willing to
do the job for less.

Until 1994, federal workers
were required to shop for their
micro-purchases—anything less
than $2,500—at small businesses,

Let's study the not-so-endangered Capitol Hill swine

As the world hurdles toward the 21st century, research is the key to the future. Yet the federal government squanders millions on silly research—money that could be better spent to advance American technology.

Federal administrators pass out grants with abandon to researchers who have studied almost everything from the habits of the hagfish to the habitat of the hackmatack. Here are just a few examples:

— The National Science Foundation gave scientists $57,770 to catch mosquitoes and study their wing shape. "This might possibly contribute to understanding their aerodynamic design," explained a spokesman.
— Another $38,000 study was commissioned to find out why people become depressed. The conclusion: "Negative events may lead to depression."
— The Army paid $6,000 for 17 pages of directions on how to by a bottle of Worcestershire sauce.
— The National Science Foundation spent $84,000 to study why people fall in love.
— The Agriculture Department spent $46,000 to discover that it takes .792 of a second to take an egg out of the refrigerator.

Washington Merry-Go-Round
December 10, 1985

even if they could get a better price at a chain store. Thus, if an
office needed pencils, it couldn't send a secretary to a discount

store. Instead, it had to buy from a locally owned office supply store for twice the price. It didn't take long for these micros to add up to one huge macro—$4 billion a year.

The ban on bargain shopping ended when Michellee Craddock, a contract specialist in the Public Health Service, questioned why. She kept questioning until her complaints reached someone high enough to do something about it. I offer this as proof that stupidity <u>can</u> be repealed.

Future shock

These are just a few ways to apply the brakes and slow down this runaway train we call the deficit. Here is the vision of the future if we don't act:

By the year 2025, federal spending will account for 44 percent of the total national economy. The amount of money that we need to borrow every year just to stay afloat will reach 23 percent of the gross domestic product. The cancerous national debt will drive all private investment out of the market. Without private investment, America will become a stagnant, Third World country.

Young people will balk at paying the bills for the elderly. Generational conflict will break out as workers see their net pay dwindling and their money going to support someone else's leisure.

It doesn't have to come to that. The road to deficit reduction has been traveled before. Several industrialized nations that are our competitors in the international market place—including Australia, Japan, Canada, Mexico, Germany and England—have managed to reduce their debt. The General Accounting Office made the rounds, seeking solutions in those countries. Only one, Mexico, had waited until it reached the brink of imminent collapse. The others, looking ahead, didn't like what they saw. None of them found a quick fix or a magic formula. Yet the solution was simple enough: They had to spend less money.

In each country, the leadership persuaded the populace that a little hardship now was better than incalculable misery later. They sought the support of opinion makers and special-interest groups.

They emphasized shared sacrifice and traded big cuts in one program for small improvements in another. Some had to cut social welfare benefits and endure the howls of the aggrieved. Those cuts were often made just by separating the benefits from cost-of-living indexes. Australia cut the pension benefits of its wealthiest citizens.

It took Canada just four years after reforms to reduce the relative deficit from second largest to the smallest of all the Group of Seven industrialized nations. Ontario now requires its welfare recipients to work for their money, and Nova Scotia stopped paying unemployment to fishermen during the off season.

Mexico and England privatized many of the industries and functions that their governments should never have nationalized in the first place. Japan imposed zero-increase budgets on some programs from one year to the next. These nations sold their unneeded assets, trimmed their bloated public work forces, and froze public salaries. It wasn't painless, but it was effective. Now all six nations are in a stronger position to clean our clock in international trade.

My 50-year vigil in Washington has taught me that our elected leaders won't adopt reforms unless we wallop them with a two-by-four, as happened to the stubborn mule in Abraham Lincoln's anecdote, to get their attention. Nor can we expect the president and Congress to agree on a prudent budget if we in America are unwilling to sacrifice. We must first tighten our own belts; we must practice sacrifice before we preach it to Washington. We cannot make a difference until we start acting differently.

CHAPTER FIFTEEN

CALL TO ACTION

On the foregoing pages, I have sought to alert America to an onrushing calamity that could drastically change our way of life. I've tried not to overstate what our political leaders habitually understate. But there has really been no need to exaggerate the danger, which is as visible as a twister whirling on the horizon. It is sweeping down upon us, threatening economic devastation that could destroy the basic cohesion of the country.

It may seem to some that I am unduly pessimistic, that I have taken too little account of silver linings. Of course, nothing in history is absolutely inevitable. Feats of rejuvenation or miracles of circumstance could possibly set back the clock, which is tick-tocking remorselessly. And to be sure, I have detected optimistic glimmers here and there.

But the timing mechanism is close to going off, triggered by the mathematics of multiplying debt and the deadly erosion of confidence in American institutions. This could start a chain reaction of economic crises. Then a long-dozing government will be compelled to rush from fire to fire, trying to stave off the damage. America will be rocked by debt explosion, dollar repudiation, credit collapse, economic plunge and a dozen stored-up reckonings that are about to erupt.

Yet no one in authority has sounded a national alarm. The politicians-in-charge have pulled so much wool over so many eyes that the stuff has gotten into their own eyes, perhaps preventing them from seeing what they don't want to see. But blinders won't prevent troubles from happening.

Enough hard facts are available to get an idea of what lies ahead in the 21st century. It's not at all what Americans would want to happen. But the only way we can prevent the future from happening is to head it off before it arrives. Here are some jigsaw pieces that reveal the bare bones of the future:

Ringing up the rungs

When Harry Homeowner goes out to buy an aluminum ladder, he can get one that'll take him as high as he wants to go for under $100. But when the Air Force's San Antonio Air Logistics Center went shopping for a ladder about 10 feet long to get a pilot into the cockpit of his A-10 fighter plane, the cost was a mind-numbing $1,676 each. Investigators for the House Defense Subcommittee boggled at the price. They found that the A-10 ladder was almost identical to the one used for climbing into the F-105—and that model cost "only" $600 apiece. One trouble may have been that the Air Force shopped at only one ladder source: The 71 ladders cost taxpayers about $120,000.

Washington Merry-Go-Round
October 12, 1982

Blueprint of the 21st Century

Decline of America. Two generations ago, the United States was the world's number one military power, economic power, industrial power, agricultural power and technological power. Number one. Then some terrible enervation began dragging America down; a creeping ineffectiveness began spreading across the land. At some point in the graph, this slippage has started to reverse, but our government is still stumbling.

Chaotic explosions of red ink, caused by Democrat spending sprees and Republican tax cuts, have sent the public debt into orbit. Unheard-of deficits and over-the-moon debt continue to soar out of control. The service charges on the debt have cancelled out recent gains in trade, fatally draining off U.S. capital—money that our industries need to be competitive.

Our only strategy against a multitrillion-dollar debt has been to let the dollar slide. But will foreign lenders, who have been funding much of our debt, continue to lend? This worries the financial editors of the Washington Post. "If foreigners suddenly stopped sending their money here," the Post warns, "the American economy would go into shock." Many foreign lenders have already stopped sending money here—because the dropping dollar reduces the value of their investment. "The United States is no longer seen as a safe haven," says Wall Street oracle Henry Kaufman.

What difference does it make whether we remain number one? A huge difference. English is the international language, the dollar the international currency, our economy the international cornerstone. Our news is disseminated, our culture imitated around the world. This would change, with severe domestic consequences, if America is dislodged from the pinnacle.

Heads in the Sand. Our political leaders, watching that economic twister form on the horizon, immediately assumed the ostrich posture. They fully understood the consequences of their actions and inactions. Yet they fostered a climate of complacency.

They refused to make decisions that might cause temporary pain, with full knowledge this would cause later, greater pain. They pushed federal deficits to the outer limits, with full knowledge that it would hobble productivity. They ignored the savings and loan problem, with full knowledge that the costs would multiply. They stood by while foreigners developed our inventions and then sold them back to us as finished products, with full knowledge this would cause a disastrous trade imbalance.

It has became obvious that some pain will have to be inflicted on the citizenry. Yet neither Democrats nor Republicans are willing to be identified as the inflictors. They blithely continue to employ budgetary deceits that have been used for years to obscure the bottom line—overblown revenue estimates; underprojected interest rates; false savings by transferring this year's costs to next year's budget; failure to count what was borrowed from Social Security or what was spent for the savings and loan bailout and the Persian Gulf War.

Meanwhile, our politicians continue practicing yesterday's politics at the expense of tomorrow. In a global economy, their focus is parochial. In the technological age, they still support archaic industries and unions. To get more for their constituents, they seek government subsidies for obsolete programs and oppose funds for future research. Admirably, our leaders have assigned first priority to social progress. But to achieve social equality, they have lowered standards, leveled the masses and de-emphasized excellence.

As for the citizens who own this country, we have basked in the political complacency, happily consuming more than we produce. This prodigious consumption has generated a false prosperity. We borrow, spend, consume; then we charge our high living to our children.

Yet the fact that we have inherited a way of life does not assure its perpetuation. We have no right to expect that the blessings of America will continue to be showered down on us whether we value them or not, earn them or not, deserve them or not. Those who expect to inherit everything *gratis* are on the way to losing what they have inherited.

The Anarchy Zone. Americans are adrift in an anarchy zone of loan guarantees, spawned by the endless quest of politicians for ways to meet the desires of their constituents and contributors without bearing the onus of raising taxes to pay for them. The savings and loan guarantee has already ruptured, causing a multibillion-dollar hemorrhage. Half a dozen other funds, all clones of the S & L, are likewise insured by Uncle Sam with only token reserves.

Other monster collapses could prove to be the force that brings down the federal government's strange financial house. Individual deposits in 15,000 commercial banks, for example, are guaranteed up to $100,000 by the federal government. At the moment, these banks are sitting on risky loans totaling hundreds of billions of dollars—potential losses that exceed their stockholders' equity and loan-loss reserves.

They are writing off bad loans by the billions each year, with billions more in hopeless Third World debt still hanging over their vaults. About half the bad loans are written off in taxes that the banks are excused from paying, thus leaving the government with less money to meet its obligations.

As if this were not enough to cause a monumental migraine, banks are also being flooded with fake $100 bills that are almost impossible to distinguish from real money. The near-perfect fakes

---

How to get rich in the hammer business

I have heard from thousands of taxpayers who are boiling at the Pentagon's spending practices. They wonder why the Pentagon would pay $91 for a 3-cent screw, $114 for a 9-cent battery, $511 for a 60-cent lamp and $436 for a $7 hammer.

I have a suggestion. Since the government places such high value on these items, maybe taxpayers should pay their taxes with 3-cent screws and 9-cent batteries. Of course, I doubt the Internal Revenue Service would give taxpayers $91 credit for a 3-cent screw.

How does the government justify paying $436 for a $7 hammer? I'll tell you how the Navy justifies it: $41 to order the hammer and figure out how to use it; $93 for "mechanical subassembly" to make sure the hammer works; $102 for "manufacturing overhead"; $37 to line up spare parts for the hammer; $3 for packing the hammer for shipment; $90 for the contractor's "general administrative cost"; $56 for the finder's fee; $7 for the "capital cost of money"; and $7 for "other expenses."

Washington Merry-Go-Round
October 10, 1984

---

are printed on the Treasury's own presses, which were given to the late Shah of Iran back when Henry Kissinger was manipulating the strings in the backrooms of Washington. He had a special passion for the Shah, who had granted multibillion-dollar oil and banking concessions to the Rockefeller interests. Coincidentally, Kissinger came to Washington from the Rockefeller camp.

While Kissinger was around, whatever the Shah wanted he seemed to get. And he wanted Iran to have top-quality currency. The U.S. mint not only shipped one of its presses to Iran—the only one ever to leave its control—but sent experts to help the Shah design his currency. Unfortunately, the presses and the technical know-how were left behind when the Shah fled Iran. Now a hostile Iran is producing phony $100 bills and scattering them around the world like autumn leaves. These counterfeit bills, with a face value of hundreds of billions of dollars, are circulating through banks that can't tell fake Iranian bills from genuine U.S. currency.

Since depositors are protected by U.S. guarantees, they have responded with massive indifference to the predicament of the banks. The buck passes to the Federal Deposit Insurance Corporation whose own reserves are a gaping question mark. Ultimately, the buck will be forwarded to the taxpayers where it stops.

Meanwhile, banks and other entities have also loaned out government-guaranteed money for housing, farmers, veterans, students and small businesses. Storm clouds are building above all these credit programs. At risk are several trillion of the taxpayers' money which stands behind these shaky loan guarantees.

The Oil Specter. Even before Iraq's invasion of Kuwait, oil analysts warned that a spark could set ablaze the rich oil fields of the Persian Gulf. The oil barrels were simply too close to the powder kegs. An explosion in this volatile area would catapult oil prices out of this world. Even if a precarious peace can be maintained, the price rise, though slower, should continue relentlessly upward. This will nullify efforts to halt the buildup of the trade debt.

Add to the oil equation the skyrocketing surge in consumption by the Pacific Rim countries. Then factor in the bad news that oil production by nonmembers of the OPEC cartel, once a safety valve, has now peaked. Clearly, conditions for Oil Shock III are at hand whether it should come about gradually or suddenly.

High oil costs have driven the inflation rate up and crimped economic activity. Peter Drucker reminds us that under the classic rules of cartels, whenever the price of a product is forced upward to monopoly heights, the price of other products in its general class must fall because, for one reason, less money is available to purchase them.

Oil is in the class of primary goods, and Peter Drucker's rule has come down with crashing force upon other primary goods—foodstuffs, cotton, timber, minerals—the prices of which have been dropping as oil prices have risen. Unhappily, these are America's biggest exports.

The Great Social Security Embezzlement. Perhaps the most devastating blow to the government's fiscal stability will be the disappearance of the only ace up Uncle Sam's sleeve—the Social Security surplus. This is the excess that comes in from the payroll tax above what is currently paid to recipients. But under current practice, instead of surplus, there will be only a pile of government IOUs.

I devoted a full chapter to this scandal earlier in the book; it's an important jigsaw piece that will help make the future clearer. So many younger workers don't believe there'll be any reserve to pay their pensions after a lifetime of payroll deductions, for the system is beginning to crumble as the understanding of it sinks in. New York's Senator Pat Moyniham openly called it "thievery," and Pennsylvania's late Senator John Heinz corrected him, saying the proper term was "embezzlement."

The Medical Monstrosity. Another important jigsaw piece that will help shape the future is the medical crisis, which I also covered in an earlier chapter. For ordinary families, the combined cost of insurance and unallowed expenses already approaches the breaking point. Medicare is projected to go bankrupt early in the 21st century. Medicaid for the tens of millions of uninsureds and medical indigents is already breaking down in state after state. There is no one around to pick up the broken parts except Uncle Sam.

Misfortunes and Miscalculations. A nation that walks the economic tightrope lives at the mercy of the law of history which decrees anything that can go wrong will go wrong—eventually. Yet Americans are conditioned to believe that the U.S. economy somehow will absorb, without collapse, the vast fiscal and trade deficits. This scenario depends upon hairbreadth calculations, which assume America will encounter only soft breezes.

It's a scenario that ignores the normal decadel turbulence and cyclical disorders that historically recur. No margin is left for any of these common adversities. What could possibly happen? The economy, instead of advancing at the official projection rate, might simply stand still. Stagnation could add another $100 billion, give or take a few billion, to the deficit. Up to this writing, official calculations have also failed to take into account a possible economic downturn; or a rise in protectionism; or a jump in world interest rates; or another oil crisis; or an outbreak of fighting; or a backlash by states and municipalities which could dump back on Washington the financial burdens it keeps dumping on them.

The hardware store of horrors

The toll of eye-popping extravagance in the Pentagon's spare-parts purchases continues to mount, despite the brass hats' assurances to Congress that the military is cleaning up its act. Here are the latest shockers:

— McDonnell Douglas was paid $2,043 for a plain round nut that could have been bought at any hardware store for 13 cents, and $145,950 for a standard computer printer that should have cost $28,840.

— Gould Simulator Systems was paid $456 for a half-inch socket worth $1.49, and $599 for a pair of drill bits worth $1.69. Gould was also paid $652 for a tool box that retails for $11.67.

— Sperry Corp. was paid $243 for a circuit breaker that could have been bought for $11.10.

— Hughes Aircraft was paid $512 for a 48-cent fuse.

These outrages were uncovered by investigators for the Senate Committee on Governmental Affairs.

Washington Merry-Go-Round
September 28, 1985

All of these pendulum swings are overdue. At least two may have already struck. Any one of them could cause America's economic acrobats to teeter on the high wire without any safety net.

Our Crumbling Infrastructure. Even if a magic wand were to smooth over all other obstacles, the rejuvenation of the economy would be hobbled by the spreading fractures at our base. Examples: the multibillion-dollar loss each year caused by delays at congested airports; the even costlier time lost in gridlock traffic, plus the extra miles to avoid road and bridge repairs; the mounting cancellations of proposed new plants because local infrastructures can't accommodate them; the multibillion-dollar hit on Southern California's economy caused by water shortages.

These are but introductions. America's road systems are inadequate; mass transit systems are overwhelmed; municipal water systems are corroding; toxic waste dumps and radioactive pile-ups must be cleaned up. But even more crucial, because it's more imminent, will be the cascade of cost explosions set off by the inevitable succession of airline crashes, bridge collapses, traffic-jam spectaculars, electricity brown-outs, nuclear waste leakages, excrement overflows and business pull-outs. These jarring tragedies and irritations will create a public rage for repairing the degeneration of three decades of neglect.

And estimators are just beginning to calculate the staggering cost of repairing and replacing municipal water systems across the nation, plus the bankrupting cost of rebuilding hundreds of thousands of low-income housing units that are destroyed year-in and year-out by vandalism, arson and demolition—while the number of poor people surges.

Unskilled Labor. Any hope we have of pushing back the tides of trade debt that threaten to engulf us depends upon our ability to match—and surpass—the competitive pace set by our more advanced rivals. When American industrial planners visited Italy to study the complex machinery in modern Italian textile plants and when other industrialists examined a high-tech bicycle assembly line in Japan, they reached the same shocking conclusion. This foreign machinery was simply too complicated for the low-cost, low-skill American labor force to operate.

Labor Secretary Robert Reich may not want to admit it, but I know he has been told repeatedly by executives of foreign firms: "We have to simplify our machinery and dumb-down our training programs for workers in the United States."

Is our productivity improving? Far from it. The capacity of our incoming workers is declining. Groups with lower scores are entering the work force in great numbers, and those with higher scores are declining. And that's only half the demographic. In the recent past, a population glut among the work-entry age group allowed employers to get by, after a fashion, by picking the best among mediocre applicants. The unfit could simply be cast aside. No more. The baby-bust generation is now providing a million fewer applicants each year.

The bottom line: There is a shortage of acceptable labor in the United States.

Divided States of America. In urban neighborhoods within our greatest cities, part of America has fallen not only off the production line but out of civilization.

This "underclass" is festering in a hideous environment— where murder is a common response to trivial irritations or wants; where the remnants of legitimate enterprises are packing up to leave; where drug pushing, theft and prostitution are the only thriving industries; where the noncriminals must be publicly supported; where children are systematically recruited for crime; where fathers feel no responsibility to their offspring; where mothers casually abandon their babies; where pregnant women heedlessly transmit the agonies of drug debilitation and venereal disease to their unborn; where the elderly live behind barricaded doors; where it is hazardous to venture into the next neighborhood or even to step outside at night.

Our big-city governments, left more and more to themselves to contain this blight, are approaching breakdown and bankruptcy. Their worst neighborhoods are starting to look like the bombed-out cities of World War II. The violence in these urban neighborhoods is also beginning to spill over into the cities proper. A while ago, a young punk slipped up behind me and bashed me over the head with a pipe. It happened in broad daylight a few blocks up busy 16th Street from the White House. The police told me that men like him prowl our city streets in search of victims. They're armed with guns, knives and blackjacks.

In many neighborhoods, the police have lost control on the streets to youth gangs. These gangs have an estimated two million members who are armed and dangerous. The barbarization of our inner cities has become so deep an inner-core illness that it can best be defined as a domestic civil war.

Getting the fax straight

Fax machines are going for bargain-basement prices, but we can't expect the Pentagon to shop garage sales. The Air Force is buying custom-made fax machines for $421,000 each. Apparently the Air Force needs something that will survive a nuclear war. And, in the meantime, Air Force personnel can fax state-of-the-art requisition orders for pizza.

Washington Merry-Go-Round
December 1, 1989

The Slow Grind. A nemesis larger than any of its parts haunts the future. This might be called the delayed-hit effect—declines in industrial output, basic infrastructure, technological progress, educational level and worker skills. It will take years before the main impact will hit the economy like a time bomb.

Free enterprise in America, meanwhile, has become less and less free. It has become entangled in government red tape and hobbled by bureaucratic encumbrances. This land swarms with petty officials, litigating lawyers and multiplying bureaucrats who create barriers that obstruct production and run up costs. Our adversarial system—the bureaucrat against the entrepreneur, the worker versus the manager, the small enterprise against the corporate giant—is bogging America down.

Even if we can clear away the obstacles and reverse the economic tide, it will take years of resurgence that will cause its own pain. To regain economic strength will require that we consume less that we produce, exporting the balance. Current resources must be drained to repair past neglect while the payoff awaits the future.

Destabilization and Disillusionment. As a dozen crises converge, the alarm bells at last will begin clamoring. An alarmed society will likely prod the lethargic government apparatus into action. There will be urgent attempts to increase revenue, to slash spending, to enforce consumer austerities, to stimulate technology leaps, to encourage better performances from students, workers and managers.

Yet last-ditch countermeasures won't be enacted unless in the nation-at-large there's a renewal of unity, discipline and sacrifice. Above all else, Americans must have faith in the country's leadership and in our system itself. But official misconduct and mismanagement has been turning Americans off, not turning them on. This threatens to tear apart the framework of citizenship and followership—to cause the disjointing, not the uniting, of our diverse society.

Downward Mobility. We have taken it as a law of nature that each American generation will do better than the one before. Yet for the majority of Americans, the 1990s will culminate in a generation of sliding downwards. We are slowly awakening to the awful recognition that it may not be just stagnation or temporary reverse that grips us but perhaps a permanent fall never contemplated in the American promise.

This downward mobility has been obscured by temporary factors that are rapidly running out—the 50 percent increase in working wives since the 1960s; the drop in the number if children per family; the delay in their birth that made per capita income seem to grow; the artificial pumping up of living standards by consuming more than we earned.

Now, alas, the remorseless trends have overtaken us. From here on, most families will start off with two earners, causing a sharp decline in real wages. The fall in the birth rate has ended, and fewer work force entrants will also tend to lower living standards and deflate the American balloon. As for the anesthetic effect of foreign credit, we will now pass from the illusions of receiving to the cold turkey of paying back.

On top of all this, the average family income won't buy as much satisfaction per dollar as it used to. State, city and county taxes, health care expenses, auto insurance, user fees—all are on the rise. These increases will swallow what used to be disposable income.

The Rising Sun. Perhaps the best way to understand the decline of America is to compare it to the rise of Japan. In the twinkling of an historical eye, Japan has caught up with the United States as a prime producer and financial power. Yet Japan is a small, tight, overcrowded island nation with few resources. In contrast, the United States is a large, expansive nation with abundant resources.

How has Japan achieved its stunning success? Lacking natural resources, it has developed its human resources. It has upgraded its schools, with emphasis on excellence. Its 120 million people have demonstrated a shoulder-to-the-wheel commitment. Its industrial managers and political leaders have learned to work together for the national good. This has enabled Japan to man its factories with the world's best-educated, most skilled, hardest-working labor force.

Then what has caused the U.S. slippage? Above all else, I would blame our consumption binge. Year after year, we have consumed more than we have produced. The Japanese have always produced more than they consume. They were willing to sacrifice yesterday for today; now they continue to sacrifice today for tomorrow.

We used to have the world's best-educated, most skilled, hardest-working labor force. That's how we surpassed Great Britain as the world's number one industrial power. We used to look forward to the great future ahead of us; now we look backward to the great achievements behind us. We used to be willing to sacrifice our comforts for the common good. Oh yes, we're still willing to sacrifice, all right; we're willing to sacrifice our children's tomorrow for our own today. That's why the me-first generation is destined to end up last—unless we change our ways.

This, then, is a last call to action. In the America we have inherited, we the people are the sovereigns. It is up to us to answer the call.

How to Prevent an Economic Collapse

If you have read this deep into the book, you should be aware that we are traveling on a superhighway to disaster. Across President Clinton's bridge to the 21st century awaits a catastrophe that will cause incalculable misery and mischief for ourselves and for our children.

Who is to blame? I accuse, above all others, the politicians-in-charge. Our current problems and future danger are the work of failed policies, self-serving politics and myopic vision. The connecting thread has been the political opportunism of the moment. But what politics can cause, politics can also cure. So let us begin a political solution.

On November 5, 1996, America's voters delivered a mandate. It was not a mandate for President Clinton. Nor was it a mandate for the Republican Congress. The voters themselves may not have realized that they handed us at Citizens Against Government Waste their mandate. The post-election analyses are quite clear about that: The voters re-elected Bill Clinton primarily because they thought he would protect their entitlements. But they also re-elected a Republican Congress primarily because they wanted to slash government spending and reduce their taxes.

How in the world can the American people keep their benefits but pay less taxes? How can they maintain government programs and, at the same time, gut the federal budget? This is exactly what CAGW has been striving to do ever since its founding in 1984. We have been preaching the solution with all our lung power—JUST ELIMINATE GOVERNMENT WASTE! But until the 1996 election, the response had been a hollow whisper.

Now the dynamics have changed. Having read the electorate's sheet music, a bipartisan chorus is suddenly singing the right tune, and President Clinton is leading the choir. If he could "accomplish only one thing" in his second term, he said, "I would pass a balanced budget . . . . " To provide the necessary wherewithal, he and his sidekick, Al Gore, are ready to do some more "reinventing" of government. They want to make government more efficient yet by eliminating waste. The GOPers on Capital Hill, not to be outdone, have also pledged to slash waste with a vengeance.

That means the fat ought to disappear quickly from the federal carcass, right? Wrong! Waste in Washington is too entrenched. Powerful coalitions form around every wasteful government program. They include the people who benefit from the program, the contractors who provide the supplies and services, the bureaucrats who process the paperwork, and the politicians who champion the program in exchange for votes and contributions. Together they lovingly embrace and protect the lard.

These special pleaders are politically active, organized and vocal. The taxpaying public is politically inactive, unorganized and silent. Yet here in America, those who govern understand that their power is derived from the governed. The state is not superior to its citizens. So it's still possible for an aroused public to prevail.

I ask you to join CAGW in warning our political leaders that the boat we're all in is heading for the reefs. If we don't change direction, we'll crash into the rocks. Those whose hands are on the helm must change course, or we will arrive at where they're taking us.

Take heed: Politicians by nature are skilled at evading issues, shifting responsibility and diverting difficult decisions to someone else. So we must unite for a confrontation with a Washington crowd who have been deaf to unwanted arguments and indifferent to unpleasant facts.

The first thing you should do is join CAGW. Just send $15 to cover costs. Address it to Citizens Against Government Waste, 1301 Connecticut Avenue, Suite 400, Washington, D.C., 20036. We already have more than 600,000 members—enough to gain the ear of our political leaders. But a membership of millions would get their undivided attention.

In your own self-interest, you should speak out. You are responsible for what you say, but you may be even more responsible for what you do <u>not</u> say. You go down with the ship if you keep silent. The most effective way for you to raise your voice in Washington is to turn it into a great chorus. CAGW will see to it that our collective voices are heard, loudly and clearly, inside the White House and upon Capitol Hill.

We'll call upon the president to keep his promise to get rid of government waste and balance the budget. Can he easily carve the fat out of the legislation that Congress submits to him easily? Yes, because Congress has now given him the scalpel to do it with. It's a sharp-cutting blade—the line-item veto. He'll be tempted to use it to gain political advantage. He could offer to spare someone's private pork in return for his/her political support. But CAGW will point an accusing finger at any fat he misses. We need your help to raise a howl if he tries to play politics with the line-item veto.

You can help us, too, to deliver the message on Capitol Hill. We ask you to contact your congressional delegation. The best way to hammer home the message is to open the dialogue with a phone call, then follow up with a letter. Your communications will have more impact if they're concise, lucid and sincere.

You can also help generate public sentiment. Share the message with your own circle of friends, then encourage them to widen the circle to include their friends. This is politics at its best— grassroots politics.

There are a few, rare, breathtaking moments in human affairs when action can be taken that will alter the course of history. A chorus of individual voices, demanding action to stop the national erosion, could reverse our dangerous course. We have it within our power to bring back the America of former glory.

You can make a difference! Too many Americans have come to feel powerless and removed from the decision-making process. Those caught in the benevolent toils of the government have become apathetic; public programs tend to produce more whiners than doers.

Tenants of public housing, for instance, may well be descendants of pioneers who cleared the wilderness. Yet they are apt to complain listlessly that weeks have passed and no one from the Housing Authority has come around to fix the toilet.

Everywhere in America, citizens are grappling with the federal octopus. Many become entangled in its tender embrace; its undulating tentacles simultaneously caress the docile citizen and restrict his/her movement. Its many tentacles make the octopus difficult to outmaneuver; instead, men and women find it easier to succumb and become its pampered captive.

This book is addressed to those who haven't yet succumbed to the monster's caresses—to Americans who won't easily surrender their sovereignty. You can help stave off the approaching calamities; yes, you can make a difference.

The cumbersome federal apparatus must be overhauled; the careless, ceaseless spending must be stopped; the piled-up accounts must be paid. Worse, yesterday's extravagances must be paid out of tomorrow's bleak prospects. The money our government has borrowed belongs to those who loaned it. This money we have spent and now owe. The debt must be paid; it cannot be wished away.

Wiping out waste will save monstrous sums and make the government more efficient. But it will take thrift and industry to get America going. We must work as hard, as inventively, as efficiently and as meticulously as do our toughest competitors. We have done it before; we can do it again. At the end of World War II, we built an entire new nation that we called "suburbia." We constructed millions of homes, with schools, churches and shopping malls to support them. We laid a vast network of roads and pipelines.

Certainly we should now be able to repair our collapsing infrastructure, revitalize our economy, and prevent disaster from happening. It would take a Herculean national effort to turn things around. But I believe we're capable of that effort.

First, we must plug the leak of dollars from our families, from our businesses, from our communities, from our government. This means we must consume less, work harder and produce more.

We can no longer count on our political leaders to act in our best interests. They have failed us in the past. Nor is there time to wait for them to get their act together. Each of us, in our own individual spheres, must contribute to the solution.

We must begin where we are with what we have. We need to seek services we can perform, goods we can produce, products we can sell. Each of us should be able to find something productive to do. America can no longer afford individuals who spend more than they make, take more than they produce, and withhold their best effort.

The future we're striving to change for the better, after all, is your future.

INDEX

If you're ready to move beyond the headlines and MAKE A DIFFERENCE I have the perfect resources for you.

A MISSION FROM JACK • 1-800-982-2455 •

Qty.	Item	Price	Can. Price	Total
	24 issues of the **Jack Anderson Confidential**	$99		
	One year membership to **Citizens Against Government Waste**	$15		
	Washington Money-Go-Round*	$28.95	$32.95	
	*$4.00 for shipping and handling of first book, $3.00 to ship each additional book at the same time.			
	*Washington residents please add 8.2% sales tax			
	Total enclosed			

Telephone Orders: 1-800-982-2455
Have your VISA or MasterCard ready.

Fax Orders: 1-206-281-1625
Fill out order form and fax

Postal Orders: Elliott & James Publishing
PO Box 19535
Seattle, WA 98119

Payment: Please Check One

☐ Check

☐ VISA

☐ MasterCard

Name: _____

Address: _____

City: _____ State: _____ Zip: _____

Credit Card: _____ Exp. Date: _____

Signature: _____

Day Time Phone: _____

Failure to lead has consequences in

Pork becomes a hot entree on Congress' menu

House bill paves U.S. i

Congress

Pentagon's brownie recipe needs reinventing

Bureaucrats milk Sunda

itary a talent for squandering money

Embarassing letters punctuate